JUST Leisure:
Equity,
Social Exclusion
and Identity

Edited by
Celia Brackenridge
David Howe
Fiona Jordan

LSA
Publication No. 72

First published in 2000 by
Leisure Studies Association

The collection as a whole © 2000 LSA
The individual contributions © 2000 the respective authors

A catalogue record for this book
is available from the British Library.

ISBN: 0 906337 83 6

21 903840

Layout design and typesetting by Myrene L. McFee
Binding by Kensett Ltd., Hove

CONTENTS

Introduction: Just Leisure, Social Exclusion and Identity
Celia Brackenridge, David Howe and Fiona Jordan v

About the Contributors x

I ⅄ EQUITY AND SOCIAL EXCLUSION 1

The Sexist State: Leisure, Labour and the
Ideology of Welfare Policy
Tess Kay 3

– Equity or Exclusion? Contemporary Experiences
in Post-industrial Urban Leisure
Euan Hague, Chris Thomas and Stephen Williams 17

What's the Score? Using Sport and Leisure as Diversion
Jonathan Long, Eddy Lloyd and Jon Dart 35

Social Disadvantage and Leisure Access:
The Case of the Unemployed
Francis Lobo 49

Just sport – Sport and the Concept of
Equal Opportunities between Women and Men
Håkan Larsson 69

Tied Together Through Sport? Sport and Social Cohesion
in New Housing Estates
Hugo van der Poel and Colette Roques 83

II IDENTITY 103

Homophobia and its Effects on the Inequitable Provision
of Health and Leisure Services
for Older Gay Men and Lesbians
Arnold H. Grossman 105

The "Goodness of Fit" in Norwegian Youth Sports
Reidar Säfvenbom 119

Identities and Subculture in Relation to Sport: An Analysis
of Teenage Girls' Magazines
Claudia Cockburn 131

Glencoe: A Case Study in Interpretation
Judith E. Brown 149

⌐ Who Are These People? And What on Earth Are They Doing?!
Lesley Lawrence 161

Other Publications from LSA 185

Just Leisure?
Equity, Social Exclusion and Identity

Celia Brackenridge, David Howe and Fiona Jordan

Cheltenham and Gloucester College of Higher Education (UK))

Introduction

A strong tradition of welfarist thinking in leisure studies has meant that issues of equity have always featured prominently in the literature of the field. In recent years, however, this approach to the leisure studies agenda has been roundly challenged from two perspectives, one theoretical and the other practical. Theoretical critique has been effected through the de-stabilising forces of postmodernism on formerly taken-for-granted social categories (age, class, gender). Practical critique has been effected through the equally destabilising forces of commercial realism on the formerly taken-for-granted emancipatory project that underpinned much leisure research.

Issues of justice, fairness and value have not been lost, however, in the turmoil of these debates. If anything, they have become even more sharply focused. As the Editors of *Just Leisure: Policy, Ethics and Professionalism* (the companion to this volume) have written, "The idea that leisure might centrally be related to matters of ethical significance is not a new one". The use of the deliberately ambiguous term 'just', then, plays nicely into both the postmodern and the commercial attacks on leisure studies, its nature and purposes. What is *just* (fair) in leisure (service provision, consumption, management or research) still concerns us as much as whether these activities are *just* (simply) leisure.

This book comprises two sections: the first addresses Equity and Social Exclusion and the second explores aspects of Identity. It might be argued that the two sections themselves are aligned with the debates mentioned above, although the distinction between them is by no means clear-cut. The chapters on Equity and Social Inclusion are concerned explicitly with the location of leisure in contemporary policy initiatives. The chapters on Identity focus much more on the place of leisure in identity politics, yet also address notions of leisure exclusion, justice/fairness and just-ness/justification. Whilst contributions to the volume come from a range of national and international perspectives, they are all European-based, including the UK, USA, Norway, Sweden and the Netherlands. Whether, together, they represent a distinctively European perspective on leisure and justice is for the reader to decide.

Equity and social exclusion

The first section of the book opens with **Tess Kay**'s examination of how state policy towards reconciling paid work and family life both impacts on men's and women's expectations of the role of paid and unpaid work and also influences individual women's experiences of leisure. Using data on employment and childcare drawn from across the European Union, she concludes that parenthood compromises women's access to social citizenship.

In their essay on post-industrial urban leisure, **Euan Hague, Chris Thomas and Stephen Williams** argue that landscape changes are closely tied to social, economic and cultural changes in urban society. They discuss the shift from production to consumption in urban spaces with reference to a case study of Festival Park in Stoke-on-Trent. Through an examination of space, place and the experience of leisure in the late-modern urban landscape, and the use of Bourdieu's concept of *doxa*, they conclude that practices of exclusion operate both implicitly and explicitly in such arenas.

Shifting our attention from leisure as consumption to leisure as social therapy, **Jonathan Long, Eddy Lloyd and Jon Dart** examine a specific scheme for addressing 'the problem' of youth crime. They use an evaluation of one specific mentoring initiative for young people, referred (voluntarily) from the youth justice system, to examine the potential benefits of leisure for social integration. They conclude that, despite the many ambivalences uncovered, the apparent separation of the scheme from the young people's everyday lives and a degree of scepticism amongst the young people themselves, small-scale benefits are discernible which can be extremely cost-effective.

The next chapter continues the theme of young people's leisure, this time in relation to employment rather than criminality. Current social policies frequently invoke the concept of citizenship in attempts to include young people and other groups as full participating members of the community. In describing his study of unemployed young people in Western

Australia, however, **Francis Lobo** shows how unemployment disadvantages young people in their leisure and contributes to their material and psychological social exclusion.

Håkan Larssen takes us on an interesting theoretical excursion as he investigates the rationale for so-called 'equal opportunities' initiatives in relation to men's and women's sport. Drawing on Foucault's concept of 'governmentality', he explores the representation of gender in sport and how sport and scientific research in sport function both in the production of women and men as objects and subjects of knowledge and as a technique or procedure for regulating male and female behaviour. Larssen argues that sport has become heterosexualised on the basis of assumed natural categories of 'maleness' and 'femaleness' and that the discourse of equal opportunities has both normalised femininity and, at the same time, problematised masculinity. The effect of these processes, he argues, is to constrain our possibilities for new ways of thinking about, and doing, sport.

The essay by **Hugo van der Poel and Colette Roques** is centrally concerned with whether leisure has a place in the spectrum of core leisure services or 'social infrastructure' and, in particular, whether sport can contribute to social cohesion in the new compact cities built in VINEX-locations in the Netherlands. Preliminary empirical work in a number of these locations reveals no direct correlation between sport participation and social bonding within the place of residence but suggests that those who engage frequently in organised club sport develop stronger bonds than those who practise 'unorganised' sport. However, with a broadening of the definition of 'sport' in modern society it becomes more and more difficult to demonstrate any measurable effects of sports participation. The authors use their findings to make policy recommendations for the planners of the new housing areas that include integral design and costing of both public and commercial sports facilities and services.

Identity

The invisibility of older gay men and lesbians in health and leisure service provision, resulting from ageism and stereotyping, is the subject of critique by **Arnold Grossman**. Evidence of exclusion, based on stigmatization and a 'discredited social identity', is presented from a number of different studies, showing that these exclusionary processes lead to a syndrome of psychological problems for older gay men and lesbians. Grossman discusses various strategies of adaptation that have been used by such individuals to cope with the barriers to service and the effects of 'othering' that confront them. He closes his essay by offering a set of practical recommendations to service providers in the fields of health, ageing and leisure services: these are aimed at eliminating the negative effects of homophobia and making services more equitable and service environments safer.

So-called 'drop out' from sport has long been a concern of policy providers and educators committed to the sport-as-personal-development school of thought. In his investigation of youth sport provision in Norway (the Adolescents in Leisure Study, ALS), **Reidar Säfvenbom** examines the interrelationships between meaningful free time activity patterns, sport context and participation amongst 'at risk' youth groups and their non at-risk peers. The author focuses on a particular component of the ALS in which respondents recorded their activity patterns and perceptions systematically throughout a seven-day period. The results show that these adolescents are faced with a narrow menu of free time activities, oriented mainly to instrumental and achievement-oriented ends. Säfvenbom concludes, therefore, that a reconceptualisation of youth sport is needed in order to address the lack of fit between these activities and young people's own constructions of meaningfulness.

Through her analysis of four teenage girls' magazines, **Claudia Cockburn** continues the theme of young people's leisure and identity. She reminds us that the needs of many girls and young women are not met by traditional sporting structures and that popular magazines for girls offer contradictory and restrictive images of beauty, sexuality and physical activity. Her content and discourse analysis reveals few alternative identities for women and emphasises the risks and trivialisation associated with active engagement in sports. Teenage girls' identities are constructed discursively through representations that both privilege heterosexuality and belittle serious engagement in sports.

Representation is also the theme of the next paper, by **Judith Brown**, this time in relation to national (Scottish) rather than sub-cultural identity. Using a range of text- and image-based tourism and heritage sources and interpretive materials, Brown analyses the way in which representations of the famous Glencoe massacre have contributed to the shaping of Scottish national identity and, conversely, how notions of Scottishness have shaped representations of Glencoe.

Star Trek fans have often been portrayed as 'anoraks, geeks and nerds' yet, in a lively and provocative final paper, **Lesley Lawrence** demonstrates how their fandom might be regarded as a paradigm case of 'serious leisure' and no less marginal than many other, more commonly accepted leisure identities. Using findings from her participatory research, Lawrence examines the apparent mismatch in 'insider' and 'outsider' perceptions from the perspective of *Star Trek* fans themselves. One basis for criticism of the fans by outsiders is their alleged adherence to the idea of a 'social utopia' characterised by 'tolerance and equality'. Ironically, as Lawrence points out, it is these very values of social inclusion and equity that feature so strongly in *Star Trek* fan identity.

Lawrence's essay is an apposite ending for this volume, in which the reader is invited to reflect on both the just-ness of social inclusion/exclusion in contemporary leisure practices and the significance of leisure in identity formation.

Celia Brackenridge
David Howe
Fiona Jordan
Leisure and Sport Research Unit
Cheltenham and Gloucester College of Higher Education
October 2000

About the Contributors

Prof. Celia Brackenridge is Professor of Sport and Leisure at Cheltenham and Gloucester College of Higher Education and Head of the College's Leisure and Sport Research Unit. She chaired the Leisure Studies Association from 1993–95, edited the journal of Leisure Studies from 1995–97 and was the first Chair of the Women's Sports Foundation in the UK from 1984–88. Celia is an accredited BASES researcher, a staff tutor for the National Coaching Foundation and a World Class Adviser for the UK Sport Institute.

Judith E. Brown is a Senior Lecturer at Cheltenham and Gloucester College of Higher Education. She has a B. A. in Arts subjects from the Open University and an M. A. in Literary, Historical and Cultural Studies from Cheltenham and Gloucester College. Her teaching includes the history of tourism and heritage tourism. Her research interests are in representation and interpretation of heritage sites.

Claudia Cockburn is a postgraduate student at the Research and Graduate School of Education, University of Southampton where she has studied under the supervision of Dr Gill Clarke.

Jon Dart was a relatively late entrant to HE and graduated in 1995 with a degree in Leisure Studies. Jon then worked for Cambridge City Council to promote the city centre before starting a PhD on the non-work lives of traditional homeworkers and modern teleworkers (from which he presented a paper at LSA 98). He is currently studying part-time, being employed as a research assistant within the School of Leisure and Sports Studies at Leeds Metropolitan University.

Dr. Arnold H. Grossman, Ph.D., C.S.W., A.C.S.W., is a professor in the Department of Health Studies, School of Education, at New York University (NYU). He is currently the co-investigator of a research study focused on the victimization and mental health of lesbian, gay and bisexual (lgb) youths. He is also the principal investigator of two new research projects funded by NYU: one focused on transgender youth and the other on caregiving by older lgb adults. He recently served as principal investigator of a study that focused on the lives of older lgb adults, and he was the project director of a grant that trained professionals about mental health and HIV/AIDS. His teaching, research, and service focus on people who experience stigmatization, marginalization, and social exclusion.

Dr. Euan Hague, B.A. (Bristol); Ph.D. (Syracuse) was formerly a Post-Doctoral Research Fellow at Staffordshire University, but is now an Associate Professor in the Geography Department at Syracuse University USA. His research interests are in the social and cultural construction of personal, place and national identities. He currently teaches on the changing spaces of the city and is researching ideas of Scottishness in America.

Dr. P. David Howe, Ph.D is senior lecturer in the anthropology of sport at Cheltenham and Gloucester College of Higher Education. His research interests include ethnographic studies of pain and injury as well as issues related to the participation in and development of the Paralympic Games and sport for the disabled more generally.

Fiona Jordan is Course Leader for Leisure and Tourism Management at Cheltenham and Gloucester College of Higher Education. She graduated from Manchester Metropolitan University with a degree in Hotel and Catering Management, has a Masters degree in Leisure and Tourism Studies and is currently studying part-time for her PhD. Fiona is a former Secretary of the Leisure Studies Association Executive Committee. Her research interests are centred around the relationship between women and tourism. She has previously published in the areas of women in leisure and tourism management and the experiences of women as solo tourists. She is particularly interested in the impacts of space, culture and identity on women holidaying alone.

Dr Tess Kay entered sport and leisure research in 1981. She worked as a research assistant at Loughborough University for four years evaluating sport projects for the unemployed and completed her doctorate on leisure in the lifestyles of unemployed people. She is now a researcher in the Institute of Sport and Leisure Policy at Loughborough University. Most recently, Tess has published on leisure and labour market issues, especially with respect to gender.

Dr. Lesley Lawrence is a principal lecturer in Leisure and Sport Studies in the Department of Tourism and Leisure at the University of Luton with main teaching areas lying in the sociology of leisure and youth sport. She taught Physical Education before undertaking a doctorate on the professional delivery of leisure in education, focusing upon teachers' perceptions. Current research interests include the interrelated areas of: volunteerism, work and serious leisure. She is co-chair of the organising committee for the 2001 LSA Conference at Luton.

Eddy Lloyd is Principal Lecturer in the School of Leisure and Sports Studies, Leeds Metropolitan University. He initially trained as a teacher of physical education, worked in residential communities for five years before entering the university. More recently he was the course leader for the PE teacher training courses while maintaining his interest in the use of outdoors as a medium for personal development.

Jonathan Long is Reader in Leisure Studies in the School of Leisure and Sports, Leeds Metropolitan University, and was previously Research Director at the Centre for Leisure Research and the Tourism and Recreation Research Unit. Continuing to research on behalf of external clients, recent projects include: racism in cricket; partnership funding for the Heritage Lottery Fund; the influence of lifestyle on outdoor recreation. Jonathan is also in charge of post-graduate research students in Leisure and Sports Studies. He has been a member of the LSA since 1976; a former member of the Executive Committee (twice), Newsletter Editor and conference organiser. He was also on the editorial board of *Leisure Studies* for 15 years, at various times acting as editor and book reviews editor.

Håkan Larsson lectures in Physical Education theory at Högskolan Dalarna, School of Arts and Education in Falun, Sweden. He is about to finish a doctoral thesis on sport and the construction of manliness and womanliness during the second half of the 20th century. The main theme of this research is equal opportunities policy as a modern way of performing sex/gender difference.

Dr. Francis Lobo is Associate Professor in the School of Marketing Tourism and Leisure at Edith Cowan University. For over ten years he has researched into unemployment of seniors and young people. With unemployment causing material and psychological deprivations, Dr Lobo has long advocated equitable solutions to enable participation in public leisure. He proposes steps and strategies for continued leisure participation for those who lose their way.

Dr.ir. Hugo van der Poel is senior lecturer in the Department of Leisure Studies at Tilburg University (Netherlands). He wrote *Tijd voor vrijheid (Time for freedom)*, a Dutch introduction to leisure studies. His research focuses on sport and leisure policy. Recently completed reports deal with the future of Dutch sport policy; sport and social integration in new towns; and sport, space and physical planning. Hugo van der Poel is vice president of the Vereniging voor de Vrijetijdsector, the Dutch equivalent of the LSA.

Drs. Colette Roques completed her Master's degree in Leisure Studies at Tilburg University and worked as research assistant at the Department of Leisure Studies. At present she holds a similar position at the Centre for Research and Statistics of the Municipality of Rotterdam.

Reidar Såfvenbom holds a postdoctoral position at The Norwegian University of Sports and Physical Education. Until last year most of his research focused upon at-risk adolescents, and the developmental potential of leisure. Until 2002 he will be working on a project funded by the Norwegian Research Council, questioning ordinary adolescents' relationships to physical activity contexts.

Chris Thomas, B.A. (Wales) is a Senior Lecturer in Geography at Staffordshire University, with interests in the social and cultural geography of landscapes, communities and transport, and in qualitative methods. As well as researching social exclusion in urban and rural spaces, he has studied the historical geography of tourist and leisure landscapes.

Dr. Stephen Williams, B.Sc. (London); Ph.D. (Wales) is a Principal Lecturer in Geography at Staffordshire University. The author of *Outdoor Recreation & the Urban Environment* (ITP) and *Tourism Geography* (Routledge), his current research concerns recreation and tourism in post-industrial cities and the conceptual understanding of tourism. He is also actively engaged on consultant research on countryside visiting and the management of Areas of Outstanding Natural Beauty (AONBs).

I

Equity and Social Exclusion

The Sexist State: Leisure, Labour and the Ideology of Welfare Policy

Tess Kay

Institute of Sport and Leisure Policy
Loughborough University (UK)

Introduction

This paper makes an initial attempt to identify how particular forms of social policy may be important influences on individuals' experiences of leisure. The paper focuses on state policy towards reconciling paid work and family life, as an area of particular relevance to leisure analysts because of its impact on men and women's expectations of the role of paid and unpaid work. Employment status has been identified in leisure research as a significant factor affecting men and women's access to leisure (Deem, 1982, 1986; Dixey and Talbot, 1982; Green, 1996; Green, Hebron and Woodward, 1987, 1990; Henderson and Bialeschki, 1991; Kay, 1996, 1998; Wimbush and Talbot, 1988), with those in employment appearing to benefit from both the practical and psychological attributes of paid work. Family-related policies that affect mothers' and fathers' labour market activity may therefore have implications for gender differentiation in leisure. The paper considers two dimensions of the influence of family-related social policy:

- the extent to which family-related social policy discriminates between men and women, fostering gendered difference in lifestyles and leisure;
- the extent to which the influence of family-related social policy is experienced differently across the socio-economic spectrum, fostering diversity and polarisation in lifestyles.

The context

The relationship between contemporary leisure and social policy must be located in its socio-economic and political context. The current time is

3

recognised as one of rapid social, political and economic change. In Europe, socio-demographic, political and economic changes have been taking place in European Union (EU) member states since the union was established in 1957. The major trends include (European Union Directorate General V, 1997):

- the growing imbalance between older and younger people;
- changes in living arrangements and family life;
- changing relationships between men and women;
- the development of the information society;
- fundamental economic transformations;
- changes in working arrangements as individual work histories become more complex.

These changes have consequences for the appropriateness and viability of existing forms of social policy (Figure 1). The core challenge for policy makers is to maintain high standards of social protection without adversely affecting growth and competitiveness. There is increasing concern among policy-makers that existing national and supra-national policies may not be effective to meet the challenges that the above changes pose. There is much evidence already of the financial problems faced by social protection systems, and of their non-sustainability in the context of social and demographic change.

The current analysis is particularly concerned with the implications of changing patterns of employment for lifestyle and leisure, and the role of social policy in shaping these outcomes. Changing patterns of employment are an international phenomenon, with increases in women's employment accounting for most of the change in labour force composition throughout

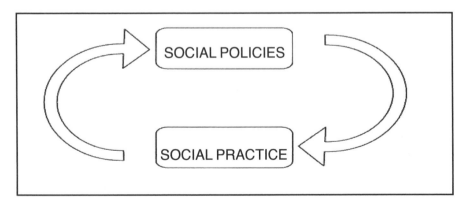

Figure 1   The relationship between social policy and social practice

the economically advanced nations. This is significant not only for its impact on women but also for how it affects households. The range of activities carried out by households, and the ways in which men and women meet the demands of those activities, are issues confronting the majority of the population (Brannen *et al.*, 1997).

It is clear that these issues have implications for gendered leisure behaviour. If nothing else, whether or not women are in employment has an impact on their leisure experiences. This impact is partly practical: women who are in paid work are more likely to have control over money for their own use, to have social networks beyond the home, and to have access to personal transport. Being employed also affects women's access to and perception of time: although employment reduces the amount of uncommitted time women have, it has the benefit of introducing a clear demarcation of 'work' and 'non-work' time. Women who have clearly defined paid work activities seem to have a stronger sense of entitlement to personal leisure than those who are involved in unpaid domestic labour, in which the boundary between 'work' and 'non-work' activities is less clear. More fundamentally, being in employment can challenge the traditional gender stereotypes that constrain women, both by removing their financial dependency on a male partner and by establishing a non-domestic area of activity as a substantial part of their lifestyle (Deem, 1986; Green, Hebron and Woodward, 1987, 1990; Kay, 1996, 1998). Whether women in heterosexual relationships are in employment or not is an important component in the way in which men and women relate to each other and, therefore, in the way in which gender ideology is constructed.

Identifying how policy affects these aspects of individual and household behaviour, and the process through which it does so, is problematic. However, there is a growing amount of research that indicates that family-related social policies are important influences on men and women's adult roles. Some of the strongest evidence of this comes from recent comparative analyses of the situation in the EU, where research has been stimulated by interest in the effect of supra-national policy-making on social practice in member countries (for example, Duncan, 1996; Kofman and Sales, 1996; Meyers *et al.*, 1998). Comparisons of family-related policies in the EU reveal very substantial differences between countries in relation to patterns of individual labour and in relation to patterns of paid and domestic labour in households. These comparisons strongly suggest that such differences reflect variations in social policy approaches. They also show that the impact of family-related social policy varies in its effects on men and women in different socio-economic circumstances. Family-related social policy therefore affects relationships between the sexes, and does so differently for different sub-sectors of the male and female populations.

Dividing the sexes: the relationship between male and female labour market participation and family-related social policy in the European Union

By the mid-1990s the main characteristics of male and female employment in the EU were as follows (see Table 1):

- On average, just over half (51per cent) of women of working age in the EU were in paid employment, but rates were highly differentiated across the EU countries. The level of female employment in Sweden, the highest in the EU, was 72per cent, more than twice as high as the lowest rate of 32 per cent, in Spain.

- Countries also varied in terms of the scale of differences between male and female employment rates. Overall, the proportion of women who were employed in the EU was 71 per cent that of the proportion of men but in some countries the gap was much wider and in some it was much smaller. Roughly speaking, the biggest differences were found in southern European countries and the smallest in the north.

- The picture was further complicated by women's involvement in part-time employment. Part-time employment is often adopted by women as a strategy for combining paid and unpaid work; for example, in Britain it is particularly common amongst mothers of school-age children. Whilst full-time work might be seen as a challenge to the tradition of the female as the home-maker, part-time work is often the opposite. For many women it is a way of sustaining the homemaker role. Most of the EU countries with the highest per cent of women in employment in 1995 did have high levels of part-time work. The EU average was 31 per cent and, of the four countries with the high female employment levels, three were well above that average.

Overall, different EU countries appear to have different expectations of the economic role of adult females. There is enormous variation in the proportion of women who do paid work, and also in the extent to which employed women may combine their employment with a home-making role. Both the practicalities and ideologies that underlie these patterns are affected by social policy.

The differences between male and female employment rates in EU countries are most evident when women become mothers. It is motherhood that leads to divergence between male and female employment patterns and household roles. In all capitalist patriarchal societies, women normally carry out the primary parenting functions for children, far beyond the biological processes of motherhood. It is in social policies that affect how women carry out motherhood that differences between EU countries emerge.

Table 1   Women's unemployment in the European Union, 1995

	% women employed	women's employment as % of men's	% of employed women working part-time (4 highest)
Spain	32	52	
Italy	36	54	
Greece	39	52	
Ireland	42	61	
Belgium	46	68	
France	53	77	
Netherlands	53	71	
Germany	54	75	
Luxembourg	56	57	
Portugal	56	75	
Austria	61	76	
Finland	60	94	16
UK	63	82	44
Denmark	68	82	36
Sweden	72	98	43

Borchorst (in Duncan, 1996) has coined the term 'political motherhood' to describe the influence that social policy has on the conditions under which motherhood is carried out. 'Political motherhood' results from mechanisms through which the political system shapes motherhood; these include legislation on marriage, benefits, children's rights, maternity/paternity leave, collective childcare, and so on. These have a practical effect on the conditions of motherhood; for example, the level of state childcare, which is free or relatively cheap, affects the ability of mothers to be in employment. However, policies are also significant because they embody ideology about the role of women within the family and the community. The way in which policies of these sorts set parameters for the daily life of men, women and families varies significantly between EU states.

Although a wide range of social policies affects motherhood, researchers tend to concentrate on the area of childcare provision as a particularly strong indicator of expectations about family roles. This is because the relative availability of childcare directly influences the work roles of mothers with younger children and has a knock-on effect on women's longer-term employment patterns. Levels of state childcare provision and schooling arrangements therefore embody assumptions about adult women's role in the family, and about employment in women's lives. However, they also clearly embody assumptions about how family households are expected to work and about how much differentiation there is to be between the roles of mothers and fathers.

Duncan (1996) has categorised EU countries according to the profile of women's employment, and the level of childcare associated with it (see Figure 2). He has identified three groupings: Group 1 countries, in which state policy supports the combining of motherhood with child-rearing; Group 2 countries, in which motherhood is combined with reduced maternal employment (for example, part-time work); and Group 3, in which the combination of the two roles is not encouraged. Typically, Group 1 countries have substantial state provision of childcare for the youngest pre-school children (age up to three), for older pre-school children (three plus) and for older children outside school hours, including holiday time. In these countries, collective childcare and paid work are part of motherhood. Countries in Groups 2 and 3 have low levels of state childcare for young pre-school children, with most so-called

Childcare policy supports ...	Pattern of female employment...	Countries
Dual role throughout working life	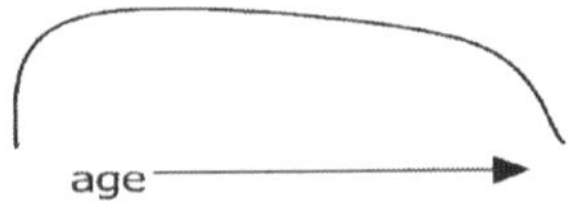 age ⟶	(Group 1) Denmark France Sweden
Dual role with homemaker/ part-time work role	 age ⟶	(Group 2) West Germany Netherlands UK
Homemaker	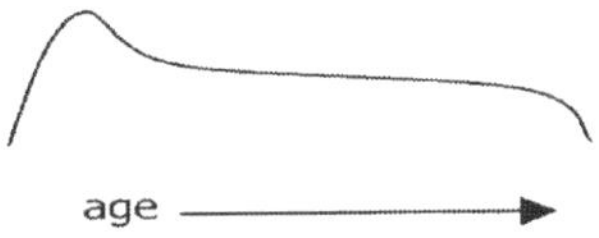 age ⟶	(Group 3) Luxembourg Belgium Portugal Spain Ireland Greece Italy

**Figure 2   Childcare policies and patterns of female employ-
ment in Europe; adapted from Duncan, 1996**

'childcare' provision coming through early entry into the schooling system. Childcare and schooling systems vary in whether they are part-time (for example, about half of Britain's provision for older pre-school children) or full-time, and in the nature of childcare. In West Germany, care for the youngest pupils takes place in the morning only with no lunch provided; in Sweden, care can cover the whole working day and include meals. There are similar differences in schooling arrangements: in France and Spain, the school day lasts eight hours, but in West Germany, only five. Thus, while in Group 1 countries schooling and collective childcare allows mothers to work full-time, in a situation such as West Germany's, childcare functions more as a support to the homemaker. Mothers can better devote a short amount of time, free from children, to domestic tasks and services.

When childcare comparisons are made, relationships emerge between levels of state-provided childcare and female employment rates. State childcare and schooling policies thus embody a broad societal consensus on the role of women during motherhood which affect mothers' labour market participation and this is one important component of how gender relations are acted out in heterosexual family units.

Another important element is obviously how men and women relate not to the labour market but to each other, through partnership. Here, we can consider the notion of the 'political family', in a similar way to how 'political motherhood' was previously recognised. Like 'political motherhood', the 'political family' is likewise defined through legislation, this time relating to ownership rights, inheritance, taxation, benefits, dependency, sexuality and so on.

Analysts of the different situation of 'the family' in EU countries have concentrated on divorce rates and rates of birth outside marriage as indicators of the relative political importance of the traditional family in personal relationships. On this basis three distinctive groups can be identified:

1. Countries with very low divorce rates and low rates of birth outside marriage; marriage is taken as a permanent relation and children are brought up within it. The countries in this category are Ireland, Italy, Spain, Portugal and Greece, the more peripheral capitalist countries with, until recently, strong religious influence on both the state and civil society.

2. Countries where marriage is no longer seen as necessarily permanent but where divorce rates are still relatively low and children are mainly brought up within marriage. This group comprises central European countries: the Netherlands, West Germany, Luxembourg, Belgium and, outside the EU, Switzerland. Here, state policy is usually used to bolster the traditional family.

3. Countries in which marriage no longer seems to provide the framework for either partnership or childbirth. These countries either have very high divorce rates, very high rates of births outside marriage, or both. They

include the Scandinavian European countries (Denmark, Sweden, Finland within the EU and Norway outside it), Austria and France. Britain appears to be in transition between Group 2 and Group 3.

From these differences we can see that social policy in different European Union countries embodies different conceptions of gender and gives different emphasis to the value of the traditional family. A more critical awareness of this may be helpful within our analyses of the interrelationships between men's and women's leisure, labour and welfare. Comparative analysis of this sort is valuable because it reminds us how specific the situation is in a single nation-state.

Dividing the women: the varied impact of family-related social policy in the United Kingdom

Low levels of state childcare provision suppress women's labour market involvement. However, social policy provisions do not have an equal impact on all sectors of the female population: while some women are heavily reliant on the state, others are better positioned to access alternative systems of support. Women vary, therefore, in how vulnerable they are to weaknesses and failings in social policy provisions. The point is well-illustrated in the case of state childcare provision in the United Kingdom, where the differential impact of social policy on different groups of women is clearly evident.

Working and mothering: the case of the United Kingdom

UK welfare policy embodies certain strongly gendered assumptions about the organisation of economic activity at the household level. Among the European Union states, Britain has long been characterised by its low levels of intervention to help parents combine employment and family life and has determinedly resisted EU initiatives that run contrary to this standpoint. State intervention to help households reconcile labour market participation and family care has not, therefore, been a policy goal for the UK. In consequence, British state childcare provision has been amongst the lowest in Europe. In 1995, only 2 per cent of British children under three were in publicly–funded daycare (Kofman and Sales, 1996), and although the figure rose to 35 – 40 per cent of children aged three to five, this was only because these figures included early entrance into the schooling system. In any case, the amount of childcare provided through early years schooling was, and remains, limited with approximately half the provision in Britain being part-time, that is available in mornings or afternoons only (Duncan, 1996). Overall, very little state childcare provision has been available to mothers of pre-school and early school-age children.

Despite this, British women's employment has been increasing, with the rise being greatest amongst mothers. Between 1975 and 1995 female employment in the UK rose from 63 per cent to 72 per cent. The most significant change was the growth in maternal employment, which rose at twice the rate for other women (by 10 per cent, from 49 per cent to 59 per cent) between 1984 and 1994, with the biggest increases among women with a child under five years old. However, this growth was very uneven: it was concentrated in the most affluent and well-educated social groups, while women in other situations experienced different or even opposite trends. Between 1984 and 1996, labour market activity increased among women with qualifications but for those without them it fell (Labour Market Trends, September 1997: p. 344).

By the mid-1990s there were, therefore, some very strong differences in patterns of maternal employment across the socio-economic spectrum. The main differences lay in levels of full-time employment. Whilst the majority of mothers were likely to be employed, there were large variations in the extent of their labour market involvement. In the lowest occupational categorisation, full-time maternal employment was very uncommon among mothers with a child under five, only 2 per cent of whom worked full-time (Pullinger and Summerfield, 1997; Office for National Statistics, 1997); the equivalent figure for mothers in professional or managerial occupations was 36 per cent. Although the full-time employment rate rose for both groups as children's ages increased, the differential remained very strong. Overall, about 60 per cent of working mothers in professional/ managerial occupations worked full-time while they had dependent children (aged up to 16), but only 10 per cent of working mothers in unskilled jobs did so. Mothers in low-status jobs had been relatively unaffected by the overall increase in UK women's employment levels during this period.

Differences in British mothers' labour market activity rates cannot be attributed solely to the availability of state childcare. Nonetheless, there is considerable evidence that the way that women compensate for the absence of state provision is an important influence on their labour market involvement. Most mothers who work part-time rely on non-institutionalised childcare to facilitate their employment, that is 'informal' care by parents or in-laws, other relatives, friends or neighbours (Ferri and Smith, 1996). Only a minority (28 per cent of those working less than 16 hours/week) use formal provision while they have a pre-school child in the household, and even smaller proportions do so when their youngest child has reached school-age (2 per cent of those working <16 hours, and 10 per cent of those working 16–34 hours). For the great majority of mothers working part-time, "the immediate or extended family [is] a crucial source of support in balancing the demands of employment and parenting" (Ferri and Smith, 1996: p. 23).

However, the amount of care provided in this way appears to be limited. For practical or emotional reasons, mothers who rely on relatives and neighbours to care for their children, while they themselves do paid work, are extremely unlikely to work full-time.

The situation is very different for mothers who do work full-time, who tend to be well-qualified women in higher status jobs. These women are usually partnered by men in similarly favourable employment situations and are more likely to use commercially-provided childcare (Brannen *et al.*, 1997). Such services are unlikely to be affordable for women working in low-paid and/or insecure occupations, who are equally likely to be partnered by men in broadly equivalent employment sectors to their own. The lack of state childcare provision therefore appears to be of considerable importance in constraining the labour market potential of mothers and households in the least affluent sectors of society.

In the UK, state policy towards pre-school childcare provision produces divergent experiences for women (Brannen *et al.*, 1997; Ferri and Smith, 1996; Kay, 1996, 1998). The practical consequences of such divisions are evident: they affect the financial resources and the individual and collective activity patterns of family households. However, these policy divides are also important for their ideological significance. They are most clear-cut in the contrast between employed and non-employed women although researchers have argued that the contrast between whether a mother is in full-time and part-time employment is also significant. Part-time employment for women does not necessarily challenge the maternal role to the same extent as full-time employment does, and may hardly challenge it all. For many women, part-time employment is a way of sustaining, rather than substituting for, the responsibilities of motherhood. Part-time employment may therefore confirm the female role as one of service to the household unit, with an emphasis on the traditional female responsibilities for domestic labour, childcare tasks and emotional sustenance. Her economic contribution is likely to be regarded as a relatively minor aspect of this, rather than a defining one.

The significance of welfare policy for analyses of leisure and gender

It has been argued here that the significance of welfare policy in influencing the way in which gender relations are played out in the home should be incorporated in the study of leisure, gender and the family. To date, the welfare policy context of gender relations has been given less attention in Leisure Studies than in the non-leisure literature on gender and family, where attention has been directed to the implications of rising maternal employment for state support of families combining paid and unpaid work roles. It is becoming apparent that there are measurable, if imprecise, relationships between these policies and family employment profiles, and that particular types of policy can have an important impact on the way in which the paid and unpaid work activities of households are distributed between men and women.

Nation-states vary in the extent to which they support families combining paid employment and caring, with the consequences of this being more directly borne by women. This is evident in the way that 'family' policies affect the economic activity of the sexes very differently. Male employment levels across countries are universally high regardless of the specific content of family policy whereas mothers' employment patterns in states with different approaches towards maternal employment contrast quite sharply. Women are, therefore, more vulnerable than men to the practical impact of state systems of support for families. What may be of equal or even greater importance, however, is that these policies do not *only* exert influence through their practical effects; they are also a particularly powerful medium for delivering an ideological message about a nation's current consensus on its social institutions. In the case of 'family' policies, the ideological message contains a powerful discourse on the preferred construction of contemporary motherhood and womanhood. Whether this emphasises traditional views of the complementary roles of the sexes, or more liberal conceptions of symmetry, may be significant in affecting whether women see themselves primarily as caregivers within the family unit, or as citizens with individualised rights.

Prevailing ideologies of motherhood and womanhood have been extensively recognised as fundamental influences on women's leisure (Green, Hebron and Woodward, 1987, 1990; Freysinger, 1997; Kelly, 1997; Shaw, 1997). Researchers have, however, tended to concentrate their more detailed analyses on the significance of social networks (relatives/friends/kinship networks) and on the mass media in perpetuating traditional ideologies of motherhood. It has been suggested here that fuller attention could also be directed to the role that state policy plays, which may be a particularly important influence because of the way it combines a direct practical impact with its ideological message. It is therefore important to recognise the practical and ideological content of welfare policy as one of the range of influences on lifestyle and leisure in present-day heterosexual family households.

Conclusion

Because child-rearing responsibilities are concentrated on female parents, social policies which affect how women carry out motherhood have a disproportionate significance for how the household, as a unit, combines child-rearing with economic activity. Levels of state childcare provision and schooling arrangements therefore embody assumptions about adult men's and women's roles in the family and about employment in men's and women's lives.

This paper has identified ways in which the influence of family-related social policy contributes to the construction of the gendered adult roles of heterosexual men and women that are recognised as influential discriminators in their experience of leisure. It has argued that:

1. State policies affect employment patterns for couple households, particularly impacting on women through policies towards state provision of childcare. The outcome is that women's labour market activity is affected much more than men's. This will impact on leisure through the direct relationship between leisure and employment, and through the implicit ideology of womanhood that such policies uphold.

2. Social policy fosters divides within, as well as between, the sexes. The impact of state policies is experienced differentially by women within the same nation-states:

- Women who are most dependent on state provision are more vulnerable to both the ideological and practical consequences of state policy in this area. These women are typically those with the lowest income, which is also related to the lowest educational qualifications and other indices of relative and absolute disadvantage.

- Conversely, women with least dependency on state mechanisms face more choices about the organisation of family life during the years of intensive parenting. The high incomes of highly-qualified women and their households provide a certain level of protection against inadequacies in public provision. In this way they may access adult experiences that are both less bound practically by, and themselves challenge the ideology of, state policy.

We can see that nation-states' family-related social policies embody conceptions of gender and the value of the traditional family. The ideologies of motherhood and womanhood, that are so widely recognised as influences on women's leisure, reflect very different cultural expectations and, through social policy, have very different practical manifestations. In comparison with men, women are likely to be more affected by this situation because of their more complex and multi-statused experience of the welfare state. In addition to, and often to the exclusion of, their participation in market activities, women continue to be the primary providers of unpaid caring and domestic work in the home. Women, therefore, have multiple roles and are far more likely than men to encounter the welfare state both as needs-bearing clients and as rights-bearing citizens and consumers (O'Connor, 1996; Orloff, 1993).

More fundamentally, Meyers, Gornick and Ross (1998) have suggested that policies that affect maternal employment have important implications for women's social citizenship. They argue that opportunity to participate in the labour market is a 'necessary condition' of social citizenship (Meyers *et al.*, 1998); as O'Connor puts it, "independence is the key to citizenship and in the democratic welfare state, employment is the key to that independence" (O'Connor, 1996: p. 78). Whether family-related policies encourage women to see themselves primarily as caregivers within the family unit or as citizens with individualised rights is likely to affect both their sense of entitlement to personal leisure and their ability to access it. From this perspective parenthood can be said to compromise women's access to social citizenship.

References

Brannen, J., Moss, P., Owen, C. and Vale, C. (1997) *Mothers, fathers and employment: Parents and the labour market in Britain 1984–1994.* Research Report No. 10, Department for Education and Employment. London: HMSO.

Central Statistical Office (1995) *Social trends 25.* London: HMSO.

Deem R., (1986) *All work and no play? The sociology of women and leisure.* Milton Keynes: Open University Press.

Deem, R. (1982) 'Women, leisure and inequality', *Leisure Studies* Vol. 1, No. 1: pp. 29–46.

Dixey, R. and Talbot, M. (1982) *Women, leisure and bingo.* Leeds: Trinity and All Saints College.

Duncan, S. (1996) 'The diverse worlds of European patriarchy', in M. D. Garcia-Ramon, and J. Monk (eds) *Women of the European Union.* London: Routledge, pp. 74–110.

European Commission (1996) *Employment in Europe.* Brussels: European Commission.

Ferri, E. and Smith, K. (1996) *Parenting in the 1990s.* London: Family Policy Studies Centre and Joseph Rowntree Foundation.

Freysinger, V. J. (1997) 'Redefining family, redefining leisure: Progress made and challenges ahead in research on leisure and families', *Journal of Leisure Research* Vol. 29, No. 1: pp. 1–4.

Green, E. (1996) 'Gendered cultures of time: Does a more flexible female workforce mean less available leisure time for women?'. Paper to the international Conference on New Strategies for Everyday Life; Work, Free Time and Consumption, Tilburg University, December 1996.

Green, E., Hebron, S. and Woodward, D. (1987) *Gender and leisure: A study of Sheffield women's leisure.* London: Sports Council/Economic and Social Research Council.

Green, E., Hebron, S. and Woodward, D. (1990) *Women's leisure, what leisure?* London: Macmillan.

Henderson, K. A. and Bialeschki, M. D. (1991) 'A sense of entitlement to leisure as constraint and empowerment for women', *Leisure Sciences*, Vol. 13: pp. 51–65.

Kay, T. A. (1996) 'Women's work and women's worth', *Leisure Studies* Vol. 15, No. 1: pp. 49–64.

Kay, T. A. (1998) 'Having it all or doing it all? The construction of women's lifestyles in time-crunched households', *Leisure and Society* Vol. 21, No. 2: pp. 438–454.

Kelly, J. R. (1997) 'Changing issues in leisure-family research – again', *Journal of Leisure Research* Vol. 29, No. 1: pp. 132–134.

Kofman, E. and Sales, R. (1996) 'The geography of gender and welfare in the European Union', in M. D. Garcia-Ramon, and J. Monk (eds) *Women of the European Union*. London: Routledge, pp. 31–60.

Labour Market Trends (1997) 'Working households, unemployment and economic inactivity', *Labour Market Trends* September: pp. 339–345.

Meyers, M. K., Gornick, J. C., and Ross, K. E. (1998) 'Public child care, parental leave, and employment', paper presented to the First Workshop of the Network on Working and Mothering: Social Policy and Social Practice, TSER (Targeted Socio-Economic Research), Lund.

O'Connor, J. (1996) 'From women in the welfare state to gendering welfare state regimes', *Current Sociology* Vol. 44, No. 2: pp. 273–296.

Office for National Statistics (1997) *Living in Britain: 1995 General Household Survey*. London: The Stationery Office.

Orloff, A. S. (1996) 'Gender in the welfare state', *Annual Review of Sociology* Vol. 22: pp. 51–78.

Pullinger, J. and Summerfield, C. (eds) (1997) *Social focus on families*. London: Office for National Statistics, The Stationery Office.

Shaw, S. M. (1997) 'Controversies and contradictions in family leisure: An analysis of conflicting paradigms', *Journal of Leisure Research* Vol. 29, No. 1: pp. 98–112.

Wimbush, E. and Talbot, M. (eds) (1988) *Relative freedoms: Women and leisure*. Milton Keynes: Open University Press.

Equity or Exclusion?
Contemporary Experiences
in Post-industrial Urban Leisure

Euan Hague, Chris Thomas and Stephen Williams

Community, Identity and Participation Research Group,
Geography Division, Staffordshire University (UK)

Introduction

The urban landscape has always been dominated by change as much as
continuity. The expansion and contraction of the physical edifices of industry,
commerce, dwelling and recreation have impacted hugely upon the fabric
of urban spaces throughout the world. Such landscape changes are closely
tied to social, economic and cultural changes in urban society. In the late-
modernist, post-industrial world of Britain, at the turn of the twentieth and
twenty-first centuries, our cities are changing shape, perhaps more rapidly
than at any time since the industrial revolution. Industries which had taken
a century or more to grow have contracted and disappeared in a decade. As
'regeneration' becomes the zeitgeist of the late-modern age, industrial sites
are rapidly transformed to residential and retail developments, or quickly
filled by new high-tech industry and sports stadia, with little if any referent
remaining of their former significance. Names that might have offered clues
to erstwhile factories, steelworks or collieries are replaced with topographic
neologisms that hint at a less industrial past than is actually the case, such
as Meadowhall in Sheffield, or Festival Park in Stoke-on-Trent, which we
examine in this paper.

Perhaps the most significant component within this emergent urban
landscape of late-modernity is leisure. Boosted by the release of space and
time which was previously occupied in the main by work, the world of leisure
is more obviously present and seemingly more inclusive than ever before
within the urban landscape. Meanwhile, new technologies such as personal
computers, satellite and cable television reconstruct the notion of leisure at
home. At the same time, multiplex cinemas, fast food restaurants and retail

parks redefine the choice of discretionary leisure behaviour outside the home. For example, on retail parks, Do It Yourself (DIY) stores bridge the gap between public and home-based leisure.

Within this paper we argue that such expanded leisure opportunities and activities are far from the inclusive arenas that their ubiquity might suggest. Rather than being accessible to all, many of these 'new' opportunities and activities of the expanded leisure market are inherently exclusive. Whilst progressive constructions of inclusive leisure are often presumed, the spaces, places and experiences of leisure in the late-modern urban landscape are structured by practices of exclusion that operate both implicitly and explicitly.

Current debate in Britain regarding 'exclusion' focuses upon processes of social exclusion. This conceptualisation centres on social inequality, marginalisation, poverty, disadvantage and deprivation. These concerns form the basis of research by the government's Social Exclusion Unit (SEU), founded in 1997 (for example, SEU, 1997; 1998a; 1998b; 1998c; 1999a; 1999b; 1999c). Within this context, political debate about 'social exclusion' has encountered leisure but rarely investigates this as a relevant area for further detailed research. Unlike issues of housing and unemployment, for example, there is little discussion of how leisure provision may alleviate social problems or indeed why exclusion from leisure is considered to be problematic (Aitchison, 2000; Coalter, 2000).

Drawing from recent field research investigating leisure exclusion in urban areas of North Staffordshire, this paper discusses some basic conceptualisations of exclusion from leisure opportunities and facilities. We concentrate on the extent to which exclusion may be conceived as working in a diverse range of ways and affecting groups that would not normally be considered to be 'socially excluded' nor likely to be identified as 'disadvantaged' by traditional indicators. The leisure patterns of such groups may be expected to reflect notions of equity. Nevertheless, our research suggests that these people experience a wide range of exclusionary practices in the construction of their everyday leisure lifestyles.

The paper is arranged in two parts. First, we set out some basic observations on the nature of leisure, equity and exclusion in the 'postmodern city' (Scraton and Watson, 1998) and outline a typology of exclusionary contexts influential in shaping leisure patterns within such places. These contexts will affect both individual and communal experiences of leisure and help to highlight the divergent and often unseen channels through which practices of exclusion may operate. Secondly, a brief and preliminary investigation is undertaken of the extent to which some of the different forms of exclusion are revealed in usage of the post-industrial leisure location of Festival Park. This is an entertainment and retail complex located in Stoke-on-Trent. Evidence gathered from site observation and household surveys is used to argue that not only is this supposedly public site of leisure actually highly exclusive, but also that this exclusivity is a strategic aspect of the construction of such contemporary spaces of leisure.

Equity or exclusion in post-industrial urban leisure?

Since 1970, public leisure provision has been founded on principles of equality that is welfarist. The *Sport for All* campaign is arguably the most memorable and explicit articulation of this approach (see, for example, Sports Council, 1982; 1988). Even though such indiscriminate direction of policy has been questioned (see, *inter alia* Williams, 1995) and more recent policies for sectors such as sport have revealed shifts towards a more focused pattern of investment, political motivations for leisure provision still tend toward the notion of equity (Aitchison, 2000). Yet, the vast differences in people's lifestyles mean that many people do not fit within these structures of leisure provision (Coalter, 2000), not least because of the substantial changes in the physical, economic and social composition of Britain's urban areas over the same period. These 'post-industrial' or 'post-modern' transformations of urban space (see, *inter alia*, Castells, 1991; Dear and Flusty, 1998; Hall, 1996; Lash and Urry, 1994; Sassen, 1991, 1994; Soja, 1989, 1995) have seen facilities like multiplex cinemas, shopping malls, theme pubs and relocated football stadia fundamentally alter the geography of urban areas and their associated leisure opportunities. Despite the apparent benefits of utility and accessibility, these new leisure spaces are not as all-inclusive as some of their developers claim. Leisure facilities are defined by many rules governing whom has access and what behaviours are appropriate therein. Consequently, leisure spaces are 'policed', sometimes quite literally, but often in more subtle ways, to determine who is an appropriate user.

The rapidly changing post-industrial city accentuates the relationships between equity and exclusion that constitute the leisure experiences of many people today. However, rather than looking at *equity* as the standard by which leisure opportunities are measured, a better way of framing and directing leisure policy is to focus upon *exclusion* from leisure. The complex philosophical questions and presumptions that impinge upon notions of equity suggest an approach that will largely provide conflicting and potentially unproductive forms of intervention. In contrast, the concept of exclusion enables the researcher to recognise that what may appear equitable is typically exclusive in effect.

Exclusion is both materially and discursively constructed (Samers, 1998). Practices of exclusion in one of these fields typically generate exclusionary processes in the other. As Kirby (1996: p. 13) makes clear: "patterns of belonging and excluding may function in the first instance only to divide conceptual space, but they finally operate materially, structuring physical spaces". Discursive exclusions can, therefore, have material effects. Whilst taking heed of this dualistic division of exclusionary practices, we suggest a more particular conceptualisation for the investigation of leisure exclusion. This builds different types of exclusion into a framework that differentiates exclusionary effects according to how exclusion is experienced.

As we indicated above, participation in leisure is regulated, licensed and policed by individuals and institutions and leisure activities are culturally and socially structured. Processes of socialisation or '*habitus*' (Bourdieu, 1986) allow some people in some contexts to accept situations of exclusion unquestioningly or even unknowingly. Other exclusions are openly recognised and contested.

To attempt to frame these fluid and uncertain dimensions of exclusion, we adopt, and adapt, Bourdieu's notion of '*doxa*' (Bourdieu, 1977; 1986; 1990a; 1990b; 1992; 1993; Bourdieu and Eagleton, 1992). *Doxa* refers to the societal realm of that which is "undiscussed" and "undisputed" (Bourdieu, 1977: p. 168), defining areas of experience that are taken for granted, the "unquestioned social conceptions that acquire the force of nature" (Fowler, 1997: p. 92). The concept of *doxa* understands people just accept things as they are without really thinking about them, rather than being misguided by an authorial ideology. Eagleton, amongst others, has criticised this conceptualisation suggesting it leaves no room for "dissent, criticism and opposition" and maintains that *doxa* asserts a "natural" state of affairs that renders repression invisible (Bourdieu and Eagleton, 1992: p. 114). This is, of course, Bourdieu's point. *Doxa* is the realm of things that are taken for granted and incorporated unconsciously. They may be repressive, but this is made invisible as people do not even consider contesting them. Precisely because *doxa* is not thought about, it cannot be articulated and opposed in the same conscious manner as an ideology. Consequently, as the relations of *doxa* are unquestioned they are, by implication, legitimate.

People do not acknowledge *doxa* until they confront its barriers and boundaries. Bourdieu makes this evident in his diagrammatic explanation of the relationship between the taken for granted *doxa* and an adjacent area of contest (orthodoxy and heterodoxy), the "universe of discourse and argument" (Bourdieu, 1977: p. 168) (see **Figure 1a**). Yet, despite Bourdieu's demand that this model is flexible, his concept appears to be rather static. The boundary between the taken-for-granted and the contested seems either solid or crossed in an instant. We propose that an area of ambiguity, a liminal space, should be added to this visualisation — a zone of transition between the contested and uncontested (see **Figure 1b**).

Superimposing notions of inclusion and exclusion on this model suggests there are clear polarities of inclusion and exclusion that are either never

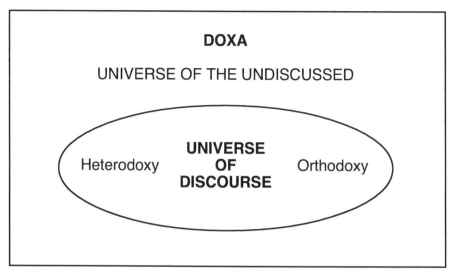

Figure 1a

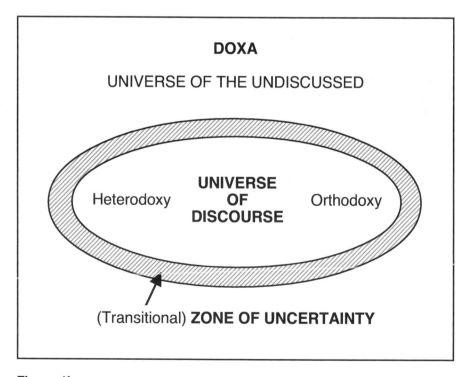

Figure 1b

challenged or are regularly contested. In addition, there is an area of uncertainty in which exclusionary practices impinge, with varying degrees of clarity and force, upon an individual's experiences. By using this augmented version of Bourdieu's concept, we propose the following three discrete forms of exclusion:

- *embedded exclusions* that are probably permanent or, at least, long-term. Located within *doxic* societal realm, these are neither consciously identified nor, if they are identified, questioned;

- *evident exclusions* which lie with Bourdieu's 'universe of discourse' and which are therefore obvious, contested and debated, having been actively acknowledged and questioned;

- *episodic exclusions* that occur within the transitional area between these two other realms of experience. Their impact upon the consciousness of a subject is variable and largely contextual. They are likely to be short-term and consequently so is the extent to which they are questioned. They may be produced by minor shifts in the taken-for-granted realm and its temporal, spatial or social parameters of experience, for example, through the pursuit of a familiar form of leisure activity in an unfamiliar location or a familiar location occupied by an unfamiliar social event or group.

In association with this tripartite division of exclusionary processes as 'embedded', 'evident' and 'episodic', we have identified six *contexts* through which exclusion can be experienced. These may operate alone or in combination to produce their exclusionary effects. We understand them as follows:

Legal exclusion includes statutory laws, legally binding regulations on individuals or institutions, written or unwritten codes of practice. Leisure is one sector in which legal constraints are prevalent creating exclusionary situations. Examples include the widespread use of legal licensing (such as for the sale and consumption of alcohol, the performance of entertainment); regulation of leisure sites (for example, fire and safety regulations) and the imposition of non-statutory 'rules' (for example, designation of no-smoking zones or the use or dress codes at venues such as night-clubs).

Accessibility exclusion relates to site access. This can include the effects of distance and transport costs and the physical ability to access a location. Issues of disability access and exclusion have been discussed by, amongst others, Kitchen (1998b). With leisure facilities increasingly clustered at locations such as retail and entertainment parks that are typically found on the outskirts of urban areas, transportation increasingly governs access to urban leisure. Those who are immobile, or relatively so, find their leisure opportunities restricted.

Financial exclusion reflects the inability to pay for leisure goods and services, or to access financial services (such as credit — see Leyshon and Thrift, 1995) that are becoming more essential to the purchase of leisure goods and services. Leisure is increasingly a commercial enterprise in which the ability to pay is central to questions of access and exclusion. This is not necessarily a consequence of poverty and may occur in other parts of the community with greater disposable income.

Technological exclusion refers to the trend in many areas of contemporary leisure for participation to be dependent upon technological skills and knowledge. Nowhere is this more apparent than in access to the leisure worlds of cyberspace and virtual realities. The 'computer age' is often heralded as an era where equality will dissolve conventional barriers that cause exclusion. However, not only do hardware and software command substantial fees, but cyberspace is a socially constructed "space dominated by white, middle class males from Western nations who can converse in English and are generally in their late teens or early twenties" (Kitchen, 1998a: p. 112). Technological competence and confidence are always selectively focused and there will always be significant portions of society who do not feel comfortable using new technologies.

Identity exclusion occurs in situations of outright discrimination against individuals on the basis of their social identity — for example, age, race, gender, sexuality, class, religion, etc. It is well understood that leisure participation is fundamentally shaped by issues of identity. In the post-industrial world, leisure is now replacing more traditional influences, especially work, on the construction and projection of personal and collective identities (see, *inter alia*, Kelly, 1983; Crouch and Tomlinson, 1994; Rojek, 1995).

Cultural exclusion arises in situations based upon real or perceived cultural differences between groups, or prevailing views of certain cultural groups as being "out-of-place" in particular spatial or social contexts (Cresswell, 1996; Hague *et al.*, 2000). The exclusion of many black citizens from leisure sites in the British countryside is one example (see Sibley, 1995). In cities, the occupation at night of central entertainment zones by teenagers and young adults may exclude others for whom such a cultural milieu is distressing.

It is important to stress that this conceptual typology is neither exhaustive nor mutually exclusive. At times many of these exclusions overlap, reinforce each other, or are brought into play by other contextual factors. For many people, therefore, even if they are relatively affluent and unencumbered by constraints of physical mobility, exclusion from leisure spaces and activities can occur in a range of ways.

The influence of agency is a final element that needs to be taken into account in conceptualising exclusion in leisure. In other words, some people will be *doing* the excluding, whilst others are *being* excluded. Furthermore, exclusion may be a consequence of the actions of others as *external* influences on the leisure choices that we make. Alternatively, it may be a form of *self-exclusion* in which we exclude ourselves as a result of our own perceptions and apprehensions of particular leisure sites, activities or situations (Hague *et al.*, 2000).

Case study: Festival Park, Stoke-on-Trent

To illustrate how these theoretical proposals translate into everyday patterns of exclusion we turn now to the case of Festival Park in Stoke-on-Trent. Here, we aim to illustrate how this post-industrial leisure space is a site of multiple exclusions. Some of these are stipulated by the producers of leisure at the site, others are created by the behaviours, circumstances and attitudes of consumers. All act to exclude people and constrain the opportunities for leisure in this post-industrial landscape.

Festival Park covers approximately sixty-four hectares in Stoke-on-Trent and is primarily located on part of the former industrial land of British Steel's Shelton Works. The majority of the area was reclaimed for the National Garden Festival in 1986 and has since become a centre for business, retailing, entertainment and, most recently, residence (Thomas and Hague, 2000). Leisure facilities on site include a commercial leisure pool with flumes and wave machines, an artificial ski slope, a multi-screen cinema, an amusement arcade, a laser-quest game, a ten pin bowling centre, a bingo club, a snooker club and various pubs and restaurants, including major fast food retailers. All the facilities are, at most, ten years old. There is also a system of nature trails together with some gardens and areas of open space retained from the Garden Festival, that together account for twenty-six hectares. One unusual aspect of the facilities at Festival Park is that although they are common to a host of similar edge-of-town developments, the site is within one mile of Stoke-on-Trent's city centre.

The incidence of exclusion at Festival Park was investigated through a combination of methods. Initial observations carried out at the site itself were supplemented by eliciting the views and opinions of a sample of one hundred residents from the Trentham Park ward of the city, an area of good-quality housing with significant concentrations of 'middle-class' residents (see **Figure 2**). This survey contained a wide range of questions concerning the leisurely uses and non-uses of a diversity of sites across the city as a whole, and a section dealing specifically with Festival Park. The profile of the respondents suggested an essentially established community (with over 40 per cent resident in the area for more than twenty years), with a majority falling within middle and older-age groups. The sample revealed a predominance of professional, white-collar occupations and mobility levels were high with car

Indicator	Trentham Park
Population	15,588
Percentage of Stoke-on-Trent's total population	6%
Population change (1981– 1991)	+13.4% *
Age profile: Children under 15 years	19.9%
Age profile: Young people 16– 29 years	18.8%
Age profile: Adults 30– 60 years (women) and 30– 65 years (men)	43.6%
Age profile: Pensioners (men >65 years; women >60 years)	17.7%
Number of households	6,072
Level of owner-occupation	85.6% *
Level of council tenancies	9.2% **
Level of privately rented housing	3.8%
Level of Housing Association housing	0.7% **
Number of pensioner households	31.4%
Households without a car	21.5% **
Lone parent households	2.0% **
Male economic activity (16– 65 years)	88.6% *
Female economic activity (16– 60 years)	74.5%
Unemployment	5.4% **
Households with residents having long term illness	22.6% **
Occupations: Class I and II (professional/managerial)	42.7% *
Occupations: Class III (skilled manual)	32.9%
Occupations: Class IV and V (partly skilled/unskilled)	12.7% **
Educational achievement: Those with diploma or degree	15.6% *

*   Highest ranked ward in Stoke-on-Trent for this indicator
**   Lowest ranked ward in Stoke-on-Trent for this indicator

Figure 2   **1991 Census data pertaining to Trentham Park ward in Stoke-on-Trent. (There are currently twenty wards in Stoke-on-Trent).**
(Source: City of Stoke-on-Trent, 1991)

ownership at 87 per cent. Levels of ownership of leisure goods were also high suggesting, in most cases, a 'leisure-rich' lifestyle (Bernard, 1988).

Outwardly, these advantages translated into quite extensive patterns of usage of the Festival Park site by residents sampled within the survey. However, in some cases it became clear that usage was shaped by a perceived lack of choice or, more complexly, by exclusion from other leisure places, which lead to the use of Festival Park. The supermarkets, discount and DIY stores were used by over 40 per cent of the people interviewed, the multiplex cinema by 61 per cent of the sample and the various fast-food restaurants by an average of 29 per cent. Other leisure facilities such as the leisure pool and the ten-pin bowling complex also attracted significant levels of use. Across all categories, visits tended to be made at relatively extended intervals, with over three quarters of the sample stating they visited only once a month or less.

Many of the respondents expressed favourable opinions of the development. The absence of charges for car parking and the proximity of parking areas to the main facilities compared favourably with other city centre shopping and leisure areas. The environmental improvements that had accompanied the conversion of a derelict site to a major zone of amenity which included landscaped greenspace also drew considerable positive comment. However, although the attraction, ease of use and convenience of the site appealed to some users, several of the contexts of exclusion that we have hypothesised in the first sections of this paper became evident in the context of Festival Park.

First, legal exclusions stemmed from the private ownership of Festival Park. Like many commercially-oriented leisure spaces, the public is allowed to use the facilities provided at the behest of a developer who imposes 'regulations' concerning usage. These apply especially to the open spaces within the site, where two roadside signs (neither of which are located beside the main retail and leisure buildings) detail conditions of use (**Figure 3**). Note the 'small print' at the bottom of this sign which states that, "access to this area is given by kind permission... No public right of way is granted". Although this leisure and retail complex proposes itself as public space that is accessible to all, it is in fact private land which could be controlled, and access restricted, as the owners demand. There are direct parallels with indoor shopping malls which occupy deceptive, anomalous positions as 'private-public' spaces (Shields, 1989).

Secondly, complex sets of exclusions relating to accessibility are evident. The access to the site is principally afforded by high-capacity, dual-carriageways, with the inevitable result that cars dominate travel to the site, with an additional public transport presence. There are greater risks attached to gaining access by walking or using two-wheeled vehicles (especially bicycles), with such vehicles deliberately excluded from the open spaces of

Access to open space.
Please help to maintain the quality of this open space for the enjoyment of all by observing the following regulations.
Please keep to pathways.
Leave no litter.
Keep all dogs on lead.
No cycles motorcycles.
No camping.
No fires.
No access during hours of darkness.
Access to this area is given by kind permission of St. Modwen Developments. No public right of way is granted.
Thank you for your co-operation.

Figure 3   Signpost at Festival Park, Stoke-on-Trent

the development (see **Figure 3**). This creates access conditions that encourage particular types of visitor, namely car users. Such a scenario is repeated at other shopping centres in the English Midlands, such as Merry Hill (Dudley) where 85 per cent of the users visit by private car but only 60 per cent of the population in this area actually have cars (Mintel, 1996; OPCS, 1992).

The privileging of car owners is emphasised through deficiencies in the levels of public transport access to the site. As well as the paucity of walking routes, scrutiny of bus timetables reveals that the frequency of services is often poor. The best level of service is once every twenty minutes and the worst offers just one journey per day. Furthermore, on several scheduled bus routes, the last buses run before the entertainment facilities at the site close for the evening, especially the cinemas. The lack of direct bus services to more distant parts of the city (such as Trentham Park) is also an issue, as split journeys take longer and cost more. Many respondents in the survey area expressed frustration at the lack of access by public transport. They understood Festival Park to be out-of-the-way and inaccessible, even though it is only a mile from the central business district of the city and approximately four miles from Trentham Park. One middle-aged woman explained: "From Trentham there is no direct bus to Festival Park. You need to get two buses and go via Newcastle[-under-Lyme] or Hanley" (Female, 35–44 years). A younger man also commented:

> Not enough buses go to [Festival Park] from the city centre, it's too far out of the way. You need a car really. We would go to shop there and we would go there more, if we had a car. (Male, under 25 years)

Accessibility issues also deterred and excluded people who otherwise enjoyed the mobility of a private car. Traffic congestion, particularly entering and leaving the site, was described repeatedly as a discouragement, as was the fact that the road system seems to be poorly designed and minimally sign-posted. Car parking was described by one person as "hideous" and by another as "grim".

Although it is possible to walk to Festival Park along a canal tow-path, respondents suggested that the poor maintenance of this route, its lack of tarmac and lighting makes such a journey unattractive. One man stated: "The canal path is excellent for cycling, but maintenance is very poor and in the winter it gets very muddy" (Male, 35–44 years). The same person who commented on the infrequency of buses continued: "The canal walk isn't really nice and it's not considered safe. There's old iron and industrial works all along there and it's not pretty" (Male, under 25).

Negative perceptions of the safety of the access systems were also identified. An elderly respondent encapsulated the views of many of the older residents when she stated:

> I stopped going to the cinema there as they stole my wheels and hub caps from my car and you can't do anything about it. My neighbour's car was stolen from the car park there. I've stopped going there because while I'm enjoying the film, my car is being damaged while I'm inside. (Female, over 65)

A member of the city police force commented:

> You can't really get out of the car park, and you get boy-racers belting up and down the roads there if the roads are not closed in and blocked. There's a bad atmosphere at night, with young kids drunk and hanging around. I wouldn't want my kids to be down there at night. (Male, 35–44 years)

This remark signals the presence of forms of cultural and/or identity-based exclusion. One interpretation of the developers' preference for car-based travel and the limitations placed upon two-wheeled vehicles, especially when combined with the type of retailers and entertainment facilities at Festival Park, is that the site is constructed with the intention that families are a domi-nant user group. However, the routine use of the area for unapproved forms of leisure, for example by the groups of youths hanging-out after dark, creates alternative forms of identity for the site. As the preceding quote makes clear, this encourages forms of self-exclusion. Even the younger respondents (under 25 years old) often mentioned feeling 'out of place' at Festival Park, particularly in the evenings when the 'illicit' forms of leisure tend to come to the fore.

Identity exclusions varied with age. Many people over thirty-five felt cut off from the entertainment facilities offered at Festival Park which are strongly skewed towards more youthful sectors of the leisure market. The result was that many older people, particularly pensioners, did not visit Festival Park at all. They often mentioned they had visited once when the site first opened in the late-1980s and had decided not to go back.

Although the sample was composed of predominantly affluent groups, some people mentioned what we interpret as financial exclusions associated with the Festival Park facilities. Certain shops and leisure facilities, in particular a fitness centre and the leisure pool, were highlighted as particularly expensive. Those commenting on the inconvenience of the bus routes also noted that having to get two buses increased the cost of travelling to Festival Park, particularly as the main bus companies do not offer transferable or through tickets.

Conclusions: The exclusivity of urban leisure

Our paper has concentrated on views offered by comparatively affluent, mobile people. These are subjects who would not normally be associated with problems of 'social exclusion' or exclusion from leisure. Nevertheless, they were able to identify a range of factors that conspired to discourage or exclude their participation at this major leisure site. Festival Park, as a shopping and entertainment complex, emerges as a place which both attracts and deters members of the public. Exclusivity is built into the geography of Festival Park in a number of ways: the 'legal' controls over approved activities; through a consciously fostered pattern of access and accessibility that privileges certain sectors of the community; the blending of facilities to form a particular identity for the site and hence, its users; the pricing policies within the individual enterprises that encourage use from more affluent groups whilst excluding those whose leisure exists within more limited budgets.

The comments of the survey respondents also provide evidence of the presence of embedded, episodic and evident forms of exclusion. For some people there were *embedded* forms of exclusion from Festival Park that map directly onto Bourdieu's doxic realm of the taken-for-granted. This is especially true of elderly respondents who felt there was little or nothing of interest to them at Festival Park and, consequently, the facilities of the site were never consciously considered when making leisure choices. *Episodic* forms of exclusion also emerged, especially amongst respondents who sensed a temporal shift in the social dynamics of the site that rendered the night-time environment threatening, risky or inappropriate. We might hypothesise that the 'boy racers' and youth gangs whose presence may prompt the episodic exclusions of others, could be understood to be contesting the 'taken-for-granted' constructions that surround the *evident* practices of exclusion at the site.

Leisure is, therefore, not 'just leisure' either in terms of equality or of being merely or solely 'leisure'. Leisure is considerably more complex and leisure activities that one does not do, that one feels excluded from, are as important to understanding this sector as the activities that one does practice. Leisure is, of course, a cultural system. It is filled with symbolic meanings and motives that engage people in its pursuit. We agree with Rojek (1995) that ideas of 'escape', 'choice' and 'freedom', and even equity, are far too often assumed as inherent in the practice of leisure. But leisure is not necessarily equal and access to leisure sites can be highly policed or constrained, restricted or, ultimately, denied. This is often not explicit, and something as simple as a financial cost can often determine unequal access to leisure. "The further we probe into the matter of what leisure is, the greater is our appreciation of the part played by cultural mores, distinctions and conflicts in establishing the parameters of debate and also what occurs in leisure time and leisure space" (Rojek, 1995: p. 2).

Leisure spaces such as Festival Park market themselves as locations for 'exclusive entertainment' and they are, quite literally, exclusive. The owners of the businesses do not want to permit access to certain people, behaviours are proscribed and requests for compliance are politely enforced. Exclusion is, therefore, created within a flexible and multi-dimensional framework in which the forms and contexts of exclusion may intersect and produce situations of 'multiple exclusion', or run in parallel and consistently affect certain individuals or communities.

As our brief examination of Festival Park illustrates, some forms of exclusion are externally imposed, some by the circumstances under which people live, others being self-imposed through the perceptions and apprehensions that we form around particular leisure sites. Utilising Bourdieu's concept of *doxa*, we have argued that societal norms and social discourses structure processes of leisure exclusion. These, in turn, produce the kinds of disparate and sometimes unpredictable effects that we have attempted to conceptualise through our delineation of evident, embedded and episodic forms of exclusion and our illustration of a range of exclusionary contexts.

References

Aitchison, C. (2000) 'Leisure and urban exclusion: Developing leisure geographies and geographies of leisure', *North West Geographer* Vol. 3, No. 2: pp. 13–20.

Bernard, M. (1988) 'Leisure-rich and leisure-poor — leisure lifestyles among young adults', *Leisure Sciences* Vol. 10, No. 2: pp. 138–153.

Bourdieu, P. (1977) *Outline of a theory of practice.* Cambridge: Cambridge University Press.

———— (1986) *Distinction: A social critique of the judgement of taste.* London: Routledge & Kegan Paul.

———— (1990a) *In other words: Essays towards a reflexive sociology.* Cambridge: Polity Press.

———— (with Boltanski, L., Castel, R., Chamboredon, J-C. and Schnapper, D.) (1990b) *Photography: A middle-brow art.* Cambridge: Polity Press.

———— (1992) *The logic of practice.* Cambridge: Polity Press.

———— (1993) *The field of cultural production: Essays on art and literature.* Cambridge: Polity Press.

Bourdieu, P. and Eagleton, T. (1992) 'In conversation: Doxa and common life', *New Left Review* No. 191: pp. 111–121.

Castells, M. (1991) *The informational city: Information technology, economic restructuring and the urban-regional process.* Oxford: Blackwell.

City of Stoke-on-Trent (1991) *Stoke-on-Trent in the nineties: An atlas of the 1991 Census.* Stoke-on-Trent: Policy and Information Group of the Department of Planning and Architecture.

Coalter, F. (2000) 'Sport and social exclusion — a lot of balls?'. Paper presented at the Annual Conference of the Leisure Studies Association, Glasgow Caledonian University, July.

Cresswell, T. (1996) *In place / out of place: Geography, ideology and transgression.* Minneapolis: University of Minnesota Press.

Crouch, D. and Tomlinson, A. (1994) 'Collective self-generated consumption: Leisure, space and cultural identity in late modernity', in I. Henry (ed) *Leisure: Modernity, post-modernity and lifestyles* (LSA Publication No. 48). Eastbourne: Leisure Studies Association, pp. 309–321.

Dear, M. and Flusty, S. (1998) 'Postmodern urbanism', *Annals of the Association of American Geographers* Vol. 88, No. 1: pp. 50–72.

Fowler, B. (1997) *Pierre Bourdieu and cultural theory: Critical investigations.* London: Sage.

Hague, E., Thomas, C. and Williams, S. (2000) 'Leisure and exclusion: power, identity and the boundaries of participation', *North West Geographer*, Vol. 3, No. 2: pp. 3–12.

Hall, P. (1996) *Cities of tomorrow: An intellectual history of urban planning and design in the twentieth century*. Oxford: Blackwell.

Kelly, J. R. (1983) *Leisure identities and interactions*. London: George Allen and Unwin.

Kirby, K. M. (1996) *Indifferent boundaries: Spatial concepts of human subjectivity*. New York: Guildford Press.

Kitchen, R. (1998a) *Cyberspace: the world in the wires*. Chichester: John Wiley.

——— (1998b) 'Out of place — knowing one's place': Space, power and the exclusion of disabled people', *Disability and Society* Vol. 13, No. 3: pp. 343–356.

Lash, S. and Urry, J. (1994) *Economies of signs and space*. London: Sage.

Leyshon, A. and Thrift, N. (1995) 'Geographies of financial exclusion: financial abandonment in Britain and the United States', *Transactions of the Institute of British Geographers (New Series)* Vol. 20, No. 3: pp. 312–341.

Mintel (1996) *Leisure shopping*. London: Mintel International Group Ltd.

Office of Population Censuses and Surveys (OPCS) (1992) *1991 UK Census — County Report West Midlands*. London: HMSO.

Rojek, C. (1995) *Decentring leisure: Rethinking leisure theory*. London: Sage.

Samers, M. (1998) 'Immigration, "ethnic minorities" and "social exclusion" in the European Union: a critical perspective', *Geoforum* Vol. 29, No. 2: pp. 123–144.

Sassen, S. (1991) *The global city: New York, London, Tokyo*. Princeton: Princeton University Press.

——— (1994) *Cities in a world economy*. Thousand Oaks (CA): Pine Forge Press, Thousand Oaks.

Scraton, S. and Watson, B. (1998) 'Gendered cities: Women and public leisure space in the postmodern city', *Leisure Studies* Vol. 17, No. 2: pp 123–137.

Shields, R. (1989) 'Social spatialization and the built environment: the West Edmonton Mall', *Environment and Planning D: Society and Space* Vol. 7, No. 2: pp. 147–164.

Sibley, D. (1995) *Geographies of exclusion: Society and difference in the West*. London: Routledge.

Social Exclusion Unit (SEU) (1997) *Social Exclusion Unit: Purpose, work priorities and working methods*. London: Cabinet Office.

——— (1998a) *Rough sleeping*. London: The Stationery Office.

——— (1998b) *Truancy and school exclusion*. London: The Stationery Office.

——— (1998c) *Bringing Britain together — A strategy for neighbourhood renewal*. London: The Stationery Office.

——— (1999a) *Teenage pregnancy*. London: The Stationery Office.

————— (1999b) *Bridging the gap: New opportunities for 16–18 year olds not in education, employment or training*. London: The Stationary Office.

————— (1999c) *Review of the Social Exclusion Unit*. London: Cabinet Office.

Soja, E. (1989) *Postmodern geographies: The reassertion of space in critical social theory*. London: Verso.

————— (1995) 'Postmodern urbanization: the six restructurings of Los Angeles', in S. Watson and K. Gibson (eds) *Postmodern Cities and Spaces*. Oxford: Blackwell, pp. 125–138.

Sports Council(1982) *Sport in the community: the next ten years*. London: The Sports Council.

————— (1988) *Sport in the community: Into the 90s*. London: The Sports Council.

Thomas, C. and Hague, E. (2000) 'Steel blooms — Exploring the symbolic landscape of Etruria', in T. Edensor (ed) *Reclaiming Stoke-on-Trent: Identity, leisure and space in the Potteries*. Staffordshire University Press.

Williams, S. (1995) *Outdoor recreation and the urban environment*. London: Routledge.

What's the Score? Using Sport and Leisure as Diversion

Jonathan Long, Eddy Lloyd and Jon Dart

School of Leisure and Sports Studies,
Leeds Metropolitan University (UK)

Introduction

Amid widespread concern with youth crime, very different initiatives have been developed to address 'the problem'. These have varied from pernicious curfews to schemes that have been caricatured as rewarding bad behaviour with fun and holidays. Schemes that seek to use involvement in sport and leisure as a means of diverting young people from crime and anti-social behaviour now abound.

We have recently been involved in the evaluation of an initiative devised as a multi-agency project, led by the local authority, to provide a fast and innovative response to the issues identified by the *Misspent Youth* report (Audit Commission, 1996). As the initial bid for funding explained, the main aim of the *Menthol*[1] project was to be "to guide young people at risk into constructive use of leisure and legitimate activities through the use of volunteer mentors". This newly-established project works with young people referred from the youth justice system (though their participation is voluntary)[2]. They are introduced to mentors recruited and trained by *Menthol*, who engage them in sport and leisure activities, working on a one-to-one basis with them; it is the closeness of this relationship which is perhaps the most unusual aspect of the scheme.

The purpose of this paper is not to form a judgement on whether or not the scheme is a success (that will be done elsewhere), but to use evidence from the scheme to address some of the claims and counter-claims surrounding diversionary projects. In particular, we shall be drawing on data from qualitative interviews conducted with both mentors and young people. This is a very deliberate attempt to learn from the personal experiences of those at the heart of the project. Rather than dwell on the issue of reoffending we shall be more concerned here with examination of issues relating to the establishment of relationships, self-esteem, confidence and overcoming disinterest.

Ours is essentially an outsider's view; those more closely involved may well have a different story to tell. Throughout though we have tried to provide a dispassionate account and give voice to some views that have been offered to us *because* we are 'outsiders'.

Learning from elsewhere

Some initiatives are applied as a preventive or prophylactic measure to forestall problems (a); others are more targeted at individuals who have already encountered the justice system (b).

a) An example of the former is the *Reczones* project in Bolton (Morgan, 1998) where there is a strategy to provide sports development work in the community which has recognised that previous attempts at youth diversion projects have been undermined by lack of suitable infrastructure. Consequently, four multi-use games areas are being provided in conjunction with the sports development work.

b) Perhaps the best known example of the latter is *Solent Sports Counselling*, which has taken many different forms through its now quite lengthy life (it was incorporated into the Hampshire Probation Service in 1987). The overall aim was of "developing an interest in sport amongst offenders and those clearly considered to be at risk, aged over 17". Staff worked with clients to draw up a diet of activity with an emphasis on establishing personal relationships with each client, both in terms of counselling and development of the activity programme (Hampshire Probation Service, undated).

It should be noted that many of the projects receiving national attention have much greater resources than *Menthol*.

Little has changed since Glyptis (1989: p. 153) argued, in another context, that "virtually all provision had been made on the basis of assumed need and assumed benefit" and concluded that claims of assumed benefits were rarely backed up by evidence. However, although still limited, there is now a growing literature presenting attempts to evaluate the success of such schemes. It would still be true to say, however, that there are mixed views about the effectiveness of sport and leisure in diverting young people from crime and anti-social behaviour. Coalter (1989) maintained that none of the studies he reviewed succeeded in establishing a causal link between low incidence of 'delinquent behaviour' and participation in sport. Quite the reverse was argued by Begg *et al.* (1996), who suggested that those involved in sport were *more* likely to be delinquent. However, evidence from North America (for example,

Farrell *et al.*, 1995; Witt and Crompton, 1997) and from *West Yorkshire Sports Counselling* (Nichols and Taylor, 1996) is much more positive. Participation in WYSC was associated with a significant reduction in re-offending rates. Evaluating the *Midnight Basketball Leagues*, Farrell *et al.* (1995) claimed that, beyond the headline 30 per cent reduction in crime rates in the target area, participants and fans not only had a safe haven where they could engage in positive social activities and channel their energies, but also increased their educational and career aspirations.

While there may be an expectation that the outcomes of projects should reveal big changes Coopers and Lybrand (1994) have suggested that relatively small changes would in fact be sufficient for a project of the scale of *Menthol* to repay its outlay. Most of the projects they examined would only need to keep two or three young people from reoffending for a year to 'pay their way'. It should be noted that those calculations do not take account of very important qualitative benefits that cannot be quantified in monetary terms, for example avoiding the psychological damage to 'victims'.

In an earlier paper, Segrave (1983) sought to identify the major theoretical perspectives that have been used to try to address the relationship between sport and juvenile delinquency, dividing them into psychological perspectives ('recapitulation', surplus energy, personality, and stimulus seeking) and sociological perspectives (boredom, sub-culture, strain, and control). In practice, policy initiatives tend to pick and choose a convenient combination of beliefs from this range of perspectives.

In summary, our reading of the existing literature indicates that the advocates of using sport and leisure based 'diversionary' schemes seem to invoke five main types of reason why such schemes may reduce offending and anti-social behaviour generally:

- occupying time (busy-ness preventing the Devil finding work for idle hands) and offering diversion;

- providing a safety valve of acceptable activity in more worthwhile pursuits which may also satisfy 'stimulus seeking' desires — also known as sensation seeking (Zuckerman, 1994);

- offering something positive in and amongst the negative – associating their lives with reward and encouragement rather than purely punitive action;

- enhancing self-esteem – through the development of skills that allow them to be seen to be successful;

- improving the ability to construct inter-personal relationships (both with peers and adults).

These tend to presume the therapeutic value of sport and leisure (Coalter, Long and Duffield, 1989) and are associated with processes of socialisation.

However tenuously, they can be attributed to various theoretical traditions in the development of youth studies (see, for example, Roberts, 1983) that have drawn attention to issues such as psychological processes of adolescence, weak social control, learned failure and 'labelling'. Thus, although the issue of self-esteem is currently associated with issues of identity formulation, this has long been part of bio-psychological theories of adolescents trying to redefine their identity in the transition to adulthood (for example, Rapoport and Rapoport, 1975). Similarly, the concern with interpersonal relationships can be seen to be a modern development of the earlier emphasis on conflict between generations. The idea that such programmes can offer a safety valve might be questioned because of the essentially sanitised nature of what they offer, activities unable to replicate the risk found in the activities from which 'society' wishes to divert them. They do not compensate for "the moral and sensuous attractions in doing evil" (Katz, 1998). Indeed Lupton (1999: p. 149) draws attention to an alternative ideal of the self that celebrates "sensual embodiment and the visceral and emotional flights produced by encounters with danger". In this context the very nature of sport and its rules and structures may stop many of the target group becoming involved.

Some of the difficulties in assessing the contribution of schemes have been attributable to a rather monolithic interpretation of sport, what it is and what it offers. Although this may persist in terms of evaluation, many of the more recent practical projects in particular have sought to adopt a client centred approach, and indeed to expand beyond sport (or outward bound) to a broader approach based on 'leisure counselling'.

For community-based intiatives, as in other areas of evaluation, the pursuit of a scientific model of evaluation may be inappropriate and something more than purely quantitative measures is required (Lightfoot, 1994). Moreover, our methodology had to be one that was sensitive to the political and ethical issues surrounding the *Menthol* project (Long and Dart, forthcoming) in an example of 'real world research' (Robson, 1993). Our involvement was to provide evaluation that would be as comprehensive yet unobtrusive as possible. To this end, we were able to analyse data from the project's own monitoring forms (for example, for sessional reviews and mentor supervision review) and other records, and to conduct interviews with both mentors and young people. We rejected the idea of using standardised questionnaires because we decided that they were unlikely to be well received by our respondents, which would have consequences for response rates and data quality. We also considered that it would be difficult to design a single questionnaire suitable for the range of age, maturity, assurance and intelligence of the young people on the programme. In line with the spirit of the project, we opted for something that would allow respondents to have some influence on the agenda, feeling that the rigidity and formality of questionnaires might compromise the establishment of a relaxed and productive relationship between the respondents and the research team.

The qualitative interviews were administered differently for the two sets of respondents. The interviews with the young people in the programme were conducted face-to-face in as informal a manner as possible in a neutral, safe environment. The interviews with mentors were conducted by telephone shortly after we had attended a mentors' support meeting to discuss their involvement in the evaluation.

Overcoming boredom

Boredom and associated lack of motivation were identified as characteristic of the lives of many of the young people on the scheme. All reported being encouraged to suggest activities they might enjoy, but Damien's (age 14) response was "I don't want to do anything".

> [Mentor] has suggested things to do ... go-karting — I could go to new places and do new things if I wanted, but I'm not interested. We meet outside the library ... talk for about 15 minutes. If it's raining then we go inside. Sometimes I don't go ... I'm in bed [at 3 in the afternoon].

At the very least the scheme's activities offer something to do: McDonald's, swimming, paintballing, go-karting, cinema, scuba diving, touring the shops, scratching (with motor biking and snow-boarding eagerly anticipated). Alan (age 14) recognised he had done new things and gone to new places – "things that I wouldn't have done otherwise". This matched responses from the mentors:

> The feedback I've had is that it's 'something to do'. In certain circumstances there's nothing else available, so it's well worth giving it a go really... 'cos the young man I'm assigned with, initially he was under a bit of pressure on all fronts, so it was a means of him doing something, and other people seeing him do something.

Alan was very enthusiastic about the scheme because he no longer had to steal to get money to do things; he got to do them for free through *Menthol*. Although less enthusiastic, Rick (age 14) thought his friends might get involved in crime just to get on the scheme so they could do things they might not otherwise have access to (not what the *Menthol* Steering Group wants to hear).

Mentors were cautious in their assessment of their ability to overcome the problems of boredom:

> For the length of the session yes, but the situation they were in, any suggestion I made about what they might do when they went home — boredom mode, real boredom mode. Any suggestions I made were

shrugged off. While they were at the session that was fine, but beyond that...

One of the mentors suggested:

> I'm not entirely convinced that informal activity could end up being really enough by itself to make that transition from getting involved in trouble to finding something better and getting involved in something diversionary — I'm not sure it's enough. I think it's a really brilliant idea and offering them these activities does occupy them. But by itself... I think it needs to dovetail in with some other more formal structure. For the type of young person that's getting involved in this, I don't think the options that are available are going to help them out of what they're caught up in...It's very easy to dip in and out — do the activity and go home...you need something much more formally structured.

Although they probably knew to expect it, mentors tended to be frustrated by the unwillingness of the young people to make any kind of commitment and get involved. Efforts were made to persuade them to move from casual swimming to life saving classes, courses were discussed and other activities suggested that would involve regular attendance.

> Ideally I would have liked to get their agreement to start some lessons in life saving or something like that so that there was some progression, more involvement and commitment. I came up against quite a bit of resistance. Anything with a level of involvement, there was a real blockage there. Anything like a longer term course was blocked.

> I was looking for something that would give a challenge and some time to reflect... Because of his interest in bikes I tried to push him towards a club so that he'd have something to carry on with, but he made it clear he didn't want that kind of involvement.

Relationships

The variety of activities is both a strength and a weakness of *Menthol*. The activities are the attraction for some of the young people to get involved in the scheme and different activities can be chosen depending upon their appeal week by week. This provides the opportunity for a relationship to be established with an adult, but because the activity may change from week to week (McDonald's, swimming, cinema) this is comparable with a separated father/ mother turning-up at the weekend to treat their child. A lack of purpose, commitment, development or progression in the participation means there is not likely to be anything inherent in the activity that will induce positive or reflective change. As a consequence, this throws the entire burden for the success of the scheme onto the relationship; this is an onerous responsibility for volunteers. The nature of this relationship is complex.

Perhaps not surprisingly those who agreed to be interviewed appeared to get on reasonably well with their mentors and were probably more committed to the scheme. In some cases this was because of similar interests; for example, Adrian (age 16) and his mentor both like doing active things. However, not having things in common did not preclude a good relationship.

> I don't think I've anything in common with [mentor] ... but that's not really a problem ... but if [mentor] was older then it might be.

Even Damien who, at the height of his enthusiasm, commented, "Didn't expect owt so I'm not disappointed", had said yes [to being on the scheme] "cos it was an answer" and went on to note that *Menthol* had given him a chance to "meet 'normal' people — people who aren't teachers like". One mentor, thinking it through, suggested that the young person saw him as a bit of a pain but a safe haven: "I don't think he feels he needs me. I'm someone who's there though if things go wrong". Two others commented:

> Certainly not a mother. I was cool apparently — cooler than parents — she wasn't embarrassed to be with me, she wanted to play her music for me. We sometimes met people she knew and I was just introduced as Linda.

> My role is to support a young person in crisis without dwelling on the past — not to probe — just be there for them. I concentrated on the activities side to start with and then over the period tried to get his confidence, gradually share things... He brought his music with him in the car — perhaps you don't share that with your mother...but he was very respectful of me because I was that bit older. At the end of the day it's got to be a professional relationship. You've got to be yourself, otherwise you wouldn't come across as genuine, but rules or guidelines to follow are useful.

In such circumstances, mentors need guidance on whether they should be expected to encourage the young people to reflect on what brought them to be on the scheme, or to emphasise a new start, building for the future. Either approach might be perfectly legitimate but it is an onerous responsibility for a volunteer mentor to decide which is likely to be more successful in diverting a young person from crime. From the perspective of the young people involved in the scheme, in some relationships offending was up for discussion and in others it just never occurred:

> I have talked with [mentor] about getting into trouble, and why I've
> not to get into more trouble. It does get a bit boring talking about it
> ... I don't really see the point, it's not like it's useful or anything.

On the other hand, Adrian, who said that if the scheme ended he would miss
chatting with his mentor (not just the activities), seemed more prepared to
talk with his mentor about the original reason for being on the scheme. This
is intertwined with how the nature of the relationship evolves over time:

> Initially I did find it very difficult to chat with him. I wasn't sure sort
> of what were the right and wrong things to say, you know, what topics
> it was all right to talk about and how hard I should press him... He
> knows that I'm not a threat to him — sees me more like a friend —
> it's easy to converse and he knows I'm not going to disclose anything
> he tells me. The training said to challenge swear words and things
> like that, but I found it easier to let it ride to start with. Once I got a
> relationship going I was able to start to challenge some of his attitudes.

In some cases progress was felt to have been compromised by insufficient
contact. This is fairly obvious when the young person has failed to show-up
(not always the fault of the young person who may be dependent on a lift
from other adults to get to the meeting place). But even when they did show
up, some mentors felt that one relatively short meeting a week did not provide
enough time to develop a close relationship.

Many of the diversionary projects using sport and leisure have recognised
the crucial role of keyworkers, and in other contexts use mentors: for example,
there are befriender schemes in Croydon, Milton Keynes and Powys; and a
mentoring project in Hammersmith and Fulham (Institute for the Study and
Treatment of Delinquency, 1997). But the use of mentors in a 1:1 relationship
focused on sport and leisure makes *Menthol* unusual and potentially of interest
to the rest of the country. Mentors were attracted by the idea of working 1:1
with a young person but tended also to view the prospect with trepidation,
which was one of the reasons why the training was so warmly received. Having
experienced this style of working, mentors were divided over whether it was
the best way to proceed, or whether better results might be achieved through
groupwork. More of them had experience of groupwork and so felt more
comfortable with that kind of model.

Two mentioned having to deal with the issue of whether or not friends
should be allowed to join in the activities (contrary to the principles of 1:1
working). More of them mentioned that friendship networks had a far greater
influence on the young person than they as mentors could realistically expect
to have; one respondent referred to this in terms of having difficulty in *breaking
the delinquent link*.

Confidence and self-esteem

An evaluation of SPACE (a project in Leeds that uses group work alongside a programme of 'challenging activities' to encourage young people at risk to examine their attitudes and behaviour) concluded that the project had been successful in enhancing self esteem and improving attitudes towards committing crime (Lumsden, 1998): the evidence, however, is unconvincing. Its significance here is that improving confidence and enhancing esteem is central to the *Menthol* project. From one perspective some of the young people in the project are not lacking in confidence; indeed, the actions that got them into trouble in the first place need 'confidence' (or bravado?). The incentive offered for them to attend the 'de-briefing' with the researchers held little value for some, with one young person saying he could go out and steal a record rather than attend an 'interview' and collect a token. This kind of confidence, however, is not necessarily readily transferable. Certainly mentors commented that, at the outset, the young people lacked the confidence even to suggest activities they would like to try. While engaging in activities to improve self-esteem might have been valued as an objective by those running the scheme, it has to be set against peer pressures as alternative calls on time and loyalty. Lacking self-confidence, some of the young people felt uncomfortable about admitting to friends that they were on the scheme.

Some of the *Menthol* mentors attributed improved relationships to greater confidence on the part of the young people they were working with and this was reciprocal: as the relationship improved so confidence was gained. Confidence also came through tackling new challenges and operating in different environments away from the locations of their crimes and misdemeanours. New activities allowed an escape from preconceived behaviour patterns as the shake-up takes the young person out of their norm. In one sense, then, the sport or leisure activity is almost incidental: it is the process that is important, and this is what mentors need to be sensitive to. The full benefits, though, are only likely to be obtained if there is an investment in 'reviewing' to allow interpretation of what happened (Priest, 1990; Greenaway, 1993). When working well this focuses on the more meaningful experiences and is conducted so that the young person comes to understand what they have done without feeling that they have been interrogated.

However, as implied above, the nature of the activities did have significance. Many of the activities were not 'new' but were quite ordinary, thereby perhaps unduly elevating the significance of the relationship between the young person and their mentor. Although the mentors were willing to organise and plan 'big events', a combination of apathy and unreliability on the part of the young person made sure that this did not happen very often. Unusually, funding was not the major inhibitor; that proved to be the challenge of getting the young people more involved. Our proposition here is that this would have been easier had the young people been more confident but that may be a misplaced assumption. We concluded that the confidence of the young people might have been better improved had there been a greater element of challenge (rather than the everydayness of going shopping or eating at McDonald's). Alternatively, similar outcomes might have been provided by a more sustained commitment to an activity (rather than the pick-and-mix approach) but, as already noted, mentors perceived major resistance to such commitment. The 'big' activities (like paintballing, go-karting and snowboarding) were enjoyed and probably offered more potential for enhancing self-worth and confidence. However, these activities were typically undertaken as a group and not in the 1:1 format, which may have implications for the underpinning principles of the project.

As noted above in a different guise, even if it is possible to develop confidence in doing an activity, there is no guarantee that the confidence can be transposed to other areas of the young peoples' lives. At issue then is: 'Confidence for what?' There is a world of difference between knowing how to snowboard and relating to an adult who is not going to 'judge them' and/ or becoming a better citizen.

Conclusions

Classically, this project proved to be full of ambivalences, in relation not just to whether or not it was successful but also to the nature of the relationship between the mentor and the young person, the relationship between the past and the future, and levels of obligation and challenge. Mentors were divided in their views on issues of compliance and enforcement. It is difficult to see what benefits can accrue without attending the scheme (or how it could be seen as part of the solution in such circumstances) but any obligation to attend/ remain on the scheme might be self-defeating. Non-engagement, however, ought to trigger a review of their contract with the state.

We have already drawn attention to the importance of the nature of the activities selected. Although they may not initially be the watchwords, we believe it would be appropriate to review periodically both challenge and commitment. Moreover, it is hard not to question how realistic are the expectations of the scheme given that it operates (when things are going well) on approximately two hours contact a week. The mentor is separated from the rest of the young person's life. On the one hand this is a strength of the scheme because the mentor can remain apart from the normal agents of repression that the young person experiences. At the same time, however, the lack of linkages is a shortcoming as the major benefits are likely to derive from connection between the project and the mainstream of the young person's life.

Typically, both young people and mentors were ambivalent about the outcomes. For example:

> ... keeps me out of trouble 'cos it's doing things ... I don't think it's made a difference to me what I do. (Adrian)

> I'd be getting into more trouble if I weren't on the scheme ... I don't think it's helping me achieve anything. (Damien)

Although it is important to enthuse mentors at the outset, it may be necessary to make sure that they have their sights lowered without 'turning them off'. Not all the interventions will be successful; they just cannot be, nor do they need to be to justify the project. However, to ensure that the benefits are maximised there needs to be further training of mentors to support them in how to do the 'reviewing', such that non-judgmental reflecting secures the learning by the young people they are working with.

One of the major frustrations for the project workers is that they feel they rarely have the time necessary to effect any real change. As the Coopers and Lybrand study indicates though, even apparently small-scale benefits can be extremely cost-effective. A sustained positive relationship with an adult can be a significant benefit in its own right. Beyond that we were also able to record feedback on positive attitude changes, increased self esteem, more thoughtful reflection on behaviour and constructive use of leisure time through exposure to fulfilling activities.

Notes

[1]   As might be expected this is a pseudonym.

[2]   The nature of the respondents' 'crimes' is not serious, therefore making it easier for us to work with them than might have been the case had the tariff been higher. Despite Tidwell's (1994) argument that they might be considered not to be 'at risk', but to have arrived, they are clearly 'at risk' of re-offending and encountering a series of consequent damaging effects. We are mindful though of the argument of some social anthropologists that identifying them as being 'at risk' justifies social coercion and a requirement to conform to moral values (Lupton, 1999).

References

Audit Commission (1996) *Misspent youth: Young people and crime*. London: The Audit Commission.

Begg, D., Langley, J., Moffitt, T. and Marshall, S. (1996) 'Sport and delinquency: An examination of the deterrence hypothesis in a longitudinal study', *British Journal of Sports Medicine* Vol. 30: pp. 335–341.

Coalter, F. (1989) *Sport and anti-social behaviour: A literature review*. Research Report No. 2. Edinburgh: the Scottish Sports Council.

Coalter, F., Long, J., and Duffield, B. (1989) *Recreational welfare*. Aldershot: Avebury/Gower.

Coopers and Lybrand (1994) *Preventative strategy for young people in trouble*. London: Prince's Trust.

Farrell, W. C., Johnson, J. H., Sapp, M., Pumphrey, R. M. and Freeman, S. (1995) 'Redirecting the lives of urban black males: An assessment of Milwaukee's Midnight Basketball League', *Journal of Community Practice* Vol. 2, No. 4: pp. 91–107.

Glyptis, S. (1989) *Leisure and unemployment*. Milton Keynes: Open University Press.

Greenaway, R. (1993) 'Reviewing adventure activities', *Journal of Adventure Education and Outdoor Leadership* Vol. 10, No. 1: pp. 11–12.

Hampshire Probation Service (undated) *Sports counselling information pack*. Hampshire County Council.

Institute for the Study and Treatment of Delinquency (1997) *The ISTD Handbook of community programmes for young and juvenile offenders*. Winchester: Waterside Press.

Katz, J. (1998) *Seductions of crime: Moral and sensuous attractions in doing evil*. New York: Basic Books.

Lightfoot, J. (ed) (1994) *Towards safer communities: Community development approaches to crime*. London: Community Development Foundation.

Long, J. and Dart, J. (forthcoming) 'Opening-up: engaging people in evaluation', *International Journal of Social Research Methods*.

Lumsden, J. P. (1998) *A Study on SPACE*. Unpublished report available from Leeds City Council.

Lupton, D. (1999) *Risk*. London: Routledge.

Morgan, D. (1998) '*Sport off the Streets*' — *a preliminary analysis of the need for 'Reczones' in the 3Ds area of Bolton*. Paper presented to the Sport v. Youth Crime Conference, Bolton, 19th November.

Nichols, G. and Taylor, P. (1996) *West Yorkshire sports counselling — Final evaluation report*. Leisure Management Unit: University of Sheffield.

Priest, S. (1990) 'The adventure experience paradigm', in J. C. Miles and S. Priest (eds) *Adventure Education*. State College, PA: Venture Publishing.

Rapoport, R. N. and Rapoport, R. (1975) *Leisure and the family life cycle*. London: Routledge.

Roberts, K. (1983) *Youth and leisure*. London: George Allen and Unwin.

Robson, C. (1993) *Real world research: a resource for social scientists and practitioner-researchers*. Oxford: Blackwell.

Segrave, J. (1983) 'Sport and juvenile delinquency', *Exercise and Sport Sciences Review* Vol. 11: pp. 181–209.

Tidwell, R. and Corona, S. (1994) 'Youth at risk: In search of a definition', *Journal of Counselling and Development* Vol. 72 (March/April): pp. 444–447.

Witt, P. and Crompton, J. (1997) 'The at-risk youth recreation project', *Parks and Recreation* Vol. 32, No. 1: pp. 54–61.

Zuckerman, M. (ed) (1994) *Behavioral expressions and bio-social bases of sensation seeking*. Cambridge: Cambridge University Press.

Social Disadvantage and Leisure Access: The Case of the Unemployed

Francis Lobo

Edith Cowan University, Perth (Western Australia)

Introduction

This chapter examines how unemployment disadvantages young people in their leisure. Through analysis of qualitative and quantitative data, the study conducted in Western Australia shows that young people are materially and psychologically deprived in their leisure. Unemployment adversely affects the leisure of many, in and out of the home. Outside the home, activities for fitness, sociability, and entertainment are reduced in quality and quantity. Membership of clubs and associations is likewise affected. Current social policies use the concept of citizenship to include young people within the community as full participating members, ensuring that they are not exploited or abused and that their welfare is sustained and supported: but this study shows that unemployment socially excludes young people.

Unemployment leisure and disadvantage

The psychological consequences of unemployment are not homogenous (Fryer, 1995). There is considerable individual variation in the severity of the psychological impact of unemployment. Two theories dominate. They are the deprivation and the personal agency approaches.

Arguing from the deprivation approach, Jahoda (1992) suggests that employment promotes well-being by providing people with a time structure, social contacts, a collective purpose, a sense of identity, and regular activity. These five 'categories of experience', as she terms them, are important adjuncts to the manifest consequence of earning a living. When people are unemployed

49

they are deprived of both access to these categories of experience and the manifest function of earning a living in the social institution of employment.

Ideas and concepts of the personal agency theory (Fryer, 1995) have been summarised on two grounds. First, people are socially embedded agents, actively striving for purposeful self-determination, attempting to make sense of, initiating, influencing and coping with events in line with personal values, goals and expectations of the future, in a context of cultural norms, traditions and past experience. Secondly, whilst personal agency is sometimes empowered in interaction with labour market social settings and systems, agency is frequently undermined, restricted and frustrated by formal and informal social forces. Thus, unemployment is prolonged, leading to multidimensional disadvantage, which is of substantial duration and which involves dissociation from the major social and occupational milieux of society (Room *et al.*, 1993). Two decades ago, Townsend (1979) recognised the need to include leisure activities in the definition of poverty because deprivation includes different spheres of life — in work, at home, in travel, and in leisure time activities. Alcock (1997) states that leisure has become a source and site of inequality. The correlation between income and participation is borne out by statistics that show a decline according to occupational status (Office of National Statistics, 1998).

Australian research on the effect of long term unemployment on young people shows three general impacts (Crooks, 1996). First, it forces people into a subsistence lifestyle where a limited social security payment is spread watchfully over rent, food, fuel bills, transport and children's clothing. Secondly, it causes a painful contraction of personal networks and social life as people withdraw from mainstream activity. Ironically, one of the few constant links to others is through what is perceived by many unemployed people to be a demeaning and ritualistic visit to the employment agency or the social security department. Thirdly, there is less security and more uncertainty in the lives of unemployed people. They sense the futility of a training programme if there is no job at the end of it; uncertainty dominates their emotions; they do not know how they will be managing in a few years time or whether they will have any security in the rest of their adult life; their spirits take a battering; they feel angry and bitter towards the nation's leaders; and yet, they are determined not to go under. These general impacts exclude young people, socially and economically, as full participating members within the community. As a consequence, they are relegated to what Morris (1994) referred to as an underclass, a category of disadvantage.

Young people have rights. These include regular access to some form of structured social activity and rights to health protection and health promotion (Coles, 1995). Brownlee (1992) notes that leisure is one of the basic human rights safeguarded by the United Nations Declaration of Human Rights which, in Article 24, states that everyone has the right to rest and leisure, including reasonable limitation of working hours and periodic holidays with pay. Article 2 of the Sao Paulo Declaration (World Leisure, 1998) states that all persons have the right to leisure through economic, political and social policies that are equitable and sustainable. However, these rights have been eroded by policies to keep leisure facilities as units of economic viability. Further, breaches of rights do not warrant a remedy in the courts as they cannot be viewed in a true legal sense. Thus, rights are interpreted as standards (Roche, 1997) which are often ignored. While in paid employment, young people have the means to satisfy their physiological and social needs at leisure outlets but how can these needs be fulfilled when they are materially and socially disadvantaged through unemployment?

In recent times, various schemes have been implemented to increase access to leisure for disadvantaged groups such as the unemployed. Collins and Kennett (1998) have reviewed the use of leisure cards for the poor but note that financial accountability and the increased need for better economic outcomes by leisure providers has pushed into the background social object-ives of providing leisure opportunities to the public. Inability to pay for services and the movement away from concessionary group leisure cards excludes those who are unemployed. Haworth (1997) suggests that social inclusion through participation in work programmes may enhance participation in leisure activities and produce more social activity in contrast to withdrawn, isolated lifestyles. This view is supported by MacDonald (1997), whose work on employment assistance programmes for unemployed young people shows that they have resulted in improved self-esteem, extended networks and friendships, as well as training and work experience which lead to accredi-tation and further training. Special sports counselling programmes for young offenders have helped them to refrain from crime. Nichols (1997), for example, has shown how sporting activities can provide a medium for a change of self-concept, involving a rejection of offending behaviour (see also Long *et al.*, in this volume). Thus, the role of leisure could lead to a positive approach to a new lifestyle.

Leisure and its effect on unemployment are mixed. One view is that leisure is regarded as a vital contributor to quality of life. Schemes for the unemployed have stimulated new participation and recruited back into sport a number of lapsed participants but have failed, for most, to sustain participation (Glyptis, 1994). For committed unemployed participants, sports leadership schemes counteract many of the problems of unemployment (Kay, 1994). Studies of young unemployed adults by Evans and Haworth (1991) and Haworth and Ducker (1991) show that engagement in activity is associated with enhanced well-being but at lower levels than for a matched sample of employed people.

The opposite view, that leisure does not fulfil functional alternatives for work, is espoused by a number of researchers. Jahoda (1981) comments that leisure activities, from TV to sports and self-improvements, are fine in themselves as complements to work but that they lack the compelling manifest function of earning a living. Guerin's (1984) research, on a sample of young unemployed persons (aged 19–25) with little or no qualifications, concluded that unemployment led her respondents into social isolation and made them unable to invest in any kind of personal project, including leisure activities. Roberts (1992) says that leisure may add to the quality of life for people in employment but that it seems fundamentally incapable of providing an alternative for people without jobs. Leisure activity may help preserve psychic well-being during unemployment but it is not, then, a long-term substitute for employment (Roberts, Brodie and Dench, 1987).

Roberts (1997) reports that the leisure of young people is impoverished as a result of unemployment. The range of activities is not reduced but the frequency of participation decreases because of having lesser income. Similar conclusions are reached by Gallie, Gershuny and Vogler (1995) who found little evidence of any general tendency amongst the unemployed to withdraw into inactivity. As a consequence, activities in pubs and clubs are undertaken less frequently and often performed at lower cost (Roberts, 1997); or, when participation in activities is unaffordable, they may be substituted by no- or low-cost activity (Lobo, 1996). Being disadvantaged in leisure is thus associated with material and psychological deprivation.

Over the past fifty years, leisure service delivery has been characterised by several approaches. Meyer and Brightbill (1948) commented that recreation was a community service and an important governmental function. This approach characterised leisure service delivery in the United States, United Kingdom and Australia during the 1960s and the 1970s. It was known as the community development approach since recreation was regarded as a human service and an essential function of government (Neipoth, 1983). The 1980s witnessed a change in the prevailing philosophy to a more commercial orientation to service delivery. A declining tax base, inflation and increased operating costs made it necessary for governments to make dramatic cutbacks in expenditure, seriously affecting leisure services. Leisure services adopted a more business-like approach (Howard and Crompton, 1980; Crompton, 1987) and public sector marketing took on a hybrid approach by using commercial strategies, either because of limits to subsidy or to help facilities pay for themselves (Torkildsen, 1992). In Australia reforms in the name of economic rationalism have failed to increase choices for people but, instead, economic policies have caused massive unemployment. Joblessness not only causes economic disadvantage to the children of the unemployed but they also experience the psychological trauma that their parents are going through

(Langmore and Quiggin, 1994). The recreation of these children is also adversely affected (Lobo and Watkins, 1995). Young males and females are restricted in their leisure as a result of material, psychological and social deprivation (Lobo, 1997). They are placed at a social disadvantage and comprise the new underclass. The questions addressed in this research are, therefore:

1) What leisure losses or gains result as a consequence of unemployment?

2) How can equity and accessibility be achieved for those disadvantaged as a result of joblessness?

Theoretical underpinning

The conceptual framework utilised in the study is one developed by Kelly (1980). He generated a gain-loss-attachment-detachment model (GLAD) by adding a cognitive component to a traditional affective gain-loss model. The Kelly framework presents four different orientations to transitions:

Attachment gain — where the individual perceives the transition as closing the gap between his or her ideal world and the world as it is. The transition results in the receipt of more of some existing outputs that are desired and/or receiving some completely new output that is desired.

Detachment gain — where, again, the individual perceives the transition as closing the gap between his or her ideal world and the world as it is. In this case, the transition results in receipt of less of some of the input that is not desired.

Attachment loss — where the individual perceives the transition as widening the gap between his or her ideal world and the world as it is. Here, the transition results in the receipt of more of some outputs that are not desired.

Detachment loss — where the individual perceives the transition as widening the gap between his or her ideal world and world as it is. The transition here results in the receipt of less of some of the output that is desired.

According to Hayes and Nutman (1981), analysis of the literature suggests that unemployment is overwhelmingly seen in terms of both detachment and attachment loss and rarely in terms of gain. The few who voice detachment or attachment gain are either glad to have left behind things that they are glad to get away from, or have acquired new outcomes that they value. This confirms that people who hold positive attitudes towards unemployment are a small minority. The majority is left with severe decrements, particularly with the loss of status and identity.

Methodology

82 young people attending labour market programmes between the ages of 18 and 30 volunteered to be interviewed. They consisted of 49 (60 per cent) males and 33 (40 per cent) females. Of the males, 33 (67 per cent) were between the ages of 18 and 24 years, and 16 (33 per cent) between 25 and 30 years. Among the females, 25 (76 per cent) were between 18 and 24 and 8 (24 per cent) between 25 and 30 years.

Educational levels were categorised as:

• lower secondary, which is up to Year 10 of high school;

• upper secondary, Year 12, the final year of high school; and

• tertiary, which included technical and further education beyond high school or university studies.

The number of males with lower secondary education was 23 (47 per cent), upper secondary 14 (29 per cent) and tertiary 12 (24 per cent). Among the females, the proportions were 11 (33 per cent), 10 (30 per cent) and 12 (37 per cent) respectively. Of the total of 82 participants, three, all females, had university bachelors degrees.

On a self-perceived financial scale from comfortable to very poor, males rated themselves in the following way: comfortable 15 (31 per cent), poor 26 (53 per cent), and very poor 8 (16 per cent). Among females the proportions were: comfortable 10 (30.5 per cent), poor 13 (39 per cent), and very poor 10 (30.5 per cent).

Previous employment history was categorised as intermittent, steady and no previous employment. Among the males, 23 (55 per cent) had intermittent, 17 (40 per cent) steady, and 2 (5 per cent) had no previous employment. Proportions for females were: intermittent 13 (42 per cent) and steady 18 (58 per cent). There were no female cases of no previous employment.

Questions asked of the young people focused on the effects of unemployment on leisure both in- and out-of-home. Out-of-home categories included activities for fitness, sociability, and entertainment and membership in clubs and associations. Data from a previous study (Lobo, 2000) were transformed to show gains and losses in in- and out-of-home leisure. High levels of activity in the home were categorised as gains and low levels as losses. Likewise, being active towards fitness was categorised as a gain and being passive, a loss. Social involvement was seen as a gain, but uninvolvement a loss. Frequent entertainment was classified as a gain, but infrequent a loss. Retention of membership in clubs and associations was categorised as a gain, but discontinuation a loss.

Results

Home-based activities

Both males and females engaged in a wide range of home-based activities before unemployment. Eleven most frequent activities are listed in Table 1.

Table 1   Leisure activities in the home before unemployment

	Frequency			
Activity	Males	Females	Total	Per cent
Television	40	32	72	36
Gardening	15	13	28	14
Videos	9	10	19	9. 5
Reading, writing	10	12	22	11
Cooking/home/car maintenance	8	7	15	7. 5
Board/tables games	6	3	9	4. 5
Listening to music	10	6	16	8
Electronic hobbies	6	2	8	4
Swimming (home pool)	1	3	4	2
Playing musical instrument	1	1	2	1
Modelling/craft-work	4	1	5	2. 5
	110	90	200	100
	N=49	N=33		

The six most popular home activities were television viewing, gardening, videos, reading/writing, cooking/home/car maintenance, and listening to music. Five other activities, which were ranked lower, were board/table games, electronic hobbies, swimming (home pool), playing a musical instrument and modelling and craft work.

Each response on participation in home-based activities was categorised on a before and after basis. Responses that indicated a substantial amount of time spent on recreation activities in the home were categorised as *gain*. Responses that indicated that very little was done in the home were categorised as *loss*. The frequencies of before and after unemployment home-based recreation activities are shown in Table 2.

Table 2   Leisure gains and losses at home

Home Gains and Losses	Frequency		Total	Per cent
	Males	Females		
Gain–Gain	31	24	55	67
Gain–Loss	9	6	15	18
Loss–Loss	7	—	7	9
Loss–Gain	2	3	5	6
Total	49	33	82	100

Table 3   Fitness activities before unemployment

Activity	Frequency		Total	Per cent
	Males	Females		
Organised sport	41	21	62	43
Walking	9	12	21	15
Gym/aerobics	6	13	19	13
Surfing/skiing	8	1	9	6
Swimming	3	5	8	5. 5
Bike riding	8	2	10	7
Golf	5	—	5	3. 5
Jogging	4	2	6	4
Tennis	1	2	3	3
Total	85	58	143	100

The data reveal that high proportions of participating males *and* females (67 per cent) had gains in home activities before and after job loss. A substantially lower number of participants of both sexes (18 per cent) had changed from gain to loss in the home. Among the males, seven who had losses in home activity before unemployment showed no change after job loss, while there were no females in that category. A small proportion of males and females (6 per cent) had changed from loss to gain, indicating engagement in more activities in the home after unemployment.

Several reasons were given for gains in the home after job loss. These included: more time to do things of interest (9 responses); taking on more home roles (6); parents asked to do chores (4); good to keep busy (3); more help from friends; more independent living; find strategies to do things cheaply

(1). Reasons for losses of activity were: boredom and lack of motivation (9); wanting to be alone; outdoor oriented; lack of money for home interests (2); and ill-health (1). The data in Table 2 show that females tended to be more involved at home than males, though reasons for gain and loss involvement after unemployment are equally stated by both sexes.

Out-of-home recreation for fitness

Young males and females were asked to state the activities they participated in for fitness before unemployment. The activities included organised sport, gym/aerobics, surfing/skiing, swimming, bike riding, golf, jogging and tennis. These are included in Table 3.

Activities for fitness during employment and after job loss were categorised on a before and after basis. Those who participated regularly were classified as gain. Those who entered a 'no' response or said they did nothing were classified as loss. Before and after job loss comparisons on frequencies and percentages are listed in Table 4.

Table 4   Fitness gains and losses

	Frequency			
Fitness gains & losses	Males	Females	Total	Per cent
Gain–Gain	25	16	41	50
Gain–Loss	20	15	35	43
Loss–Loss	4	2	6	7
Total	49	33	82	100

The data in Table 4 reveal that half of the males and females (50 per cent) maintained gains in fitness before and after job loss. However, there were substantial proportions of both sexes (43 per cent) that had losses after unemployment, having had gains before job loss. There were several reasons for losses but the major reason was the inability to afford participation in an activity. Thirty-eight respondents stated that they could not afford participation; this included 20 males and 15 females. Losses were also induced in four males and two females by depression and the lack of motivation. Injury caused three losses and not being a sporting person (1) and lack of transport (1) were also stated as losses. Reasons for gains were: to release anger and frustration (7 — all males); more time for fitness (13 — male 6; female 7); and, continuation of activity because of low cost (4 — male 3; female 1).

Out-of-home recreation for sociability

When asked about out-of-home recreation for sociability, common responses
included: visiting friends and family; pubs, parties and dinners; and picnics
and barbecues (Table 5). Visiting family and friends was by far the most
popular social activity (56 per cent). High rates were also noted for pubs,
parties and dinners (35 per cent). Very small proportions went on picnics and
barbecues (9 per cent).

Before and after unemployment comparisons were made on the basis
of being gains and losses. Those who visited friends and relatives regularly
were categorised as gains. Those who let their friends drop off or who did
not mix with others were categorised as losses. Before and after responses
resulted in frequencies presented in Table 6.

Data in Table 6 reveal that high proportions of males and females (51
per cent) who had gains before unemployment indicated losses after. High,
but lesser proportions of males and females (41 per cent) continued with gains

Table 5   Social activities before unemployment

	Frequency			
Activity	Males	Females	Total	Per cent
Visiting friends and relative	37	21	58	56
Picnics and barbecues	4	5	9	9
Pubs, parties and dinners	20	16	36	35
Total	61	42	103	100

Table 6   Social gains and losses

	Frequency			
Social gains & losses	Males	Females	Total	Per cent
Gain–Gain	20	14	34	41
Gain–Loss	24	18	42	51
Loss–Loss	4	—	4	5
Loss–Gain	1	1	2	2
Total	49	33	82	100

after unemployment. The two cases of one male and one female who indicated loss before, but were gains after, were so because they lived away from home during their working life and returned home after job loss.

Ten responses indicated that the main reason for gains was because they had more time to visit and mix with friends. Five of the females still mixed with friends, not in the pub as formerly but in homes. There were individual cases of males who mixed with their unemployed mates, or with the same sports group before job loss, or because seeing friends was cheaper than going to the movies. Twenty-five responses, 15 male and 10 female, indicated that the lack of money was the reason for not socialising with friends. Depression and social discomfort were also cited as reasons for not mixing with others. Four responses indicated that former friends were those at work, which resulted in reduced socialising.

Out-of-home recreation for entertainment

The data in Table 7 illustrate that, before unemployment, young males and females went to movies and the cinema very frequently and high levels of attendance were noted for night clubs and discos. Both sexes ranked movies and cinema ahead of night clubs and discos. There were lesser frequencies for bands and concerts and visiting arcades and pool parlours.

Table 7   Entertainment activities before unemployment

Activity	Frequency			
	Males	Females	Total	Per cent
Movies/Cinema	26	18	44	51
Night clubs/discos	11	12	23	26
Bands/concerts	9	2	11	13
Arcades and pool parlours	6	3	9	10
Total	52	35	87	100

Before and after comparisons were made on a gain and loss basis. Those who stated that they attended some form of entertainment regularly or once a month were categorised as gains. Those who stated words like "rarely", "occasionally" or "not at all" were categorised as loss. The before and after responses are presented in Table 8 (page following).

Unemployment affected the entertainment of large proportions of females and males (48 per cent). Twenty-one percent still attended their entertainment activities, with the proportion of males being higher than females.

Table 8   Entertainment gains and losses

Entertainment gains and losses	Frequency		Total	Per cent
	Males	Females		
Gain–Loss	25	23	48	59
Gain–Gain	12	5	17	21
Loss–Loss	9	4	13	16
Loss–Gain	2	—	2	2
Unclear response	1	1	2	2
Total	49	33	82	100

The reasons for gains in entertainment after unemployment were: possession of equipment by males (4); cheaper entertainment (males 3; females 4); more time for entertainment (males 2); still go to night clubs but do not drink much (males 1; females 1). Losses were indicated by 40 responses (males 23, females 17) of lack of finance, 5 lack of motivation (males 3; females 2) and one male felt that the entertainment available was not appealing.

Membership of clubs and associations

Young people were asked whether or not they were members of clubs and associations. Of the 82 participants in the study, 47 were members of clubs and associations. Membership frequencies and percentages before unemployment are listed in Table 9.

Table 9   Memberships of clubs and associations before unemployment

Before Unemployment	Frequency		Total	Per cent
	Males	Females		
Membership	27	20	47	57
No Membership	22	13	35	43
Total	49	33	82	100

Before unemployment, young people belonged to sporting (59 per cent), special interest (18 per cent), social (16 per cent) and service (7 per cent) clubs and associations. Some people had memberships in more than one club or association. Therefore, the total number of responses exceeded the number of respondents. Frequencies and percentages of membership in clubs and associations are listed in Table 10.

Table 10   Types of clubs and associations before unemployment

Activity	Frequency		Total	Per cent
	Males	Females		
Service	3	1	4	7
Sporting	20	13	33	59
Social	4	5	9	16
Special Interest	7	3	10	18
Total	34	22	56	100

The responses of members in clubs and associations were categorised on a gain and loss basis. If membership was continued after job loss, the response was classified as a gain. If membership had lapsed or was terminated, the response was classified as a loss. The frequencies of gains and gains and losses of membership in clubs and associations are listed in Table 11.

Table 11   Club and association gains and losses

Club/Association gains and losses	Frequency		Total	Per cent
	Males	Females		
Gain–Gain	15	7	22	47
Gain–Loss	12	13	25	53
Total	27	20	47	100

Forty-seven per cent of those who had membership in clubs and associations indicated gains by retaining membership after job loss. Fifty-three per cent had losses in membership. Three reasons were given for the gains. Seven young people (5 males, 2 females) had already paid their memberships. Eleven (males 7, females 4) found the membership low cost and cheap. Two (male 1, female 1) were voluntary members of special interest associations, which had no membership fee. The major reason for loss was the lack of finance. Fourteen young people, 7 males and 7 females, said that they could not afford membership fees. Lack of motivation was also given as a reason by five respondents (males 4, females 1). Two other responses for losses were change in residence and injury.

Conclusions

Leisure losses and gains

The first research question was: What leisure losses and gains result as a consequence of unemployment? It was found that, for the majority of young people, the quantity of home-based leisure after unemployment was the same or had increased. These were leisure gains in the home. For a small proportion, which included those who were psychologically adversely affected, the quantity and quality of their leisure activities were reduced to losses as consequences of lack of motivation and apparent boredom. Thus, psychological deprivation disadvantaged certain individuals from participation in the home. Fitness activities were diminished in quantity but disengaging also caused losses of quality of the leisure experience. The major reason for losses in many fitness activities was the impact of economic disadvantage. Social losses were adversely affected, quantitatively and qualitatively. Lack of money was again cited for reduced social engagement with friends at venues such as pubs. Qualitatively, it was found that social networks were restricted to other unemployed friends who were 'in the same boat' and who had mutual understanding of the deprivations of job loss. In some cases, social discomfort in the company of others led to self-imposed isolation as a result of losses in social networks. Entertainment was seriously affected quantitatively by the lack of money. Without certain forms of entertainment, it could be inferred that the quality of the social and leisure worlds of individuals was diminished. The extent of losses (although not universal) experienced in the home, for fitness, sociability, entertainment, and with involvement in clubs and associations, shows the inability of young people to maintain social contracts because of either material or psychological deprivation or perhaps both. Thus, for many, unemployment causes disadvantages in the various domains of leisure.

Leisure equity and accessibility

The second research question was: How can equity and accessibility be achieved for those disadvantaged as a result of joblessness? It was found that many in the sample were disadvantaged in the various domains of leisure. These disadvantages were the lack of money and psychological deprivation characterised by the losses in motivation and engagement in leisure activity. These losses may be viewed, respectively, as being externally and internally controlled.

With the lack of money, the concession card, which allows free or reduced entry, seems to be the simplest method of restoring inclusion. People who are unemployed can be granted free or discounted entry on the production of their card from the benefit agency. It has been suggested (Collins and Kennet, 1998) that such a mode of entry imposes stigma on the entrant. This may be so but, in real terms, equity is built into the scale of leisure card entry charges. In these schemes social objectives take precedence over financial ones. The provider acts inclusively taking in a wide community, sensitive to the needs of those with an inability to pay. However, providers are also under pressure to make the facility economically viable and are therefore prevented from granting reduced entry fees. There are some providers who would allow lower rates at off-peak times. There is merit in this approach, since the unemployed have more free time than their employed counterparts. However, off-peak times are also periods which coincide with job searches, job training and work experience activities. This makes it difficult for the unemployed to utilise facilities at quiet times. There is also a strong likelihood that the community at large views leisure participation by the jobless at off-peak periods with disdain. The view taken is that 'dole bludgers' are utilising facilities at times when they should be looking for work. The jobless are highly conscious of this construction of themselves by society and many choose to stay at home.

A strategy utilised to get around the use of facilities where no concessions are available at public outlets is that of 'social action'. Edginton, Hanson, Edginton and Hudson (1998: p. 39) describe the strategy in the following terms:

> It presumes that there is a disadvantaged population, great injustice, and a need to force the system, institutions, organisations, and agencies to change the ways they are distributing resources, hence services.

The main attribute of social action is advocacy. This essentially means to champion a cause or group. Edginton *et al.* (1998) believe that a leisure service agency can serve as agent for social change in several ways. How would this strategy work for the unemployed? It is suggested that, given the heightened self-esteem of participants in work programmes (Haworth, 1997; MacDonald, 1997) and counselling sports programmes (Nichols, 1997), they should be issued with vouchers for leisure facilities in the area to enable them participate at whatever time they choose. The leisure provider can then be reimbursed with the full cost of their leisure activity from the job training or work programmes agency. This is a good example of partnership and 'common cause' relationship between governmental, business and social action organisations. The foregoing solution is administratively simple and feasible but applies only to those attending job training programmes. What about those who have adequate qualifications, do not need job training but are surplus to the employment market? The social action strategy could be put into place for pensioners, disabled people and other marginalised groups in much the same way as it is for the jobless.

The problem of enticing participation amongst those who are psychologically adversely affected, and who consequently lack motivation to participate, is not easily solved. There are difficulties in identifying people who drop out of participation. It is suggested, therefore, that local authorities with responsibility for the public leisure resources should be made aware of the special measures taken for residents who are socially and economically disadvantaged. These measures may include the use of public utilities at concessionary and discounted rates. In the voluntary sector, clubs and associations with registers of former participants who have dropped out because of job loss, could use these to keep in contact with such people and to inform them that their participation problems can be sorted out. Steps taken may include: low or no cost participation rates; a social arena to allow mixing with friends; a casual orientation; and, opportunities to be more than a player, by volunteering. Such strategies are inclusive and will combat social exclusion, which unemployment may tend to impose.

This study shows that unemployment psychologically, socially and materially disadvantages and excludes young people by rendering their needs unmet and their rights ignored. The chapter recommends steps and strategies for continued leisure participation for those people who lose their way. These must address the needs of the unemployed, as well as protecting them from exploitation, harassment and social exclusion. An important implication for leisure policy and policy implementation is the strategy of social action where advocacy for the unemployed and partnership with leisure providers and other agencies is fostered in pursuit of a common cause.

References

Alcock, P. (1997) *Understanding poverty.* 2nd ed., London: Routledge.

Brownlee, I. (ed) (1992) *Basic documents on human rights.* Oxford: Clarendon Press.

Coles, B. (1995) *Youth and social policy: Youth citizenship and young careers.* London: UCL Press.

Collins, M. F. and Kennett, C. (1998) 'Including poor people in leisure services without stigma: leisure cards in the UK', *World Leisure and Recreation* Vol. 40, No. 4: pp. 17–22.

Crompton, J. L. (1987) *Doing more with less in the delivery of parks and recreation services.* State College, PA: Venture.

Crooks, M. L. (1996) *The price we pay: Young people poverty and long-term unemployment in Australia.* Hobart, Tasmania: National Clearing House for Youth Studies.

Edginton, C. R., Hanson, C. J., Edginton, S. R. and Hudson, S. D. (1998) *Leisure programming: A service-centred and benefits approach.* Boston, MASS: WCB McGraw-Hill.

Evans, S. T. and Haworth, J. T. (1991) 'Variations in personal activity, access to categories of experience and psychological well-being in unemployed young adults', *Leisure Studies* Vol. 10: pp. 249–64.

Fryer, D. (1995) 'Social and psychological consequences of unemployment: From interviewing to intervening?', in R. Hicks, P. Creed, W. Patton, and J. Tomlinson (eds.) *Unemployment Developments and Transitions.* Brisbane: Australian Academic Press, pp. 58–76.

Gallie, D., Gershuny, J. and Vogler, C. (1995) 'Unemployment, the household and social networks', in D. Gallie, C. Marsh and C. Vogler (eds.) *Social Change and the Experience of Unemployment.* Oxford: Oxford University Press, pp. 231–263.

Glyptis, S. (1994) 'Leisure provision for the unemployed: imperative or irrelevant?', *World Leisure and Recreation* Vol. 36, No. 4: pp. 34–39.

Guérin, C. (1984) 'Insertion professionelle difficile et socialisation des jeunes: Les jeunes chômeurs on-ils des loisirs?', ADRAC. *Actes du Congrès Mondial de Recherche sur le Temps Libre et le Loisir*, Mary-le-Roi, Sept 24–28, Vol. 111, No. 5: pp. 16–20.

Haworth, J. T. (1997) 'Variations in lifestyle, access to categories of experience and well-being in young unemployed people', *World Leisure and Recreation* Vol. 39, No. 4: pp. 14–17.

Haworth, J. T. and Ducker, J. (1991) 'Psychological well-being and access to categories of experience in unemployed young adults', *Leisure Studies* Vol. 10: pp. 265–74.

Hayes, J., and Nutman, P. (1981) *Understanding the unemployed: The psychological effects of unemployment.* London: Tavistock Publications.

Howard, D. R. and Crompton, J. L. (1980) *Financing, managing, and marketing recreation and park resources.* Dubuque, IA: Wm. C. Brown.

Jahoda, M. (1981) 'Work, employment and unemployment: Values, theories and approaches in social research', *American Psychologist* Vol. 36: pp. 184–191.

———— (1992) 'Reflections on Marienthal and after', *Journal of Occupational and Organisational Psychology* Vol. 65: pp. 355–358.

Kay, T. (1994) 'When great expectations reach their journeys end: Accepting the limits of leisure provision of the unemployed', *World Leisure and Recreation* Vol. 36, No. 4: 9–33.

Kelly, G. (1980) *A study of the manager's orientation towards the transition from work to retirement.* Unpublished PhD thesis, University of Leeds, Leeds, UK.

Langmore, J. and Quiggin, J. (1994) *Work for all: Full employment in the nineties.* Carlton, Victoria: Melbourne University Press.

Lobo, F. (1996) 'The effects of late career unemployment on lifestyle', *Loisir et Société* Vol. 19, No. 1: pp. 167–194.

—— (1997) 'Young people, leisure and unemployment in Western Australia', *World Leisure and Recreation* Vol. 39, No. 4: pp. 4–9.

—— (2000) 'Young people unemployment and leisure: A gender perspective', in J. Andersen and L. Lawrence (eds) Gender issues in work and leisure (LSA Publication No. 68). Eastbourne: Leisure Studies Association (forthcoming).

Lobo, F. and Watkins, G. (1995) 'Late career unemployment in the 1990s: It's impact on the family', *Journal of Family Studies* Vol. 1, No. 2: pp. 103–113.

MacDonald, H. (1997) 'Assisting young unemployed people: Directions for employment assistance programs', *World Leisure and Recreation* Vol. 39, No. 4: pp. 27–30.

Meyer, H. D. and Brightbill, C. K. (1948) *Recreation administration: A guide to its practices.* Englewood Cliffs, New Jersey: Prentice-Hall.

Morris, L. (1994) *Dangerous classes: the underclass and social citizenship.* London: Routledge.

Neipoth, W. F. (1983) *Leisure leadership.* Englewood Cliffs: N. J. Prentice-Hall.

Nichols, G. (1997) 'The role of sports counselling for unemployed young people on probation', *World Leisure and Recreation* Vol. 39, No. 4: pp. 23–26.

Office of National Statistics (1998) *General household survey 1996.* London: HMSO.

Roberts, K. (1997) 'Work and leisure in young peoples lives', in J. T. Haworth (ed) *Work, leisure and well-being.* London: Routledge, pp. 143–164.

—— (1992) 'Leisure theories in the field of youth', paper presented at the Congrès Mondial Loisirs et Jeunesse, INJEP, Marly-le-Roi, November 17–20th.

Roberts, K., Brodie, D. and Dench, S. (1987) 'Youth unemployment and out-of-home recreation', *Leisure Studies* Vol. 10, No. 2: pp. 281–294.

Roche, J. (1997) 'Children's rights: participation and dialogue', in J. Roche and S. Tucker, (eds). *Youth in society.* London: Sage and the Open University, pp. 49–58.

Room, G., with Sada, G. A., Benington, J., Breda, J., Giannichedda, M. G., Guillen, E., Henningsen, B., Laezko, F., Madiera, J., Mylonakis, D., O'Cinneide, S., Robbins, D. and Whitting, G. (1993) *Anti-poverty research in Europe.* Bristol: SAUS.

Torkildsen, G. (1992) *Leisure and recreation management.* London: E&FN Spon.

Townsend, P. (1979) *Poverty in the UK: A survey of household resources and standards of living.* London: Penguin.

World Leisure (1998) *Sao Paulo Declaration.* Adopted October 30, 1998 in Sao Paulo, Brazil, at the *5th World Congress of the World Leisure and Recreation Association* (WLRA), held in conjunction with Servico Do Comérico (SESC), Sao Paulo, and the Latin America Leisure and Recreation Association (ALATIR). Vol. 12, No. 2: pp. 3–4.

Just Sport – Sport and the Concept of Equal Opportunities between Women and Men

Håkan Larsson

Högskolan Dalarna, School of Art and Education
Falun (Sweden)

Introduction

This paper is concerned with sport and the construction of sexual difference. It is about ways of seeing and speaking, about sex/gender in sport and about ways of performing sexual difference as an object of thought. Importantly, the paper considers what constitutes, discursively, manliness and womanliness in the field of sport towards the end of the 20th century? Drawing from the work of the French philosopher Michel Foucault, and in particular his concept 'governmentality' (Foucault, 1991), the paper will explore the representation of gender in sport. 'Governmentality' implies the meta-series linking the serial histories of the *practices of the self* with those of the *practices of government* (Dean, 1994). In other words, besides its meaning of control and guidance, governmentality might be seen as referring to a certain mentality that is willing and able to be governed (Simola, Heikkinen and Silvonen, 1998: p. 68). How does sport and scientific research in sport function, on the one hand in the production of women and men as objects and subjects of knowledge, and on the other as a technique or procedure for regulating male and female behaviour? I am therefore interested in the history of the "different modes by which, in our culture, human beings are made subjects" (Foucault, 1983: p. 308), and more specifically concerned with how gendered subjects are made. The particular focus of this paper is on competitive sport and the concept of equal opportunities between women and men in sport as a new way of creating sexual/gender difference.

Over the last fifty years there has been a gradual change in our ways of thinking about sex/gender differences. Whilst previously based on *practice* (what women and men do; labour division), sex/gender constructions nowadays tend to be based on *body* (how bodies look; bodily appearance and bodily experience) and *meaning* (how women and men feel doing this or that, and what they mean by doing it). These winds of change can also be traced in the discourse of the social sciences, for example in the transition from mainly positivistic to mainly phenomenological or cultural studies, and from quantitative to qualitative studies. The concept of equal opportunities between women and men has a practical value, that is to guarantee women and men the opportunities to do the same things (to do sports, to have the same kind of work, with the same salary etc.). On the other hand, the concept fixes a view of the sexes as 'naturally opposite' or, at least, 'naturally different'.

Over the last century, both formal and informal possibilities for women to participate in competitive sport have increased. Women do not compete together with men since the sexes compete in two different classes, a development which could be viewed as a *heterosexualisation* of sport. Since the 1960s there has been an ever-growing discussion in sport about equal opportunities between women and men but the concept is interpreted in slightly different ways depending on the kind of sport:

- Women and men are separated from each other in competition in almost all sports and events (which is not the case in many other parts of society, such as in labour, but is indeed the case when it comes to such things as locker rooms and so on, in other words anything that has to do with our ideas about [hetero] sexual desire and shame in the presence of the opposite sex).

- In some sports (such as gymnastics), women and men do different events and are judged according to different criteria, which differentiates them qualitatively. In other sports (athletics), women and men do the same events and are judged according to the same criteria but with different standards (for example, women have lighter throwing implements and lower hurdles, or men have heavier throwing implements and higher hurdles depending on whose perspective is adopted). In the latter cases the sexes are differentiated on quantitative criteria. In still other sports (such as football), women and men do the same events, judged according to the same criteria and with the same standards (but still separated from each other): the sexes are thus 'equally divided'.

The concept of equal opportunities leads to different practical solutions for those participating in sport. What is important here is to understand, through the discourse of sport, the development of the concept of equal opportunities as a way of governing the behaviour of men and women and their ways of reflecting upon themselves. It is my contention that women's increased participation in competitive sport is a result of the concept of the female individual as a ('gendered') political subject, at the same time assuring the maintenance of heteronormativity, that is the idea that male – female (sexual) relations is a 'natural' base for social organisation. This gives rise to the birth of a *female subject*, in relation to the traditional notion of a universal, autonomous, reasonable and (supposedly) 'gender neutral' subject, or the Cartesian transcendental subject. This whole project can be seen as a part of a new political rationality, or governmentality, where the focal point is government in the name of equality between women and men. This point of departure relies on another hypothesis, that modern sport is inextricably linked to the idea of the autonomous individual, rational in mind and in sovereign control of 'his' body and his surroundings.

Subject – body – sex/gender

Before I turn to the discursive construction of sexual difference in sport, I will briefly address issues concerning the construction of the subject, sexual difference and the body, as objects of thought. These three modes of thought are linked to three modes of government, constituting three different governmentalities. However, they must not be seen as a kind of historical development. It might be posited that they dominate scholarly and political thinking in three consecutive historical periods but my main argument is that they are always potentially accessible to us and even, potentially, present in our thought.

What follows draws on the writings of Foucault (1994, 1966, 1991), Laqueur (1994) and Illich (1985).

1. Turn the woman's [sexual organs] inside out, turn, so to speak, the man's outside in, and fold them twice, then you will find the same in both in every aspect. (Galen of Pergamon, ca. 130–200, quoted in Laueur, 1994: p. 39)

The first mode of thought is a world of analogy, resemblance and similitude, revolving in a cosmic unity. In this world, there exists one body, one sex: this is the male sex/body. The female body is merely a less perfect male one, carrying the sexual organs on the inside. The border between the sexes is not fixed. Transgression is possible but only in an 'upward' direction, towards a more perfect body. The social organisation of the sexes (gender) is, in general, fixed. However, even here it is possible for women to, at least temporarily, hold a male social position, for example if there are no male heirs (in order to safeguard the interests and belongings to the family or dynasty). Both sexual and gender differences are analogous signs of another order, will or reason, that is divine reason. The body has no ontological status as a source of explanation: God has. God is the ultimate subject of action and thought and, through him, are his earthly representative [*företrädare*]: spiritual ones (the priests), and worldly ones (the princes).

2. Every part of her body explicates the same difference: everything
    gives to her the expression of a woman: the forehead, the mouth, the
    ears, the chin, the cheek. If we turn our attention to her inside, and
    with the aid of the scalpel uncover [frilägger], the organs, the tissue,
    the threads, then we meet, in every aspect ... the same difference.
    (Brachet, 1847: quoted in Laqueur, 1994: p. 18)

The second mode of thought is of a twofold nature. Here, difference, autonomy
and specificity form the constitutive base. Two bodies constitute two sexes,
totally different in every aspect, with a fixed and clear-cut border, not really
comparable to each other. The body has gained an ontological status, as a
source of explanation, concerning sexual difference. God has abdicated as the
ultimate subject. The subject of action and thought resides, instead, within
every individual. This movement, from God to the individual, is manifested in
philosophical thought through the Cartesian *cogito* and the Kantian
autonomous subject, as well as in religious thought with the rise of individual
salvation. Under the influence of the dichotomy between 'nature' and 'culture',
it seems that manliness and male subjectivity is connected to culture, a
producer of culture, while womanliness is connected to nature, a *reproducer*
of nature. Thus we have a relation between, on the one hand, spirituality,
reason and autonomy (subject) and between, on the other, matter/body,
intuition and dependence (object). The female individual/body (object) exists
only through the male individual/subject: the father, the husband, or another
man. In scientific and political thought the man does not appear as a gendered
individual, which is another effect of the nature/culture dichotomy. He
(subject/reason) is 'gender neutral', while the woman (object/body) is 'gender'.

3. The third, and last, mode of thought is neither holistic nor twofold to its
nature, it is fragmentary and bottomless. Old dualisms seem, at least at first
glance, to disintegrate, to give rise to new ones. In this seemingly floating and
evasive world, the body turns out to be that around which identity and
subjectivity is built. But the body has no ontological status in itself. Quite the
contrary: it is moulded and fashioned by the will of the individual. It is, indeed,
a never- ending spiral. The individual is continually forced to produce him-
or herself, his or her body, his or her biography. Since the body does not
constitute identity, nor does it constitute *sexual* identity. It is up to the
individual to choose what sex he or she wants to live, even anatomically
speaking, and there are no longer just two sexes. American biologist Anne
Fausto-Sterling speaks about at least five sexes but eventually it turns out
that there are as many sexes as there are individuals (Fausto-Sterling, 1979).
    It might be tempting to think that this development in thought is a
development from a dizziness of myths and superstition to an ever more valid

and objective truth. However, it may be more constructive to analyse these transformations in relation to governmental change. Here, I will limit the discussion to the development of the gendered political subject through the politics of equal opportunities between women and men. The three modes of thought, or typology, serve as points of reference in relation to which we can analyse discourse in sport.

Gymnastics and sport

It is difficult to use the term 'sport' in a Swedish context. In the Nordic countries, an old Norse word, 'idrott', was reinvented in the nineteenth century. 'Idrott' means the synthesis between the tradition of Swedish gymnastics (which of course has many links to other traditions of pedagogical gymnastics in 18th and 19th century Europe) and the tradition of sport as it was developed in the English public schools. The sports movement in Sweden still bears significant traces, on an organisational level, from this coalescence of gymnastics and sport some hundred years ago (for example, Gustavsson, 1994).

Swedish gymnastics grew strong in Sweden, as in other parts of Europe, in the 19th century, partly I would suggest as a result of what Foucault has termed biopolitics,

> ... the endeavor, begun in the eighteenth century, to rationalize the problems presented to governmental practice by the phenomena characteristic of a group of living human beings constituted as a population (or as a category of human beings, i.e. men and women; my note): health, sanitation, birthrate, longevity, race ... (Foucault, 1997: p. 73)

Government was no longer perceived to be 'against' the crowd, but for, or even in the name of, the population. The political subject was transformed from a subject [*undersåte*] to an active citizen. Swedish gymnastics, or Ling gymnastics[1], focused on spiritual and corporal health (a rational mind in control over a desiring body), authority, collectivity and non-competitiveness. The form of gymnastics was a closed one, carefully, and supposedly scientifically, determined in advance. Scientificity was crucial since it was in the name of the health of those who performed gymnastics that it was carried out. It was performed at first by middle class boys and young men, and later by both young women and men, in the Swedish elementary schools and at the military barrack squares. The main aim of gymnastics was to enhance manliness (and in the case of women, to enhance their qualities as mothers) and the level of performance in military activities. In a way it embodied the ideas of social engineering in late 19th and early 20th century Sweden. To this end I would suggest that the development of Swedish gymnastics is concerned with the constitution of the idea of a male bourgeois class, autonomous, rational and disciplined in body and mind. In this way, middle class men distinguished themselves from the decadent aristocracy and the disorder and poor health in the working classes (see, for example, Ljunggren, 1999).

At the turn of the century gymnastics was, at least in Sweden, replaced by competitive sport — as far as men were concerned (although it remained important in schools until the 1950s). Gymnastics was slightly modified, focusing more on aesthetics, smoothness and bodily health. The body became an object of the gaze of the other and not an object of the rational mind of the self. Gymnastics remained popular among women throughout the 20th century, in different forms (Swedish gymnastics, calisthenics for housewives, jazz dance, aerobics, etc.). This constituted the idea of women/the female sex as aesthetic, somewhat introverted, focusing on body/bodily appearance, a struggle to control women's supposedly irrational nature – in short, as a problem to be controlled and examined.

Competitive sport (or British sport as it is sometimes called) is, through very specific procedures (the production of individual results in sport), a form of individualisation. It highlights autonomy, equality, individual competition and hierarchy (even in team games), freedom of choice and the striving for excellence in an open market of achievements. It has a formally open form but relies heavily on experts as bearers of rational and objective knowledge (biomechanics, applied physiology, psychology, management etc.) to draw up an 'optimal technique' which, in effect, restricts the form (Rose, 1996: p. 11) (see Table 1).

Table 1   A general comparison of ideas related to, and developed through, gymnastics and sport (Source: Ljunggren, 1999)

	Gymnastics	Sport
Body ideal	all-round, symmetry/harmony	specific, monotonous
Movements	closed (pre-decided)	open/free (within certain limits)
Form	practice/exhibition	training/competition
Meaning	health	record/victory
Participants	public	élite
Social carrier	state/school	clubs/civil society
Context	national	international

Conceptually speaking, sport embodied the concepts of liberal democracy and economy. Sport was an activity designed for young middle class men but no one was deliberately prohibited from taking part. It was considered natural that young healthy males were the most talented sportsmen (as if sport existed as an effect of nature and not as an effect of cultural conditions). The ideals of fair play, sportsmanship and amateurism are closely linked to the forming of a culture of the gentleman. This culture constitutes the ideal of men as rational autonomous subjects (and men as more extrovert, focusing on performance and competition/hierarchy).

Sport and social change

During the second half of the 19th century and the first half of the 20th Swedish laws were changed making women equal to men, politically, juridically and economically, from the point of view of the already existing mode of government. Women were allowed to vote and to be voted into the parliament from 1923, as well as attending higher ranks in the state administration. This can be seen as the fruits of liberal feminism, not the development of a new mode of government or a new kind of governmentality *per se* but the result of the kind of government that worked through the man (the father, the husband), now enabling the rights of women. However, the political subject remained gender neutral. Large political and social/labour changes did not occur until the 1960s and the 1970s in Sweden, when women left their homes for the labour market and entered the corridors of power. This, I would argue, was part of a transformation of government or the development of a new kind of governmentality, where first women, and later men, appear as 'gendered' political subjects. Female participation in competitive sport must be related to wider social changes but there is no simple causality between these. As a result of the constitution of the gendered political subject, sport turned out to be a well-fitted cultural activity for the performing of the new female subject. By this I do not mean that sport developed as a result of governmental needs but, rather, that sport was 'exploited' and functioned as 'raw material' for the creation of the 'gendered subject'. We can speak about a new mode of government — 'government in the name of equality' — or 'governing in the name of equal opportunities between women and men'. However, if this *were* the case would not the significance of sex and sexual difference become unimportant?

I would argue that 'normal' heterosexuality/heteronormativity, or the heterosexual matrix (Butler, 1990), has been partially transformed into new forms, and this is where the concept of equal opportunities applies. Equal opportunity is not only a new way of perceiving the female subject but also a way of perceiving sexual difference. Physical segregation of men and women, such as in labour division (men paid labour/women non-paid domestic labour), or in sport (men sporting/women non-sporting), becomes less significant. Rather, meaning and body increase in significance.

> ... the most important thing for girls participating in sport is the social aspect, that is associating and having fun with each other. For boys, competition is the most important. (*Tjejer på arenan* [Girls on the arena], 1998: p. 49)

> A girl becomes a woman when she passes through puberty, when her body matures into being able to give birth. She does not need physical or mental strength to have menstruation or breasts, and perhaps not even to get pregnant. The body develops all on its own, it become womanly. (Mogren and Trosell, 1997: p. 8)

In girls and women, womanliness is said to be always there, whether you want it or not, or even whether you know it or not, always lurking deep inside the body structure, waiting to burst out. The discourse of womanliness suggests that the body is the object of the male gaze but the subject of femininity, the active force in the creation of (the 'natural') womanliness, is less important. Manliness, on the other hand, is something quite different.

> Manhood must be conquered. A young man performs, does things, to show who he is. He builds up his self-esteem by showing that he is a man, both in contrast to being a little boy and even more so, in contrast to being a woman. He is to be different from the woman, both in body and soul. (Mogren and Trosell, 1997: p. 8)

In the discourse of manliness the man-as-mind is subject and his body is his tool/object with which he conquers other bodies/objects – male ones in combat, female ones in bed – in order to achieve his manliness. His task is to create culture and in his hands lies the devastating ability to destroy culture in relation to which women occur as the defenders of morality and human virtue. While the sporting female previously was seen as a 'problem' due to the 'male norm', she is now seen as merely different, but equally normal. The kind of man referred to here is sometimes said to be vanishing but this is certainly not true from the point of view of the discourses in sport within the Swedish sports movement.

   In sport, women and men are formally divided into two classes of competition. Since men and women today do similar events this division could be viewed as a kind of divided similarity, an 'outer' sameness but an 'inner' otherness. Foucault (1977) suggested that modern power relations aim at procedures that occur inside the subject and not so much at what takes place between the subjects. In the labour market, for instance, equality is not about different 'competition classes' but rather about breaking them down (women are now allowed even in Church and Military services). In society, broadly speaking, women and men nowadays do the same things together to a large extent — or at least they are formally/juridically entitled to do the same things (although still not always morally). What used to be seen as inappropriate, women and men in the same places, or doing the same things, is now seen as normal. In sport, however, women and men do the same things, but separately. Since there is no longer a strict labour division, women and men must, in some way, be made comparable to each other in order to make sure there is no confusion about what a 'true woman' and a 'true man' is. This is one explanation for why sport remains popular in today's societies and in neo-liberal discourses of government which focus, on the one hand, on individual autonomy, achievement, freedom of choice, bodily appearance and experience and, on the other, on sexual difference (sport as 'raw material'). This hetero-sexualisation of sport is seen as more or less natural, or at least unproblem-atic, in sport science, where study after study points out the competitiveness among sporting boys and the sociability among sporting girls. Sport, and sport science, makes women and men visible as subjects and objects of knowledge, in effect it performs as the new gendered political subject.

The concept of equal opportunities

The discourse of equal opportunities between women and men in sport has been evident throughout the 20th century but its place has been in the margins of political and scientific discourse. It was not until the 1960s and 1970s that, through 'gender mainstreaming', equal opportunities gained considerable importance. Equal opportunities is said to be about equalising the conditions of action and participation in different aspects of life, and not about eradicating sexual difference as some critics maintain. The word *equal* constitutes two categories put alongside each other on a uniform basis. Explicitly, equal opportunities is grounded in the notion of two already existing categories, men and women, coherent in form and objectively and universally dividable. I would argue, however, that it is not so much about guaranteeing a 'natural' or self-evident right, inherent in the categories of women and men as 'natural'. Equality is about constructing, or performing, two distinct and clearly differentiated categories, which may be equalised but also may be perceived as an apparatus that produces and regulates sexual difference. In Sweden, as in many other Western countries, equal opportunities regulate, and even stimulate, women's possibilities to do the things that men have been allowed to do. In sport this means, primarily, women's 'right' to do (competitive) sport. Sport is constituted on the edge between social-liberal and neo-liberal political rationality, the former stressing collectivity, the latter individuality, where 'normal' heterosexuality still serves as the ground for social organisation. Strategies that emanate from the discourse of equal opportunities try to 'normalise' what was previously seen as a problem and difficult to deal with (both for men – as coaches and teachers, as well as fathers, husbands and lovers – and for women themselves); it makes 'normal' what used to be 'problematic'. "Women and men possess different types of knowledge and experiences ... Women and men have different values and different interests." (*Idrottens jämställdhetsplan* [Policy for equal sport], 1989: p. 4).

> We call for a *paradigmatic shift* that changes the perspectives, that allow women and men leaders be developed on equal terms, side by side ...
> In discussions about gender, equality, and feminism, we easily base what is said on biases and personal ideas. Everyone has an opinion on the issue. This report is aimed at avoiding this pitfall. We will attempt to reason on the basis of men's and women's concrete *experiences* of leadership within different branches of athletics, to reach conclusions, and to draw up guidelines for the future ... The social patterns of women's and men's behaviour does not only vary between individuals, but also between cultures. From a global perspective, there is therefore a further danger in nailing down truths about how women and men *are*.
> (*Ledarskap på kvinnors vis* [Leading the Female Way], 1993: pp. 5)

Interestingly, these quotes imply that 'different values and different interests' as well as different 'knowledge and experiences' must be taken as the point of departure in political matters, and not seen as the effects of power mechanisms of historical origin. To a large extent, scientific inquiry (at least in the Swedish sports context) has built upon this notion of difference and complementarity. Therefore, I maintain that the concept of equal opportunities between women and men, and the production of (scientific) knowledge on women's sport, is about the transition of the heterosexual matrix into new modes of thinking. It has resulted in girls/women often having to walk a fine line, at once being both a *woman* — or rather displaying 'proper' femininity — and an autonomous subject, thus simultaneously being morally tied to the responsibilities of both these positions.

The discourse of equal opportunities has had the effect not only of normalising femininity but also of problematising masculinity. The rising interest for masculinity and 'men's studies' in Sweden in sport research must be seen in relation to the birth of the female, or 'gendered', political subject. It is my contention that this interest is about shaping a male gendered subject as equal to the female gendered subject. The problematising of masculinity thus appears *after* the problematisation of femininity, as a necessary condition for government in the name of equal opportunities between women and men.

Conclusion

The construction of competitive sport, with increased female participation and the development of equal opportunities in sport, can be viewed as related to the transition of the idea of the two-sexed body and the one-sexed subject to the idea of the two-sexed-body and the two-sexed-subject. Women and men tend to do the same sporting events but are divided into two competition classes due to their 'natural' (physiological/anatomical/biological as well as psychological and social) differences. All of this can, in turn, be related to the institution of the heterosexual matrix in a society governed by neo-liberal discourses of power. Through sport, women and men, girls and boys, are subjectified as individuals (autonomous subjects) but are still male and female human beings and all that is signified in this strict division. Equal opportunities between women and men is related to the idea about *two* gendered categories, no more, no less. The discourse of equal opportunities occurred simultaneously with the neo-liberal discourse of individuality. The individual is the focal category but is not merely 'an individual' but also a 'gendered' individual who is actually a decidedly heterosexual individual. The concept of the fragmented body/sex, or the voluntary body/sex, may be therefore seen to be historically located in the discourse of sport.

In order to examine here how to improve equality between women and men I have attempted to avoid nailing down old truths because old truths tend to serve privileged individuals and groups in stead of challenging dominance. My perspective is of course, scientifically speaking, no truer than any other. It is very much linked to the power/knowledge relation that dominates our way of thinking about sexual difference and equality. Michel Foucault's way of doing scientific analyses is, of course not good or valid in a general sense but valid exactly in relation to the dominating power/knowledge relation, or governmentality. I am sure the moment will occur when it is time for us to say good-bye to the thinking of Foucault and move on to new ways of reasoning. In conclusion, this chapter

> refuses to search for the origins of gender, the inner truth of female desire, a genuine or authentic sexual identity that repression has kept from view; rather, [... it] investigates the political stakes in designating as an *origin* and *cause* those identity categories that are in fact the *effects* of institutions, practices, discourses with multiple and diffuse points of origin. (Butler, 1990: p. ix)

We should not strive for liberation *of* something specific that is already existent, hidden, or oppressed but instead *to* something entirely new, something that none of us knew was possible before.

Notes

1   The founder of Ling gymnastics was Per Henrik Ling (1776-1839). He was also the founder of the institute for P. E. teachers' education in Stockholm 1813, presently the Stockholm University College of Physical Education and Sport.

References

Butler, J. (1990) *Gender trouble. Feminism and the subversion of identity*. London and New York: Routledge.

Dean, M. (1994) *Critical and effective histories*. London and New York: Routledge.

Fausto-Sterling, A. (1979) *Myths of gender. Biological theories about woman and men*. New York: Norton.

Foucault, M. (1977) *Discipline and punish. The birth of the prison*. London: Allen Lane.

———— (1983)'The subject and power', in H. Dreyfus and P. Rabinow (eds) *Michel Foucault. Beyond structuralism and hermeneutics*. Brighton: Harvester, pp. 308–326.

———— (1991) 'Governmentality', in G. Burchell, C. Gordon and P. Miller (eds) *The Foucault effect. Studies on governmentality*. London: Harvester Wheatsheaf, pp. 87–104.

———— (1994) *The order of things. An archaeology of the human sciences*. New York: Vintage Books.

———— (1997) 'The birth of biopolitics', in P. Rabinow (ed) *Michel Foucault. Ethics, subjectivity and truth*. New York: The New Press, pp. 73–79.

Gustavsson, K. (1994) *Vad är idrottandets mening? En kunskapssociologisk granskning av idrottens utveckling och läromedel samt en organisations-didaktisk analys. [What is the meaning of sport? A study of its development, textbook materials and an organisational didactic analysis.]* Uppsala Studies in Education 55.

Hultqvist, K. and Petersson, K. (eds) (1995) *Foucault. Namnet på en modern vetenskaplig och filosofisk problematik. [Foucault. The name of a modern scientific and philosophical problematic.]* Stockholm: HLS Förlag.

Illich, I. (1985) *Genus. Bidrag till en historisk kritik av jämlikheten. [Gender. A contribution to a historial critique of equality]*. Stockholm: Liber.

Laqueur, T. (1994) *Om könens uppkomst. Hur kroppen blev kvinnlig och manlig.* [*Making sex. Body and gender from the Greeks to Freud.*] Stockholm/ Stehag: Symposion.

Ljunggren, J. (1999) *Kroppens bildning. Linggymnastikens manlighetsprojekt 1790–1914.* [*The fostering of the human body. The manliness-project of Ling-gymnastics 1790–1914.*] Stockholm/Stehag: Symposion.

Mogren, I. and Trosell, L. (1993) *Att spränga gränser. Små idrottsflickor blir stora.* [*Blowing the borders. Small sporting girls growing up.*] Stockholm: SISU.

Rose, N. (1996) 'Towards a critical sociology of freedom', *Nordiske Udkast* No. 1: p. 3–21.

Simola, H., Heikkinen, S. and Silvonen, J. (1998) 'A catalog of possibilities: Foucauldian history of truth and education research', in T. Popkewitz and M. Brennan (eds) *Foucault's challenge. Discourse, knowledge, and power in education.* New York and London: Teachers College Press, pp. 64–90.

Swedish Sports Confederation (1989) *Idrottens jämställdhetsplan.* [*Policy for equal sport.*] Stockholm: Swedish Sports Confederation.

Swedish Sports Confederation (1993) *Ledarskap på kvinnors vis. Ett ledarskap i tiden.* [*Leading the female way. A modern leadership style.*] Stockholm: Swedish Sports Confederation.

(1998) *Tjejer på arenan ... på våra villkor.* [*Girls on the arena ... On our own terms.*] Stockholm: SISU.

Tied Together through Sport? Sport and Social Cohesion in New Housing Estates

Hugo van der Poel and Colette Roques

Department of Leisure Studies, Tilburg University
(The Netherlands)

The practising of sport in a social context contributes to social cohesion; through sport personal contacts and social relationships are established, people build up circles of friends and social networks, and also the community spirit can be strengthened. Through this socially binding effect sport can contribute to processes of socialisation, integration and emancipation in society. (Ministry of Health, Well-being and Sport, 1996: p. 15 (authors' translation))

Introduction

We are witnesses of an increasing interest in sport, both by the national and local governments in the Netherlands. After the prosperous 1970s, the next decade was dominated by discussions of whether or not sport belonged to the 'core business' of the (local) state, whether and how to privatise sport facilities, and a focus on specific target groups, such as ethnic minorities and the disabled. But in the 1990s sports are credited with many 'values', 'meanings' and all sorts of positive impacts, leading to a higher political profile for sport policy and a doubling of the national state's expenditure on sport. The higher political profile of sport is best illustrated by the addition of Sport to the name of the Ministry of Health, Well-being and Sport (VWS) in 1994.

One of the effects or values of sport most warmly embraced is its supposed contribution to social cohesion in society. This value of sport is stressed in national policy documents on sport (VWS, 1996), as well as in national policy papers on general welfare policy (VWS, 1998; 1999). In the currently fashionable policy terminology, sport is an important element of the 'social infrastructure'. Although the conviction that sport can support processes of social integration and contribute to social cohesion is very strong, so far there is relatively little empirical research that corroborates this. To the extent that such research is carried out, it mainly focuses on the poorer areas in the bigger cities. A good and recent example is the study of Duyvendak *et al.* (1998), which aimed to investigate the role of sport in the process of social integration of ethnic minorities in Rotterdam.

In terms of Dutch national physical planning and housing policies, the crucial term is 'compact cities'. Yearly, about 80,000 new houses are added to the national housing stock. These new houses are predominantly built in so-called VINEX-locations (part of the building plan for almost one million new houses in the Netherlands). They are large-scale extensions (anywhere between 20,000 to 100,000 inhabitants) of existing middle-range and big cities. The expansion of existing cities is meant to prevent a gradual suburbanisation of the whole country, to diminish travel distances between home, work and recreation areas, and to maintain the social basis for urban provisions. VINEX-locations thus are not 'new towns' or suburban villages, nor new 'quarters' or 'neighbourhoods'. The building density is quite high (30 to 40 houses per hectare), but there are relatively few, if any, high rise buildings and/or apartment blocks ('flats'). Only 30 per cent are houses for rent, roughly 70 percent are owner-occupied. The majority of the houses have a (small) garden, many houses are semi-detached and only a few are free-standing. Although located on the edge of existing cities — but often on the other side of existing heavy infrastructure (railways, motorways and/or canals) — with a few exceptions, the VINEX-locations are certainly not (meant to be) 'edge cities' (Garreau, 1991). That is to say: the policy makers want to adhere to the notion of a 'core city' or vibrant city centre and do not invest much in urban provisions in these VINEX-locations. Instead, they want to put the money into public transport provisions connecting the new housing estates to the existing city centres. More often than not, work areas also are not an integral part of the planning for VINEX-locations.

In summary: many VINEX-locations are built as extensions of existing cities, dominated by owner-occupied, semi-detached houses and dependent on the mother-city for urban provisions such as theatres, hotels, nightclubs, pavement cafés, cinemas, luxury shopping areas fit for 'fun-shopping', restaurants, amusement arcades and all sorts of other facilities that one visits to have a good time and to meet friends out of one's home. An interesting question now is whether something of a 'social life' will develop in this type of housing estates. What about the 'social infrastructure' in these VINEX-locations; what are, could be or should be its building blocks? Is it important that the inhabitants develop some sort of bond or commitment with this new part of the city and/or a social bond with the other inhabitants? What sort of facilities might enhance a process of social integration? And what role does sport play in all this?

These questions have been central to the research on which this paper is based. Commissioned by VWS, researchers of the Department of Leisure Studies of Tilburg University have carried out a research project in four new housing estates, in order to shed more light on the planning of sport facilities for the new housing estates and the (potential) role of sport in processes of social integration and the development of social cohesion in these areas. This paper gives an idea of the work in progress on this project.

Sport infrastructure, commitment and place

Sport infrastructure

The aim of the project is to recommend to (local) governments how to make better use of the possibilities of sport to enhance commitments and social cohesion in the settings of new housing estates. In current Dutch policy terms (see VWS, 1998; 1999) this means recommendations on the improvement of the 'sport infrastructure', as part of the larger 'socio-cultural infrastructure' of housing estates.

By 'infrastructure' is meant those structural conditions for (the constitution of) social practices, which are (being) created and maintained under direct or indirect responsibility of governments, and which are meant to improve the quality of existence of all those to whom the government in question is accountable. In a liberal market-economy it is very difficult to say exactly what contributes to the improvement of the quality of life of each individual. The first and foremost task for the government in that type of society, therefore, is seen as creating the conditions (the infrastructure) for as many people as possible to take care of this by themselves. Provisions for education, meeting other people, exchanging goods and services and moving around belong to these type of conditions. Seen as such, improvements in infrastructure to a large extent imply enlarging the degree of integration or system-ness in and between social systems, by broadening the scope of (exchange) relations with others and thus providing more opportunities to reach personal goals and to improve the quality of life.

There are various types of infrastructure. The 'ecological infrastructure', for instance, is important for the exchange of genetic material, and the economic infrastructure (the monetary system, economic legislation) facilitates the exchange of labour and capital, goods and services. The socio-cultural infrastructure facilitates meeting other people and familiarising oneself with their ideas and world views, norms and values, thus broadening people's scope for social and cultural relationships. In terms of the most recent *Memorandum on Well-being* (1999-2002), its aim is "to offer individual citizens opportunities for social participation in their direct environment" (VWS, 1999: p. 6).

The sport infrastructure, as part of the larger socio-cultural infrastructure, refers to that part of the structural conditions for the practising of sport that is created and maintained by governments, either via direct provision or indirectly, for instance via subsidies or special tax regulations. Governments can and do invest in the sport infrastructure for a variety of reasons, such as the inherent values of sport, or the economic and health benefits attributed to sport participation. As such, sport facilities can also be a part of the economic or health infrastructure. The focus of this project is on the ways by which governments make use (or could make use) of the sport infrastructure to enhance participation in sport activities and to develop forms of commitment in new housing estates.

Commitment and place

One might raise the question why one should be interested at all in people's commitment to the housing estate they live in. Why would we expect such a commitment to exist, in this late-modern network society, with its high levels of mobility and vast array of media that connect us in all sorts of ways with all sorts of places, people and events all over the globe? Is it not a crucial feature of our existence in a post-traditional social order that we no longer live in a place-bound culture?

Dutch physical planning has a long history of attempts to (re-)create the community spirit of romanticised village life in newly-built city districts. However, it is clear by now that the mobile inhabitants no longer allow themselves to be restricted to these districts. For a variety of reasons, they use a far wider region to work and recreate in (see for example, Reijndorp *et al.*, 1998). Nevertheless, we see several reasons why the socio-cultural infrastructure of districts, including the newest housing estates, might still be of importance. First of all, not everybody is mobile and has access to a car. Particularly for children, the disabled and the elderly, the proximity of facilities is still relevant in terms of the use they can make of them. Secondly, taking into account the relatively high proportion of houses for sale in the VINEX-locations, it is important to note that, in terms of facilities, market research indicates a strong preference for green facilities in the direct environment, followed by shops and medical provisions and the possibility to park in front of the house (Wassenberg, 1994). Prices of houses in green settings are also significantly higher than those of similar houses in non-green settings (Stichting Recreatie, 1997). People prefer to combine a recreative and utilitarian use of the direct environment with the opportunities of a mobile society. The recreative use of the direct environment is corroborated by the high proportion of the population in this type of estates who engage in activities such as walking, cycling and street sports in public spaces such as streets and parks.

Thirdly, more social cohesion in the new housing estates is supposed to correlate positively with higher levels of well-being among the inhabitants. It should imply less loneliness, more concern for the common welfare of the inhabitants, looking after each other's children, more care for the maintenance and the keeping clean and safe of public space, etc. Whereas the (local) governments spend a lot of money on all sorts of city renewal and socio-cultural projects in the old neighbourhoods in the bigger cities, as a curative way of dealing with (youth) vandalism, crime and other forms of social unrest, the question in the new housing estates is whether the governments should not spend relatively little money on preventing such socially disruptive developments by investing in facilities that give people opportunities to meet and do things together.

Fourthly, from an ecological perspective, everything that can contribute to less leisure-related traffic is welcome. When local socio-cultural facilities can provide for the needs of the local community this may bring a reduction in car travel and associated problems (pollution, parking, traffic jams). A fifth reason to pay attention to community facilities is that, as increases in scale and functional differentiation take place in the spheres of production and consumption, secondary and tertiary education, health care and so on, the few remaining community facilities become crucial as meeting points in the new housing estates. Apart from their encounters in the street and across the fences of their gardens, primary educational facilities, basic shopping facilities, some types of socio-cultural facilities and sport facilities are about the only places left where the inhabitants of the new housing estates can meet, make friends and develop some sort of commitment,

A sixth reason to support community facilities is that community facilities cannot and should not only be for the sake of the community inhabitants themselves. These types of facilities, particularly sport facilities, not only create a meeting place for the people living in their direct environment but also do so for people living elsewhere in the city and its surroundings. In other words, these facilities may work as a kind of hinge between community and city, making the community a more integral part of the city at large.

Research design

If there still are reasons to believe that it may be useful to work on a socio-cultural infrastructure in new housing estates, what then do sport and the sport infrastructure have to offer in terms of enhancing social integration, strengthening commitment and social cohesion? Sport is very popular, health is becoming an ever more crucial issue in a prosperous and ageing society, and most sports require, by their very nature, forms of organisation and social relationships. In addition, as mentioned above, apart from primary schools, there is very little else that may bring people together in the new housing estates. However, so far all of this is 'theory' and 'abstract ideas'. But how does this work 'in practice'? Do city planners actively think about a sport infrastructure as instrumental for the establishment of social relationships in the new housing estate? Do inhabitants of these housing estates themselves see or use sport in this way? Empirical research should help us to find answers to these questions.

The research project is divided in three phases. In the first phase the main focus is on the 'supply side', that is the planning of sport provisions in the new urban expansions. In the second phase we map the 'demand side', the sporting behaviour of the inhabitants of these new housing estates and the type of bonding they develop. The third phase is intended to yield policy recommendations.

Research questions

The main questions guiding the research are:

Phase 1:

1) How does the planning of sport facilities in large-scale new housing estates take place (who is involved, what is the planning procedure, who takes decisions about what sort of facilities, etc.)?

2) To what extent are social integration, commitment and social cohesion in the new housing estates, as elements of the future social life for those housing estates, taken into account in the planning process? More specifically, do the potential social integrative effects of sport play a role in the planning of sport facilities?

Phase 2:

3) What do inhabitants of recently-built housing estates do in terms of practising sport (do they practise sport? If so, how often, using what kind of facility, etc.)?

4) What sort of commitments and relationships do people develop in these new housing estates, and how important do they think these are? Is there a difference in this respect between people who practise sport, and those who do not?

Phase 3:

5) What recommendations should be given to the various governments for the planning of a sport infrastructure and the enhancement of the (potentially) positive effects of sport on social cohesion in new housing estates?

Selection of cases

In consultation with VWS four municipalities were selected: Rotterdam (590,000 inhabitants), Tilburg (186,000), Zoetermeer (110,000) and Veenendaal (58,000). Together, the new housing estates in these cities should produce a fairly accurate picture of the VINEX-locations in general.

Rotterdam 'represents' the three 'big' cities in the Netherlands (the biggest city in the Netherlands is Amsterdam with 750,000 inhabitants). Tilburg and Zoetermeer belong to a second group of roughly 20 'middle range' cities with 100,000 – 250,000 inhabitants. In Tilburg we focus on two expansions of an existing industrial town. Zoetermeer is in fact a still-expanding new town, close to The Hague. Veenendaal is an example of a fast-growing smaller place, which profits from its location on the A 12 motorway linking the Randstad with Germany.

In each municipality there is a new housing estate being built or recently completed, of which the planning dates back to the 1980s or early 1990s, and where it is possible to carry out a survey among the inhabitants. All these municipalities are making plans for new housing estates (in most cases VINEX-locations), which befit the 'compact city' philosophy even better than the recently completed expansions.

Methods

Phase 1:

The research started with a literature search and interviews with city planners and officials.

The literature search was meant to clarify crucial concepts such as social integration and social infrastructure and to chart what is known about the planning of sport and welfare facilities. On the basis of the literature we constructed an item list for the interviews and a questionnaire for the survey.

In each city we interviewed between five and seven people, including officials from the sport and recreation department, officials involved in the physical planning of the new housing estates, people actually working in the existing housing estates (managers of sport provisions, personnel in local welfare provisions) and volunteers, such as the chairman of the big soccer club 't Zand in the Reeshof, the new housing estate in Tilburg. The main aims of these interviews were to get to know the housing estates, to find out about the underlying ideas and procedures as regards the planning of welfare provisions, and the state of affairs in terms of the development of a social infrastructure. In all of this we took a particular interest in sport facilities and the (potential) role of sport in creating forms of bonding and cohesion.

On the basis of the literature search and the interviews we can formulate answers to the first two research questions.

Phase 2:

In each municipality we distributed 400 questionnaires among the inhabitants (18 years and older) of the new housing estate that was most recently completed. The addresses were randomly picked from the 'telephone book' (via CD-rom). Financial restrictions made it impossible to conduct a separate survey among, or to do interviews with, children. However, the questionnaire included questions about the children in the household, their sporting behaviour and questions about bonding related to this behaviour. The age of 18 was chosen because, on the one hand it was expected that youth would be little interested in completing the questionnaire, and on the other, it would allow for comparison with national data that uses the age brackets 12–17, 18–24, and so on. It was financially not possible to translate the questionnaire into Turkish and/or Arabic, or to use other methods to reach different ethnic groups. However, the percentage of these groups in these new housing estates is known to be relatively low.

The questionnaire included questions about socio-economic backgrounds; housing career; sport participation and opinions on sport-related issues; experiences and activities in, and opinions on the new housing estate; commitments and various aspects of relationships; children and volunteer work. The questions about the socio-economic backgrounds and sporting behaviour were taken from the (draft version of the) *Direction Sport Participation Survey (DSS)* (Diopter, 1998), which allows for comparisons with outcomes of other (national and local) research into sport participation. Most of the other questions were based on the outcomes of the literature search.

The average response was 35 per cent and appeared to be not representative for the VINEX-locations nor for the cities where we did the survey, let alone for the Dutch population as a whole. Basically, we secured an over-representation of the well-to-do, middle aged and middle class inhabitants of the four housing estates. At the time of the writing, we have just started the analysis of the results of the survey. Below we will present some of the first findings, particularly those related to the planning process, sport behaviour and social commitment. Other issues, such as the relation of sport behaviour to background variables or the evaluation of the quality of the existing (sport) facilities by the inhabitants of recently completed urban expansions, will not be addressed here.

Phase 3:

In the third and last phase of the project we will go back to the municipalities with the results found so far. In group discussions with planners and sport officials, partly the same as those we spoke with in the first phase, we will discuss the results and the conclusions that should be drawn. The main aim is to formulate practical policy recommendations (for VWS and for the local decision-makers), which come as close as possible to actual improvements in the local planning process.

Planning sport facilities

In the first phase of the research project, focused on the planning of sport facilities in new urban expansions, we found that, in the planning of the recently-completed housing estates, relatively little attention had been given to welfare provisions in general or to sport facilities in particular. The planning process is first of all dominated by the urge to build houses and the physical infrastructure that goes with it (sewers, roads, streetlights and so on). A second and growing interest is the environment, leading to a range of issues such as enhancing the role of public transport, more sustainable forms of water management and more environmentally friendly buildings. A third and also growing interest is the 'achitectonic quality' or 'identity' of the housing estate as a whole, and the various housing complexes and the individual houses in particular. Interesting, from our perspective, is that one of the reasons given for this growing concern for architectonic quality is the wish to make the housing estate 'distinctive' from the 'mass' of new housings built around the country, and to give it a more defined character in order that the inhabitants can, and will be able to identify with, their new neighbourhood. We have not pursued this any further but it would be interesting to see whether, indeed, a more defined architectonic character of the houses or the neighbourhood as a whole (or the facilities in the neighbourhood) leads to a stronger mental bond with the place where people live.

Welfare provisions (including schools, health provisions, social-cultural and sport facilities), commercial provisions (shops, small offices) and (green) public spaces appear to 'follow' the planning of the houses and physical infrastructure. The number of public facilities is decided on the basis of 'rules of thumb' and their location is mainly dictated by the logic of the overall plan. This is particularly the case for outdoor sport facilities (mostly soccer pitches). These are normally located in 'left over areas', which are unsuitable for housing for reasons such as traffic noise or soil pollution.

The planning of the housing estates in the 1980s was dominated by financial concerns on the one hand and a rather individualistic view of the future dwellers on the estate on the other. The financial pressures on these estates meant trying to cram as many houses as possible into the estate in order to maximise income for the municipality (and for the private project developers), and to prevent or cut losses on the project by minimising spending on public facilities. This type of development policy could thrive because the city planners had (and often still have) a rather individualistic view of the future inhabitants of the new estate. Helped by market research among potential buyers of houses in these estates, the focus has been on enlarging and making the houses more luxurious, and beautifying their direct environments. What appears to be particularly attractive to the Dutch buyer of a new house is its location close to 'green' areas, including water. With all this attention on spare time at and directly around the home in the new housing estates, very little attention has been given to spare time spent further away from home, and more particularly to the possibilities for meeting other inhabitants of the new estate in a (semi-)public space such as a square, a market, sport venue and so on. Indeed, we have found very little consistent thinking about the social infrastructure of the estates where we did the survey.

With respect to the plans for new housing estates which are being made or completed at this moment, we notice a growing awareness of the importance of a good social infrastructure. There is an increasing involvement of welfare departments in the planning process, and there is attention to building more 'flexible' houses that can be made fit for working at home and/or leisure activities that require more space. Nevertheless, particularly the large outdoor sport facilities remain to be used to balance the budget. The most promising development is the clustering of public facilities around schools. In a number of plans, we see attempts to build schools, sport facilities, day-care centres and the like close together, and sometimes even close to other public and commercial facilities. This gives form to an area that may develop into something of a social centre or meeting place in the neighbourhood or the whole new estate.

Despite these developments, still one cannot conclude that the social infrastructure and future social life in the new housing estate is given much substantive and consistent thought. The position of the welfare departments in the planning process is still very weak, procedurally as well as financially. The welfare departments themselves also point out that they lack the 'hard evidence' or 'data' that could underscore the importance of good welfare provisions in these areas. All in all, we witness a sharp contrast between the various policy statements with regard to the social integrative values of sport and what actually happens 'on the ground'. We have not come across any planning of sport facilities that showed signs of well thought-out ideas about the social-integrative potential of sport. It is pragmatism and (lack of) money that still dominate the planning of these facilities.

Sport in the new housing estates

In this section we present the first results of the survey and try to answer the third and fourth research questions. As said before, we have used a standardised list of survey questions to 'measure' sport behaviour. This list is, in fact, still under development and our research project is one of the very first to use this list of standardised questions. The ideal behind the *Direction Sport Participation Survey (DSS)* is to make the results of sport participation surveys more comparable, and to make benchmarking possible (Diopter, 1998). The DSS is based on the following definition of sport:

> Sport is a human activity that takes place mostly in a specific association, but can also be practised unattached, as a rule using a specific spatial facility and/or environment, in a way that is related to the rules and customs which have been developed in an international context for the purpose of performances with an element of competition or contest in that activity. (Diopter, 1998; authors' translation)

It will be clear that this 'definition' is not very strict and allows for a growing family of 'sport-related' activities (Crum, 1991) to be included. This is both to do justice to the dynamic character of sport and the proliferation of new forms of sport, as well as to accommodate the wishes of policy makers. The latter care less about the strictness of the definition of sport, and more about the factual developments in the needs for facilities to accommodate 'movement behaviour' in public space, be it 'recreation', 'sport' or 'play'.

The DSS prescribes the use of a 'presentation sheet' which, in our survey, contains a list of 88 options to tick a particular sport (like soccer, swimming, beach volleyball, climbing, bridge, squash, etc.), to write down a non-listed sport, or to tick 'no sport'. This list, combined with questions about the frequency and location in time of sport activities undertaken, allows for various ways to measure sport participation. The most common way is to say that someone participates in sport when he or she has practised one or more of the sports mentioned on the presentation sheet, twelve times or more during the last twelve months. It is acknowledged that this includes people who, for instance, combine occasional swimming during the summer, ski-ing during the winter holiday and playing billiards every now and then. Not surprisingly, then, we have found a high rate of sport participation — three quarters of all respondents. This is 10 per cent above the national average. On the one hand, one might say that this could be expected given the over-representation of the more well-to-do, middle classes in our sample, compared with the Dutch population as a whole. On the other hand, our sample shows an under-representation of younger people, who are known to be more frequent sport participants than the middle-aged. As age is a stronger differentiating factor in sport participation than class (CBS, 1998; Van den Heuvel and Van der Werff, 1998), we conclude that sport participation in the new housing estates is somewhat above the national average.

With respect to the sport behaviour of the inhabitants of the new housing estates we found 'sporting forms of recreation' to be highly popular, as compared with more traditional forms of sport. Indeed, the top ten popular sports were dominated by activities such as swimming, walking, cycling and jogging, followed by fitness/aerobics and the like. In terms of more traditional sports, the most popular sports are racketsports (tennis, squash and badminton). Sailing and (in-line) skating/skeelering (skating on indoor and outdoor hard surfaces as opposed to ice-skating) are also popular. The most frequently-practised team sports are soccer and volleyball but their participation rates are a quarter or one fifth of that of the most popular sport activities.

In general, the results of our survey appear to reflect the national trends in a more extreme form: higher rates for recreational sports and health sports, and the same or lower rates for team sports practised in the context of a sport club. Part of the difference can be accounted for by the non-representativeness of the group of respondents, particularly the under-represented young people who practise team sport in sport clubs.

Looking forward to the issue of social integration, it is interesting to see that many of the recreational and sometimes dubbed 'individualistic' sport activities, such as swimming and walking, appear to be done by people who also participate in a more traditional sport. It is not so much a matter of 'either/or', then, as a matter of doing both. Besides, when asked in what sort of organisational context they practise their sport, 60 per cent answered that at least part of their sport participation is done in informal group settings (with friends, neighbours, colleagues from work, etc.), 46 per cent do so as a member of a formal sport club and 26 per cent make use of commercial sport facilities. In contrast, 40 per cent practise his or her sport activities alone or almost alone (for example, cycling alone in combination with playing a team sport). The most striking result, however, is the large number of people who practise sport in an informal group (groups of friends making cycling tours or preparing for the marathon of Rotterdam, etc.). Much of the so-called 'un-organised' sport cannot therefore be equated with 'individualistic' sport, and may play an important role in processes of social integration, besides the more obvious integrative role of official sport clubs ('organised sport').

A final notable result to mention here is the very frequent use of public space for sporting forms of recreation. Almost 40 per cent of the respondents use the street, and 35 percent answered that at least part of their sport activities take place in woods. These and other findings emphasise the relative importance of the possibilities for 'sporting use' of public and/or recreational spaces besides proper sport facilities, such as streets, parks, woods and playgrounds.

Sport and social integration

Concepts

Integration, used in the context of studying social systems, refers to 'the degree of interdependence of action'. It can be defined "as regularised ties, interchanges or *reciprocity of practices* between either actors or collectivities" (Giddens, 1979: p. 76; italics in original). Basically, social integration refers to the mutual influence of one actor's behaviour on the other's in a string of face-to-face interactions.

This way of conceptualizing social integration implies that social integration has to be distinguished from its effects. Social integration is a 'neutral' term, not some *a priori* 'good' (or bad). It is a dynamic concept, emphasising different levels of 'system-ness' in and between social systems and the ways this comes about through exchanges, meeting one another other and developing ties between actors, both friendly (leading to 'unity: see Elling and De Knop, 1998) and hostile (in the form of institutionalised conflicts, feuds, exclusion, etc.: see Duyvendak *et al.*, 1998). The analytical value of separating integration from its effects shows in the differences that may exist in the interpretation of the nature of the regularisation of ties between actors. For instance, 'adjustment' can be an effect of social integration that may be valued quite differently by the adjusted individual and the collectivity adjusted to.

In the questionnaire we have included questions about social integration itself (such as whether people have contacts with other people in the neighbourhood, what sort of contacts, what they think about the meeting places in the neighbourhood, where sport and other activities take place, etc.) and questions with propositions (on which the respondents can score on a Likert-scale) on the possible effects of social integration (see below). Although it must be acknowledged that social integration not necessarily has only positive effects, or that it automatically leads to a growing togetherness and more social cohesion among hitherto separate groups, the assumption here is that social integration may have positive effects and may lead to increasing commitment or bonding and social cohesion. It is this potentially positive effect in which we are most interested.

We understand the distinction between commitment and social cohesion to be gradual. In commitment, the emphasis is on the perspective of the actor, the relationships sustained by the actor and the involvement of the actor in these relationships. In social cohesion, the emphasis shifts towards the social networks of which the actors and their mutual relationships are a part. It stresses the degree of connectedness within and between collectivities, as seen in the 'thickness' of relations and the intensity of the involvement of actors in and via these relations.

We distinguish three dimensions of commitment in this project: 1) mental commitment (the identification with the new housing estate); 2) functional, physical or instrumental commitment (the use of and activities in the new housing estate); and 3) social commitment (the social contacts/relationships in the new housing estate). Put another way, we are particularly interested in how, and to what extent, social integration may lead to different forms of 'bonding' (mentally, functionally and socially) to a particular place. 'Bonding' then, from our perspective, is synonymous with commitment.

Following Blokland-Potters (1998), 'social commitment' is further subdivided into four aspects of relationships (that is, four aspects of bonding of a more or less permanent form between actors): transactions or economic relationships; interdependencies or power relationships; shared frames of meanings, norms and values (socio-cultural relationships); and bonds or affective relationships. The assumption is that social cohesion in the new housing estates will be stronger when the actors show a higher degree of commitment, following from a stronger identification with the estate, a more frequent use of the public space and facilities and a broader range of relationships there. Thus, questions were asked and propositions were presented to measure the degree of identification with the new neighbourhood, the 'use' which is made of the neighbourhood and the extent to which the various aspects of social commitment or bonding have developed.

Main results

A remarkable result, in terms of social integration, is that almost half of the respondents do not greet his or her neighbours, a third do not have occasional chats with neighbours and 40 per cent says they do not visit people living close by. It thus appears that, for a substantial group of VINEX-dwellers, social integration in their neighbourhood is fairly restricted. In terms of mental bonding or identification, only a quarter of the respondents say they identify with 'Prinsenland', 'Rokkeveen' (the VINEX-locations where the surveys were conducted) and a quarter indicate that they do not feel at home in these places. In terms of functional bonding, only a third of the respondents expect to live longer than 10 years in the house they occupy at present, and most of their volunteer work is done outside the VINEX-location in which they live. The most important aspect of social commitment appears to be exchange relations, such as borrowing garden equipment from each other.

Half of the respondents practise sport with friends they already had. For them, sport is thus one of the ways in which they can give content and continuity to the bonds with their friends. 40 per cent of the respondents indicated that they have got new friends through their participation in sport, although only 11 per cent say that they intended to make new friends via sport. This finding endorses the idea that making friends is an important yet unintended consequence of sport participation. Interestingly, these new friends are not only 'sport friends'. About 85 per cent answered that they undertake other activities, besides sport, with these new friends. Those who practise sport are significantly more often a member of a club (sport or other) than those who do not. Although this may seem self-evident (those who do not practise sport will not be a member of a sport club), it does indicate that sport enlarges the opportunities to become part of some sort of social context rather than replacing or substituting for other social contexts. This is particularly the case for children: 148 have become member of a club in the new housing estate: in 129 instances this was a sport club and 32 times another club (13 children have joined both a sport club and another club).

Although we have indications that sport has positive social effects, in terms of developing and sustaining social relationships, it is not shown in the results that those who practise sport develop stronger mental, functional or social commitments than those who do not. We should again emphasise that the sample was not representative in terms of most of the demographic background variables; but controlling these background variables has not lead, so far, to different insights. With hindsight, it is likely that those who already have some sort of commitment to the new housing estate will complete and return a questionnaire about the provisions in the housing estate much more readily than those who use their house merely as a sleeping place, with no commitment at all to the estate. In other words, the sample as a whole may be biased towards a positive commitment to the estate, both among those who practise sport and among those who do not.

To summarise, the potential for social integration appears to be limited and actual social integration in the neighbourhood or the VINEX-location as a whole is low. The overall picture seems more or less to confirm the outcomes of other research in VINEX-locations, such as that of Reijndorp *et al.* (1998). People do have social contacts but these tend to be less and less place-bound. Sport fits this overall picture: it does have integrative effects and leads to the establishment of relationships and commitment. However, the geographical component in these effects is missing: sport does not appear to lead to a stronger commitment to the place people reside.

Discussion and policy recommendations

Discussion

We are disappointed by the response to the surveys because it is low and not representative. Having seen the first results, with an over-representation of the higher income brackets and higher education brackets on the one hand, and an under-representation of younger and older people, unemployed and ethnic minorities on the other, we expected, as a combined result of all this, a sport participation rate that would not differ much from national levels. In fact it lies 10 to 20 per cent higher than the national sport participation level, depending on how sport participation is measured. Given the low response, however, we simply cannot be sure that this high participation rate is not an effect of a bias in the response group. We cannot exclude the possibility that people interested in sport and/or people that have some form of commitment to the welfare and sport facilities in the neighbourhood or social life in the neighbourhood have responded more readily than those who are more unattached to the VINEX-location in general and to sport in their neighbourhood in particular.

We do not find a correlation between sport participation and bonding with the place where people live. However, we do find that people who participate frequently in sport (more than once a week), and those who have joined a sport club, develop stronger bonds than those who practise 'unorganised' sport. This may seem logical because practising sport more often and/or practising sport in the context of a sport club self-evidently leads to more opportunities to meet other people (a higher rate of social integration), and thus to more opportunities to develop more permanent relationships, including affective bonds with others. But this logic also implies that, if one uses a definition of sport in which aspects of frequency and organisational form are diluted excessively, fewer and fewer measurable effects can be correlated with sport participation. This raises an interesting dilemma: on the one hand we see — in order to stress the popularity and importance of sport — a broadening of the definition of sport, including an ever-expanding range of sport-like activities, leading to a high sport participation rate. As an (unintended) consequence, however, sport participation becomes less and less distinctive. When, as in our survey, three quarters of the population are said to be practising sport, the differentiations within the group practising sport become more important than those between people who practise sport and people who do not.

The surveys, the interviews and the visits we paid to the sport facilities made it abundantly clear that sport provides opportunities to meet people and establish bonds between them. In the interviews we noted phrases such as 'there is nothing else here' and 'you meet people at the club', stressing explicitly or implicitly the value of the sport facilities for the local community. We think further research, preferably of a qualitative nature, is desirable to explore more deeply the geographical component in the processes of social integration and cohesion that we have encountered in this research.

Whether or not social integration via sport leads to bonding with the new housing estate, or bonding on a larger scale, the fact that it leads to forms of bonding *per se* should be enough for policy makers to take the planning of a sport infrastructure more seriously. In this regard, we experienced a lack of urgency. Although we witness an increasing awareness of this social value of sport, we think the sport officials are still too pragmatically involved in trying to satisfy the organised sport clubs and pay too little attention to more informal ways of practising sport or sporting forms of recreation. At the same time, it must be admitted that the sport and recreation departments often lack the resources, the knowledge and the personnel to be able to deal with these issues effectively. A sense of urgency is certainly lacking among city planners. They appear to have little affinity to the world of sport, and more often than not are not convinced that sport is more than just another hobby that people may enjoy during their spare time.

Policy recommendations

As indicated above, there is a third phase in this research project, in which we will return to the city planners and sport officials. We want to confront them with the results of phases 1 and 2, and discuss with them the policy recommendations that should follow from this project. We conclude this paper by summing up the recommendations that are most likely to be discussed in this third phase. Basically, all these recommendations are meant to do something about the lack of urgency on the issue and to raise the profile and visibility of sport facility planning.

A first policy recommendation will be to make the planning of sport facilities in VINEX-locations an integral part of the overall planning process and the development costs. In most development plans the costs of the physical infrastructure (streetlights, roads, sewers and so on) are paid out of the yields of the sale of the land. We propose to include in these costs the layout of the sport infrastructure, meaning that the price of the land will increase by a couple of guilders per square meter.

The second recommendation is to update the 'norms' (indicators) for sport facilities needed *per capita*. At present the municipalities do not have up to date figures about the number of soccer pitches, tennis courts, square meters of swimming water, etc. per thousand inhabitants, let alone detailed figures or index numbers for various types of inhabitants (young families, elderly, high and low income groups, etc.). These indicators should be used as input for the development plans, both to indicate the number of square meters needed per type of sport, and also the costs of realising these facilities in the new housing estate. The total sum thus accounted for should be the budget with which to start working on the building of sport facilities.

More attention should be given to the fact that much of the public space is or can be used as a venue for recreational forms of sport. Again, this is partly a matter of developing new norms but it is also a matter of creativity and making optimal use of the local circumstances. Here, VWS could stimulate exemplary projects and publish best practice. For instance, if a lot of water is part of a particular development plan, what is done to maximise its use value for swimmers, skaters, sailors, surfers and kayakers?

A fourth recommendation is to include commercial facilities in the planning of the sport infrastructure of the new housing estate. First of all, commercial supply of sport facilities should be stimulated. Secondly, to the extent that this is successful and leads to the replacement of public facilities by commercial facilities, special attention should be given to the position of sport policy target groups. If, for instance, the commercial entry prices are too high for particular groups of unemployed or the disabled, personal subsidies should be considered. Thirdly, the location of this type of commercial sport facilities should be planned, for instance in the direct environment of the public sport facilities.

A fifth recommendation is to pursue the trend of clustering (co-locating) sport and educational facilities. Additionally, we suggest that experiments should start with integrated management for these clustered facilities, to optimise the multiple use of these facilities by the local community.

References

Blokland-Potters, T. (1998) *Wat stadsbewoners bindt. Sociale relaties in een achterstandswijk.* Kampen: Kok Agora.

Boer, T.A. de and Visschedijk, P.A.M. (1994) *Gebruik en waardering van binnen- en buitenstedelijk groen.* Wageningen: IBN-DLO.

CBS (Centraal Bureau voor de Statistiek) (1998) *Sport in Nederland 1998.* Voorburg/Heerlen: CBS.

Crum, B.J. (1991) *Over de versporting van de samenleving. Reflecties over bewegingsculturele ontwikkelingen met het oog op sportbeleid.* Rijswijk: WVC.

Diopter (1998) *Richtlijn Sportdeelname Onderzoek (RSO). Achtergrond, inhoud, toelichting en vervolg.* 's-Hertogenbosch: Diopter.

Duyvendak, J.W., Krouwel, A., Kraaykamp, R. and Boonstra, N. (1998) *Integratie door sport? Een onderzoek naar gemengde en ongemengde sportbeoefening van allochtonen en autochtonen.* Rotterdam: Bestuursdienst Rotterdam.

Elling, A.H.F. and de Knop, P. (1998) 'De sociaal-integrerende functie van sport. Een kwestie van interpretatie?', *Beleid en Maatschappij* Vol. 25, No. 4: pp. 215-228.

Garreau, J. (1991) *Edge city. Life on the new frontier.* New York: Doubleday.

Giddens, A. (1979) *Central problems in social theory. Action, structure and contradiction in social analysis.* Berkeley, CA: University of California Press.

Heuvel, M. van den and Werff, H. van der (1998) *Trendanalyse sport. Ontwikkelingen in sportdeelname en organisatiegraad van de sport in de periode 1975-1995.* Tilburg: KUB/VTW and Arnhem/NOC*NSF.

Reijndorp, A., Kompier, V., Metaal, S., Nio, I. and Truijens, B. (1998) *Buitenwijk. Stedelijkheid of afstand.* Rotterdam: NAi Uitgevers.

Stichting Recreatie (1997) *Recreatie dicht bij huis.* Den Haag: SR.

VWS (Ministerie van Volksgezondheid, Welzijn en Sport) (1996) *Wat sport beweegt. Contouren en speerpunten voor het sportbeleid van de rijksoverheid.* Rijswijk: VWS.

VWS (Ministerie van Volksgezondheid, Welzijn en Sport) (1998) *Sturen op doelen, faciliteren op instrumenten. Beleidskader lokaal sociaal beleid.* Rijswijk: VWS.

VWS (Ministerie van Volksgezondheid, Welzijn en Sport) (1999) *Werken aan sociale kwaliteit. Welzijnsnota 1999-2002.* Den Haag: VWS.

Wassenberg, F.A.G. et al. (1994) *Woonwensen en de realisatie van VINEX-lokaties in de Randstad.* Den Haag: VROM.

II

Identity

Homophobia and its Effects on the Inequitable Provision of Health and Leisure Services for Older Gay Men and Lesbians

Arnold H. Grossman

Department of Health Studies, School of Education,
New York University (USA)

Introduction

Older gay men and lesbians (60 years of age and older) are nowhere near as visible as gay and lesbian teenagers and those who are in their twenties. Whilst their invisibility results, in part, from the ageism and concurrent stereotypes of older people that exist in many gay communities, it is mainly an outcome of the societal homophobia that older gay men and lesbians have lived with for many years. In fact, much of their invisibility is a choice that should be understood in the context of their history and experience with homophobia (Kochman, 1993). However, it also has to be recognised that this invisibility has contributed to a lack of awareness of their needs as constituents of older adult communities; as a result there has been an inequitable provision of health and leisure services to meet their needs.

Homophobia, originally defined as "the dread of being in close quarters with homosexuals" (Weinberg, 1972: p. 4), has since become the term used to describe that cluster of stereotypical beliefs, prejudicial attitudes, animosity, and discomfort held by most heterosexuals in reference to gay men, lesbians and bisexuals (Communication Technologies, 1994). Like racism and anti-Semitism, it is a word that calls up images of loss of freedom, verbal and physical violence, and death.

Herek (1992) defined anti-gay beliefs and attitudes in terms of the distinct social and psychological functions they serve. He suggested that individuals with anti-gay attitudes range from those for whom gay men and lesbians symbolise an important value conflict, to those for whom gay men and lesbians symbolise an "out-group" in society, or to those for whom gay

105

men and lesbians symbolise an unacceptable part of themselves. With regard to those in the last group, Herek believes that homosexuality provokes intense anxiety that can only be reduced by denying and externalising the unaccept-able aspect of themselves and then attacking it in others. Individuals who fall within this group are most likely to exhibit overtly hostile reactions to gay men and lesbians and to same-sex behaviours. These reactions have included verbal abuse, beatings, being raped, loss of housing and employment, and death.

> It is a power that is great enough to keep ten to twenty percent of the population living lives of fear (if their sexual identity is hidden) or lives of danger (if their sexual identity is visible) or both. And its power is great enough to keep the remaining eighty to ninety per cent of the population trapped in their own fears. (Pharr, 1988: p. 2)

Many in this latter group are among those who make decisions leading to the inequitable provision of health and leisure services for older gay men and lesbians.

Stigmatisation, discrimination and exclusion

Communities create stigmas about groups of people who are different. Stig-mas, reflecting the prevailing social and cultural milieu, define what is unac-ceptable in society. Stigmatisation of gay and lesbian people reflects a marked status and leads to their being assigned a discredited social identity—sometimes attributed to "nature" and at other times imputed to "nurture" (Goffman, 1963). Processes of assigning blame are employed to distance people who are assumed to have the underlying "imperfection" from community life. Prejudice and discrimination are used to set gay men and lesbians apart from the community. Negative attitudes towards gay men and lesbians are based on preconceptions and stereotypes which lead people to judge them not by their personal qualities, but by their membership in the stigmatised group (Bohan, 1996).

The stigmatisation in the form of homophobia overshadows the social identities of older gay and lesbian people in their roles as professionals, parents, partners, family members and friends. The stigma becomes the focus of attention; everything about them is understood in terms of the stigma. The resulting homophobia leads to their exclusion from mainstream community life and often results in psychological distress, feelings of isolation, withdrawal from social interaction, lower self-esteem, depression, anxiety, and negative perceptions of self (Bohan, 1996; Ungvarski and Grossman, 1999).

Growing up in a homophobic society

Homophobia places such negative messages and condemnations on gay men and lesbians that they have to struggle throughout their lives for their self-esteem (Pharr, 1988). This is especially so for those people who constitute today's older gay and lesbian populations. They lived their early developmental years prior to the Stonewall Riots of 1969 (street demonstrations that occurred after police raided the Stonewall Inn, a gay bar in New York's Greenwich Village, which marked the start of the modern-day gay liberation movement). They learned that their sexual desires and behaviors were labelled immoral, illegal, undesirable and sick (Jacobson and Grossman, 1996; Kochman, 1993). Their identities as homosexuals led to their being classified as "mentally ill," and many feared that their families would use homosexuality as grounds for institutionalising them. Medical explanations of all nonheterosexual identities had prompted the consideration of homosexuality as a pathology that was amenable to treatment. Conversion therapy was deemed the normative treatment approach for this so-called "mental illness," and it was aimed at changing sexual orientation. It was not until 1973 that "homosexuality" was removed as a mental illness from the psychiatric nomenclature of the American Psychiatric Association. Shortly thereafter, the American Psychological Association followed with a resolution that agreed with this position, and it urged professionals to take the lead in eliminating the stigma of mental illness that had been associated with homosexuality (Bohan, 1996). Subsequently, older gay men also faced the stigma associated with GRID (Gay-Related Immune Deficiency) when the first cases of AIDS, which occurred among homosexual and bisexual men, were dubbed such in 1981 (Public Media Center, 1995). The media and the public still fail to make distinctions between "gay" and "AIDS," and many older gay men who grew up during a period of intense antigay discrimination do not want to be identified with any HIV/AIDS prevention education or counselling (Grossman, 1995).

Friend (1989, 1990) found that the lifelong process of resisting or internalising society's negative attitudes associated with homosexuality resulted in a variety of images of older gay and lesbian people. He proposed a model that has two continua, one which represents the cognitive/behavioral responses, and another which is a set of corresponding affective responses. The two ends and the midpoint of the continua represent the following three adaptational styles of older gay and lesbian people.

The older gay men and lesbians found on the end of the continuum that Friend labelled "stereotypical" are inclined to believe the negative images of homosexuals promulgated by a heterosexist society. They see their homosexuality as secretive and their aging as punishment for the immoral life they have led. They remain distanced from their families of origin and friends by shame, lack of self-respect, fear, ignorance, and sometimes self-loathing. These feelings may lead to misery and despondency.

In Friend's (1989, 1990) midpoint category of adaptational styles are those older gay and lesbian individuals who are labelled "passing." These individuals are inclined to believe that some of the homophobic prejudices articulated by society are true and that heterosexuality is the superior sexual orientation. They feel valued for what others expect them to be, rather than for who they really are; consequently, they hide the stigma attached to their sexual orientation by using a "cover," such as marriage and having children. When they get older, they decide not to become agents of pain to those they love by remaining in the closet, and attempt to live in two separate, compartment-alised worlds. They sometimes have extra-marital affairs with same-sex individuals or seek anonymous sex in known cruising areas. As Friend (1990) suggested, this splitting of one's life may lead to a segmented self and a lack of genuineness in heterosexual as well as in same-sex relationships. Another outcome may be fewer opportunities for emotional support during times of crisis.

The last adaptational style, "affirmative," can be found on the opposite end of the continuum from the "stereotypical" style (Friend, 1989, 1990). The older gay and lesbian individuals in this category affirm their homosexual identity by fighting heterosexism. They challenge society's homosexual assumptions by forming long-term same-sex relationships and friendships. In forming these same-sex attachments, they often confront society's rigid services designed for them. These services tend not only to deny them the assistance they are entitled to but also to perpetuate the barriers that prevent many older gay men and lesbians from achieving their potential.

Barriers to providing services to older gay men and lesbians

Society's continuing homophobia, together with the reactions of older gay men and lesbians who have experienced it for many years, have created barriers to health, leisure and other human services for large numbers of them. These barriers are usually compounded for gay and lesbian people of colour, as a range of factors have to be considered in determining the impact of ethnic or racial identity and its ongoing, dynamic interaction with sexual orientation (Greene, 1996). Often gay men and lesbians of colour face difficult challenges as they try to strike a balance that allows them to be empowered and liberated in both of their oppressed identities (Wall and Washington, 1991). The various barriers frequently lead to social and emotional isolation, including feelings of "otherness" and rejection. They have also fostered disadvantages that have prevented some older gay men and lesbians from achieving their potential and experiencing feelings of self-fulfillment.

The greatest barrier is the one stated in the opening paragraph of this paper: the *invisibility* of older gay men and lesbians. This invisibility is enhanced in cultures (for example, Western and gay) in which youth and youthful attractiveness are privileged. Furthermore, invisibility allows stereotypes and misunderstandings to persist. As a consequence, most providers do not consider the possibility that older persons are gay or lesbian, making the assumption that all older individuals are heterosexual. When older people do identify themselves as gay or lesbian, providers tend to consider them as oddities or curiosities whose existences are atypical, and who therefore can be dismissed. Concurrent with these erroneous assumptions are those that consider older gay and lesbian people as asexual, not interested in dating, and not desiring the presence of a romantic partner (Greene, 2000). All of these scenarios, however, lead to the same result: a lack of adequate needs assessment, programme planning and service delivery for older gay men and lesbians. Until positive images of older gay and lesbian adults are portrayed, their lives will be neglected.

Lack of visibility leads to a second barrier in the provision of, and accessibility to, services for older gay and lesbian people, and that is the persistence of *negative myths* about them. The predominant myths are that the older gay man is a predator and the older lesbian is a frustrated spinster and that they both live unhappy, lonely, and sad lives. There is no mention that older gay men and lesbians have created long-standing relationships, as they are not visible in most social settings. Overall, these negative myths foster the false beliefs that older gay men and lesbians have to "recruit others to their lifestyles" to meet their needs, as well as add to their ranks. These negative myths provoke intense anxieties in providers, prohibiting them from establishing needed services and creating outreach programmes for older gay men and lesbians.

A third set of barriers consists of *fears*. The primary fears of older gay men and lesbians relate either to their sexual orientation being discovered or to their being rejected because they informed others about it. Some of these fears are based on internalised homophobia, resulting from decades of hearing negative views about homosexuality and homosexuals. Other fears emanate from having experienced rejection and other negative consequences (for example, name-calling, gay-bashing, job and housing discrimination) because they disclosed their sexual orientation. Although hiding one's sexual orientation may lead to feelings of isolation and to a lack of services, it also fosters a sense of security that coming out about one's sexual orientation tends to jeopardise. While the stress of hiding may lead to some self-destructive behaviours (for example, alcohol and other drug abuse), having to cope with the ongoing consequences of stigmatisation and victimisation may lead to similar outcomes. Only by creating safe spaces (with supporting policies and procedures) and establishing advocacy programmes can providers communicate that there is no real rational basis for many of these fears.

An important barrier to providing health and leisure services to older gay men and lesbians is the *absence of education* about them in most professional preparation programmes and a similar *lack of training* at professional conferences and in continuing education programs. While the content of programmes and conferences is increasingly addressing issues facing gay and lesbian people, it seldom focuses on the ageing members of those groups. Consequently, most agencies that address the needs of older adults and provide services to them do not acknowledge the presence of sexual-minority adults among their constituencies. Administrators and policy-makers of health and leisure service agencies must seek opportunities to provide education and training to their staff members and to provide services that are inclusive.

A powerful barrier to providing health and leisure services to older gay men and lesbians is the *limited knowledge base* about them. For the most part, we have not asked this group about their needs, and they seldom make requests of agencies in ways that make their personal lives known. In conducting a gay and lesbian gerontology review, Gabbay (1997) found only 58 articles that reported empirical findings on gay elders. This is in contrast to the thousands of studies that have been conducted about older people and that never consider that gay and lesbian people are included in their samples.

Gabbay (1997) found that both qualitative and quantitative studies had been conducted with older gay men and lesbians, with studies that used structured interviews, anecdotes and questionnaires dominating the data collection methods. Her review also discovered that a substantial portion of the studies combined gay and lesbian participants, while recognising the limitations in doing so; however, separate studies were reported. Those studies that described findings from older gay men were, almost without exception, conducted with white, middle-class, well-educated, urban-dwelling men who had some connection to the gay community. Those findings cannot be generalised to those older gay men who are nonwhite or poor, who live in rural communities, or who have few gay and lesbian friends or other ties to the gay community. Also, most of the studies had the purpose of contradicting the stereotypes and myths surrounding the men. While 43 of the studies included older lesbians in their sample, Gabbay found that only five empirical studies were exclusively focused on lesbian aging. Following the gay male studies, the empirical findings on lesbians also debunked the myths and stereotypes about them. However, they also revealed that a great diversity of backgrounds, experiences, values and relationships existed among the women in the studies and that a connection with others in a safe environment was associated with positive adaptation and effective functioning in old age. However, it was also acknowledged that being members of a triple minority—female, homosexual and old—was considered risky (Gabbay, 1997).

Results from recent studies about older lesbian and gay people

The author identified four relatively recent empirical studies that focused on older gay, lesbian and bisexual adults. Dorfman and her colleagues (1995) reported on a sample of 108 people, (55 women and 53 men) between the ages of 60 and 93 (Mean = 69.3, SD = 6.8), of which 56 were homosexuals (23 female and 33 male) and 52 were heterosexuals (32 female and 20 male). Their findings indicated that there were no significant differences between older homosexuals and heterosexuals with regard to depression and social support; and, as expected, higher social networks were associated with lower depression. However, the sources of social support varied, with gay men and lesbians receiving significantly more support from friends, while heterosexual elderly individuals derived more support from family members. The authors suggest that there is a need to redefine the concept of family to include "friendship families." Many gay men and lesbians do not have support from their families of origin that their heterosexual counterparts enjoy, and this may be especially true when they are older and in need of care or social contact. Furthermore, the absence of legal status of a relationship may have negative implications for older gay and lesbian couples, especially if one member is ill, hospitalised, disabled or in need of residential care (Greene, 2000).

Quam and Whitford (1992) studied adaptation and age-related expectations of 80 older gay and lesbian adults (39 women and 41 men) over the age of 50 living in a Midwestern metropolitan area. Participants reported acceptance of the ageing process and high levels of life satisfaction. Being active in the gay community was found to be an asset in accepting one's own ageing. Among the other findings were the following: close to 64 per cent of the participants reported that they had gone to or participated in a lesbian/gay social group; however, only 8.8 per cent reported participating in activities at a general population senior centre or club. Because lesbian/gay identity encompasses more than participation in formal organisations, the investigators asked about the sexual orientation of the respondents' friends. They found that over half of the women reported that most of their closest friends were lesbians, while only 27.5 per cent of the men reported that most of their friends were gay men. 65 per cent of the men indicated that their network of close friends included women and men, gay and nongay; while only 38.5 per cent of the women described their friendship network similarly.

From a recent exploratory study of 71 (17 female and 54 male) self-identified gay men, lesbians, and bisexuals ages 50–80 (Mean = 60.8, SD 8.31), Jacobs, Rasmussen and Hohman (1999) concluded that social support services for the older lesbian/gay population may best be provided in a lesbian/gay environment. Among their findings were that the participants used social and support groups within the gay/lesbian community and that gay/lesbian community services were significantly rated as more adequate in meeting needs in time of emotional crises than nongay/lesbian services. They also found that both men and women indicated that they would be interested in participating in social groups that were segregated by gender.

Beeler, Rawls, Herdt and Cohler (1999) conducted a study with 160 older lesbians and gay men in Chicago (49 female and 111 male) between the ages of 45 and 90 (with a median age of 51). They drew three primary conclusions regarding the planning and provision of services for older gay men and lesbians. First, they indicated that providers needed to recognise the diversity of the population, for example those single, those partnered, those with children, and those making transitions from a heterosexual lifestyle and becoming more integrated in the gay community. Second, the investigators found that it was important to consider the social context in which services are provided, for example services perceived to be catering to one section of the population but not to others. Finally, a community organising approach appeared to offer more promise in meeting the needs of the population than the direct provision of specific services, as it involves older gay men and lesbians in identifying, planning and implementing a variety of services. Additionally, the investigators found that a large majority of the respondents (89 per cent) indicated that they could turn to at least three friends for advice and emotional support if they were dealing with "a serious problem" and that 60 per cent indicated that they had six or more such friends. More than half of the respondents (68 per cent) indicated that they had a "family of choice," with whom they socialised on holidays. The authors concluded that friendship networks were among the most important sources of social support for older lesbians and gay men.

Expanding the knowledge base: selected findings from a new study about older gay, lesbian and bisexual people

Grossman, D'Augelli, and O'Connell (2000) recently completed a study of older lesbian, gay and bisexual adults that expands the knowledge about this population. A survey research design was used, and a questionnaire of existing scales was developed to measure various variables. The investigators recruited an opportunity sample of research participants through 18 groups or agencies providing social and recreation services to older gay, lesbian and bisexual adults across the United States, and through one group in Ottawa, Canada. People 60 years of age and over were asked to volunteer for the study by a co-ordinator at each site. The older adults at each site were asked by the co-ordinators to recruit other older gay, lesbian, and bisexual adults who were not members of their groups, but who were also not their partners, lovers or roommates. The responses to the questionnaires were anonymous and were returned to the coordinators in sealed envelopes. Each individual who completed a questionnaire was given $10.00 in recognition of his/her time and contribution of information. Questionnaires were received from 430 individuals, 14 of which were not useable because the participants were either under 60 years of age, heterosexually identified, or submitted incomplete information (for example, age, sexual orientation).

The final sample consisted of 416 older lesbian, gay, and bisexual adults, of which 71 per cent were males and 29 per cent females. They ranged in age from 60 to 91 years (Mean = 68.5 years). The large majority (92 per cent) identified as lesbian or gay, and 8 per cent indicated they were bisexual. More than three-fourths of the participants (79 per cent) were recruited through agencies and groups for older adults, and the remaining 21 per cent were social contacts of those who were affiliated with the agencies and groups. Although efforts were made to diversify the sample by ethnicity, most of the participants (90 per cent) identified themselves as European/Caucasian/White; 3 per cent described themselves as African American/Black, and 2 per cent as Hispanic/Latino/Latina. The remaining 5 per cent indicated "other" on the list of choices. One-third (34 per cent) of the participants lived in a major metropolitan area, while approximately another third (36 per cent) lived in a small city. The remaining participants lived in a suburb (10 per cent), a small town or a rural area (13 per cent), or another type of community.

The majority of the participants (63 per cent) reported living alone, 30 per cent indicated that they lived with a partner; while 2 per cent reported living with friends, 2 per cent living with relatives, and 3 per cent identified themselves as being homeless. Reporting their highest educational level, 21 per cent of the participants earned a high school diploma and 65 per cent had a bachelor's or higher degree; and the other 14 per cent had obtained associate degrees or various types of certificates. Most of the participants (74 per cent) were retired. However, 18 per cent said they were still working; 3 per cent received disability payments, and 5 per cent continued to work even though they had retired from other work. With regard to personal yearly income, 15 per cent earned less than $15,000, 44 per cent between $15,000 and $35,000, and 41 per cent more than $35,000. Regarding differences by gender, the men in the study were significantly older than the women (average

age 69 vs. 67). The men also reported that they had worked in higher status jobs and had higher current income. For those in the sample living with partners, men reported having lived with partners longer.

Health and physical activity indicators. Three quarters of the participants described their physical health as good to excellent, 21 per cent said fair, and only 4 per cent reported their physical health status to be poor or very poor. Although 60 per cent of the older adults stated that their physical health never or seldom stands in the way of their doing the things they wanted to do, the remaining 40 per cent indicated that it sometimes, often or very often did. More than half of the participants (57 per cent) indicated that they regularly participated in exercise activities (for example, walking, hiking, jogging, biking or swimming), while 27 per cent did sometimes, and 16 per cent never or seldom exercised. Regarding their ability to perform physical activities (such as walking, shopping, working around the house), a little more than half of the participants (55 per cent) indicated that their ability had not changed in the past five years. However, 37 per cent said it was somewhat or much worse, and only 8 per cent indicated that it was somewhat or much better. 36 per cent of the participants reported having a physical disability or handicap, and 16 per cent of those indicated that they required an assistive device. While the large majority of the participants (93 per cent) had known people diagnosed as HIV-positive or with AIDS, an equally large percentage (90 per cent) said that they were very unlikely or unlikely to be infected with HIV. However, only 48 per cent said they had ever been tested for HIV, and 40 per cent indicated that they did not expect to be tested.

Mental health indicators. Most of the participants (84 per cent) reported that their mental health was good or excellent, while 14 per cent said fair, and 2 per cent poor. Eleven percent of the older adults described themselves as having a mental disability or illness. Feelings of isolation were reported by 13 per cent of the participants, and 27 per cent reported that they felt a lack of companionship. Only 9 per cent of the sample reported using alcohol to the extent that they could be currently classified as "problem drinkers." However, no significant involvement with drugs (not including alcohol beverages) in the past year was reported by any of the participants. More than three quarters of the participants (80 per cent) said that they were "glad to be lesbian, gay or bisexual," whilst only 8 per cent reported being depressed about their sexual orientation and 9 per cent said they had received counselling to stop their same-sex feelings. However, 17 per cent said they wished that they were heterosexual. Ten percent of the sample said they had sometimes or often considered suicide, and 4 per cent said they had considered committing suicide in the last year. Of those who ever had thought of suicide, 29 per cent said those thoughts were related to their sexual orientation.

Victimisation based on sexual orientation. Over their lifetimes, the majority of participants (63 per cent) reported experiencing verbal abuse based on their sexual orientation. Many reported having been victims of violence (29 per cent) and assault (16 per cent). Eleven percent had had objects thrown at them, while 12 per cent reported being assaulted with a weapon. Twenty percent experienced discrimination in employment, while only 7 per cent reported housing discrimination. A significant percentage of the older adults (39 per cent), however, reported being victimised by someone who threatened to disclose their sexual orientation.

Computer access and use. Almost half of the participants (47 per cent) owned or had access to a computer, with most of them (45 per cent) using it for both business and pleasure, but almost one-third (32 per cent) used it only for pleasure. Of those owning and having access to a computer, 29 per cent had e-mail and 26 per cent had Internet access. However, only 8 per cent had ever used e-mail or the Internet to meet other gay, lesbian or bisexual people.

Summary. Most of the participants in this study said they were in good or excellent physical health, but 40 per cent stated that their health often or very often stands in the way of doing things that they want to do. It appeared that a majority of the participants were concerned about maintaining their physical health, as they exercise regularly. The results appeared to pay off, as a majority also reported that their ability regarding physical activities such as walking, shopping, and working around the house had not changed in the past five years. Most of the participants also said they were in good or excellent mental health, and only a very small percentage could be classified as "problem drinkers." More than three-quarters of the participants said they were glad to be gay, lesbian, and bisexual, though a large majority reported experiencing verbal abuse because of their sexual orientation. More than third of them also had been victims of violence and assault, and a similar number also reported being threatened by others who would disclose their sexual orientation. 10 per cent stated that they had sometimes or often thought of suicide, and almost one-third of those said the thoughts were related to their sexual orientation. Although almost half of the participants owned or had access to a computer, only a very small percentage used e-mail or the Internet to meet other gay, lesbian, or bisexual people.

Eliminating the inequities and creating safe spaces

As an increasing number of older adults disclose their sexual orientation as gay, lesbian, or bisexual, it is important that professionals in the fields of health, ageing and leisure services advocate for policies and programmes to eliminate the negative effects of homophobia and provide equitable services in safe environments. The following are some specific recommendations toward meeting this objective:

1. Encourage professional associations to enhance the visibility of older gay men and lesbians by including knowledge about them in educational and training programmes, conferences and symposia, and professional publications.

2. Advocate for organisations and societies focused on the ageing to plan and market programmes and services to meet the needs of older gay men and lesbians.

3. Champion the inclusion of the needs of gay and lesbian people in professional preparation programmes, incorporating the special needs of those who disclose their sexual orientation as older adults.

4. Endorse allocation of funds to support systematic research aimed at discovering the mental health, physical health, and leisure needs of gay and lesbian older adults.

5. Support the development of policy studies to determine the impact of existing laws, and institutional and programmatic policies on the quality of life of gay and lesbian older adults.

6. Endorse the creation of networks and referral services that link formal health and leisure services for gay and lesbian older adults to informal programmes and support services that exist in gay and lesbian communities.

7. Argue for the creation of programmes that minimise social and emotional isolation of older gay men and lesbians, for example support groups, buddy and home visitor programmes, transportation services.

8. Recommend the creation of advocacy programmes that assist older gay men and lesbians in having their needs met by helping them to negotiate with retirement living facilities, health care systems, skilled nursing facilities, and leisure services systems.

References

Beeler, J. A., Rawls, T. D., Herdt, G., and Cohler, B. J. (1999) 'The needs of older lesbians and gay men in Chicago', *Journal of Gay and Lesbian Social Services* Vol. 9, No. 1: pp. 31–49.

Bohan, J. (1996) *Psychology and sexual orientation: Coming to terms.* New York: Routledge, pp. 31–59

Communication Technologies (1994) *AIDS stigma and discrimination: A review of the literature.* San Francisco: Communication Technologies.

Dorfman, R., Walters, K., Burke, P., *et al.* (1995) 'Old, sad and alone: The myths of the aging homosexual', *Journal of Gerontological Social Work* Vol. 24, Nos. 1/2: pp. 29–44.

Friend, R. A. (1989) 'Older lesbian and gay people: Responding to homophobia', *Marriage and Family Review* Vol. 14: pp. 241–263.

Friend, R. A. (1990) 'Older lesbian and gay people: A theory of successful aging', *Journal of Homosexuality* Vol. 20: pp. 99–118.

Gabbay, S. G. (1997) 'Gay and lesbian gerontology review', *Outword* Vol. 3, No. 3: pp. 4, 8.

Goffman, E. (1963) *Stigma: Notes on the management of a spoiled identity.* Englewood Cliffs, NJ: Prentice Hall.

Greene, B. (1996) 'Lesbians and gay men of color: The legacy of ethnosexual mythologies in heterosexism', in L. A. Bonet and E. D. Rothblum (eds) *Preventing heterosexism and homophobia.* Thousand Oaks, CA: Sage, pp. 59–70.

Greene, B. (2000) 'Beyond heterosexism and across the cultural divide: Developing an inclusive lesbian, gay and bisexual psychology. A look to the future', in B. Greene and G. L. Croom (eds) *Education, research and practice in lesbian, gay, bisexual and transgender psychology: A resource manual.* Thousand Oaks, CA: Sage, pp. 1–45.

Grossman, A. H. (1995) 'At risk, infected, and invisible: Older gay men and HIV/ AIDS', *JANAC: Journal of the Association of Nurses in AIDS Care* Vol. 6, No. 6: pp. 13–19.

Grossman, A. H., D'Augelli, A. R., and O'Connell, T. S. (in press 2000) *Asking and telling: Findings from a study on the lives of older gay, lesbian, and bisexual adults.*

Herek, G. (1992) 'Being lesbian, gay, bisexual and 60 or older', Journal of Gay and Lesbian Social Services.

Jacobs, R., Rasmussen, L., and Hohman, M. (1999) 'The social support needs of older lesbians, gay men, and bisexuals', *Journal of Gay and Lesbian Social Services* Vol. 9, No. 1: pp. 1–30.

Jacobson, S., and Grossman, A. H. (1996) 'Older lesbians and gay men: Old myths, new images, and future directions', in R. C. Savin-Williams and K. M. Cohen (eds) *The lives of lesbians, gays, and bisexuals: Children to adults.* Fort Worth, TX: Harcourt Brace, pp. 345–373.

Kochman, A. (1993) 'Old and gay' in L. F. Farrell (ed) *Lambda gray: A practical, emotional, and spiritual guide for gays and lesbians who are growing older.* North Hollywood, CA: Newcastle, pp. 93–99.

Pharr, S. (1988) *Homophobia: A weapon of sexism.* Inverness, CA: Chardon Press, pp. 1–26.

Public Media Center (1995) *The impact of homophobia and other social biases on AIDS.* San Francisco, CA: Public Media Center.

Quam, J. K., and Whitford, G. S. (1992) 'Adaptation and age-related expectations of older gay and lesbian adults', *The Gerontologist* Vol. 32: pp. 367–374.

Ungvarski, P. J., and Grossman, A. H. (1999) 'Health problems of gay and bisexual men'. *Nursing Clinics of North America* Vol. 34, No. 2: pp. 313–331.

Wall, V. A., and Washington, J. (1991) 'Understanding gay and lesbian students of color', in N. J. Evans and V. A. Wall (eds) *Beyond tolerance: Gays, lesbians, and bisexuals on campus*. Alexandria, VA: Association of College Personnel Administrators, pp. 67–78.

Weinberg, G. (1972) *Society and the healthy homosexual*. New York: St. Martin's Press.

The "Goodness of Fit" in Norwegian Youth Sports

Reidar Säfvenbom

The Norwegian University of Sport and Physical Education,
Oslo (Norway)

Introduction

The drop out from sports and physical activity during adolescence is evident
in most industrialised countries. Research from Norway shows a significant
decrease in the physical activity level during adolescence (Wichstrøm, 1995;
Brevik and Vaagbø, 1998). Broad inductive studies of cultural orientations
(MMI, 1994), as well as a few ethnographic studies on youth sports (for
example, Alvim, 1998), confirm that organised Norwegian youth sports
generally reflect an instrumental and achievement oriented type of activity.
The drop out may indicate that this is not what the majority of Norwegian
adolescents need or want.

Most of the research which focuses on drop out from sports has urged
the pinpointing of risk factors that may explain the drop out. A more positive
search for mechanisms which serve the sport interaction process and which
contribute to adherence and motivation for continuing participation has not
been that salient in sport research. A consequence of this is that we know
more about why adolescents drop out of sports than we do about how to
prevent that drop out. We may know why they leave but not why they stay.
We also do not know why some return after leaving.

From the world view of contextualism (Bronfenbrenner, 1979; Houts,
1991; Lerner and Tubman, 1991; Pepper, 1942; Silbereisen and Todt, 1994;
Wozniak and Fischer, 1993) it can be argued that participation in youth sports
and physical activity relies primarily on a 'goodness of fit' (Lerner, 1982)
between the participant and the sports context (Figure 1, page following).
From this perspective, dropping out from sports during adolescence may be
analysed as a relatively sudden change in a person's behaviour caused by

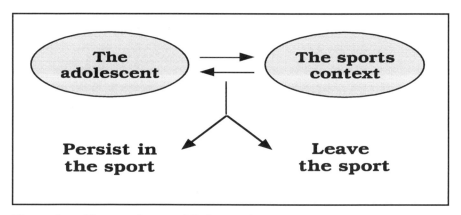

Figure 1   The goodness of fit in youth sports

some kind of interactional mismatch. Leaving the sport indicates that the sport interaction does not contribute to the quality of the adolescent's everyday life as it once did. It indicates that the adolescent does not find the emotional and social payoffs which had been rewarding in their earlier sporting years. Needs and values change as we mature; therefore, for a teenager to remain in sports the sport environment must provide the psychological, physical or emotional experiences which the teenager will value. Sports must provide experiences which are, as Garbarino wrote (1993: p.9), "compatible with his or her needs as they exist at a specific point in his or her developing life". It would appear, then, that an adolescent's participation in a particular sport depends on how the context of that sport fits into the everyday life of that adolescent. In other words, it depends on the adolescent's "readiness" for the experience offered by the local sports club (see Garbarino, 1993; Jessor and Jessor, 1977).

The adolescents in leisure study

In the absence of specific studies reflecting Norwegian youth's needs and desires regarding their free time, and particularly with regard to their sport and physical activities, data from the Adolescents in Leisure Study (Säfvenbom, 1998) provides appropriate information. The primary task of this study was to compare the use of free time of those 'at risk' adolescents who live in youth protection institutions with that of their non-institutionalised peers. The comparison was made in order to determine both differences in activity pattern perceptions of the free time contexts and also determinants for the experience of meaningful free time activities. (See Säfvenbom, 1998; Säfvenbom and Samdahl, 1998, 2000 for further details.)

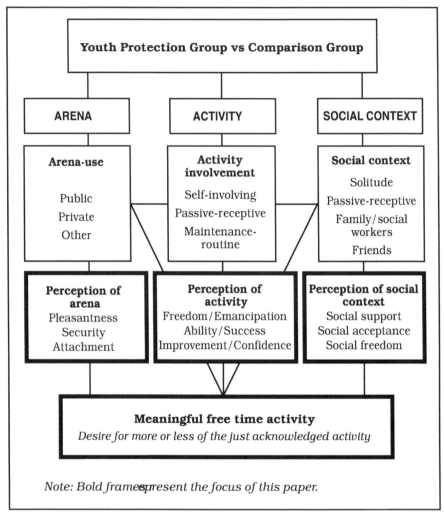

Figure 2   Conceptual model for The Adolescent in Leisure Study
(Säfvenbom, 1998)

During the research process the notion of 'meaningfulness' appeared as a key concept. One study analysed the relationships between adolescents' perceptions of components of the total free time context with one variable indicating the adolescents' perception of the free time activity's meaningfulness. This study investigated how an individual's experience of a meaningful free time activity was affected by his or her perceptions of the activity interaction itself, the social context of the activity, and the arena where the activity was performed (Figure 2 above).

As will be shown, the analysis revealed only minor differences between the two groups of adolescents participating in the study. This indicated that some common needs and desires regarding leisure experiences were being experienced, even among a rather disparate group of adolescents.

Data collection

The data for this study were collected using the Experience Sampling Method (ESM) (see Csikszentmihalyi, Larson and Prescott, 1977). Each participant in the study received a booklet containing 30 identical questionnaires and a wrist watch programmed to sound 30 signals over the seven days of the study. They were told to complete one questionnaire each time they received a signal. Each completed questionnaire served as one report. The participants were in the study for seven days, beginning on Monday morning and ending on Sunday night. Because the study focused on the adolescents' free time, signals were sent only after school and on weekends. The method captures a random sampling of experiences for the participating adolescents throughout this time period. In total, 1220 reports (86% of the total number of signals) were completed by the final sample of the 47 participants, who ranged from 14 to 18 years of age.

The main purpose of the study was to examine a broad array of perceptual factors linked to activity, social context, and arena as possible experiential determinants for the experience of meaningful free time activity. A model of the dimensions and variables included in the presented study can be seen in Figure 3.

Measurements

The adolescent's perception of the activity, placed in the centre of the model (Figure 3), was measured through a seven point semantic differential scale involving ten items. A factor analysis of the ten items resulted in a reduction to three main dimensions of activity which can be seen in Figure 3: perception of *freedom/mental emancipation in the activity* (for example, emancipation, routine, need for release, boredom) $(\alpha = .73)$, perception of *ability/success in the activity* (for example, success, ability, challenge) $(\alpha = -.67)$, and *perception of improvement/confidence enhancement in the activity* (for example, improvement, confidence enhancement, importance) $(\alpha = .70)$. The perception of social context, placed to the right in the model, was assessed through ten items addressing how the individual related to the other people in that situation. The ten items were factored into three significant factors which were labelled *social support* (motivation, challenge, give/receive support, social control) $(\alpha = .59)$, *social acceptance* (acceptance, solidarity, security) $(\alpha = .80$

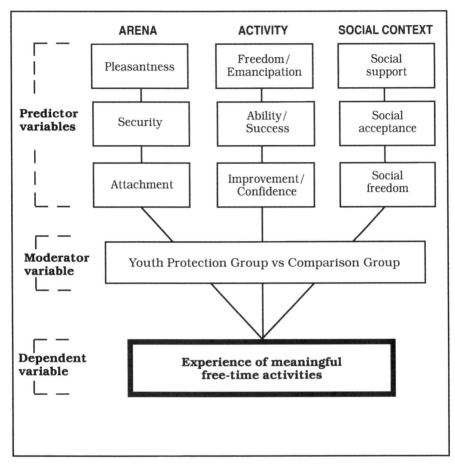

Figure 3   Meaningful free time activities: hypothesised experiential determinants

), and *social freedom* (no need for release, boredom) ($\alpha = .71$). Finally, the perception of arena, seen to the left in Figure 3, was assessed through items measuring pleasantness, security and attachment to the arena.

The dependent variable (Figure 3) indicating the experience of meaningful free time activity was, in this study, assessed through one single question; *Is this an activity you would like to do more often or less often than you do?* The participants responded on a three-point scale indicating "less often", "neither more or less often", and "more often". This question reflects an overall assessment capturing the perceived quality, significance and intensity of that situation compared with the adolescents lived experience. The immediate on-site response claiming "I'd like to do this more often" captures many factors including the person's past experience and present or future expectations. Thus, it is assumed to represent an ecologically valid measure of an individual's experience of meaningfulness not biased with normative standards or self-presentation (see Veenhoven, 1991).

As shown in Figure 4, the relationship between the predictor variables and the dependent variable was controlled for the two groups of youth that participated in the study (adolescents from social agencies vs. "ordinary" adolescents).

Results

Regression analyses were conducted to examine the relationship between the adolescents' perception of the various dimensions of the free time contexts and the dependent variable indicating experience of meaningful free time activities. Preliminary analyses were conducted to exclude negligible variables from the final analyses.

As can be seen in Figure 4, these analyses revealed that five of the nine predictor-variables entered into the analyses qualified for the next step in the procedure. Perception of *freedom / emancipation* in the activity, perception of *ability / success* in activity, perception of *improvement / confidence* in activity, perception of *social support*, and perception of *arena security* all were shown to be significant predictor variables in one or more of the subgroups.

The preliminary results revealed minor differences between the two groups of adolescents regarding the influence of the identified determinants for the experience of meaningful free time activities.

The final regression revealed that *perception of freedom / mental emancipation within the activity* represented *the* variable determining meaningful leisure time activities. In the comparison group the variable explained 43% of the variance in the dependent variable. Independently of whether the activity was categorised as a passive-receptive, consumer-oriented activity, or as a self-involving activity, the perception of freedom/emancipation within the activity appeared to be the most powerful and significant predictor for the experience of meaningful free time activities. In addition to this variable, perception of social support played a less but still significant role in the analysis for both groups. In the comparison group this variable explained another 6 % of the variance in the variable indicating meaningful free time activities. As can be seen from the beta values in Figure 5, only minor differences were seen between the two groups of adolescents. In addition to the two variables discussed, perception of ability contributed to explain the variance in the dependent variable in the youth protection group, whilst

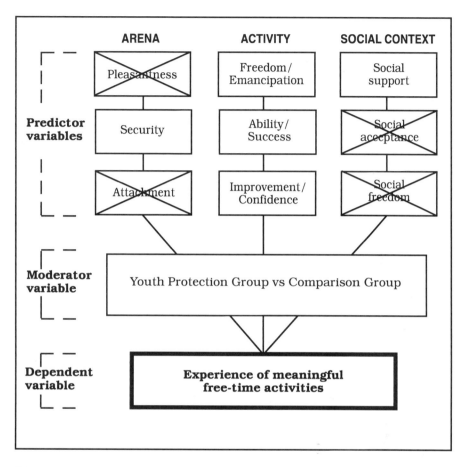

**Figure 4   Meaningful free time activities: main experiential
determinants**

perceived security at the arena for the activity had a negative effect among
the comparison group. Both variables explained less than 1% of the variance
in the dependent variable.

Based on the results a four-cell matrix indicating high and low perceived
freedom/emancipation in activity, and high and low perception of social
support was created (Figure 6).

According to the results *high perception of freedom/emancipation in the
ongoing activity and high social support* should represent "meaningful
activities". As can be seen from Figures 5 and 6, the additional analyses
showed that a high match (high/high) between perception of *freedom/
emancipation* in activity and perception of *social support* was most commonly

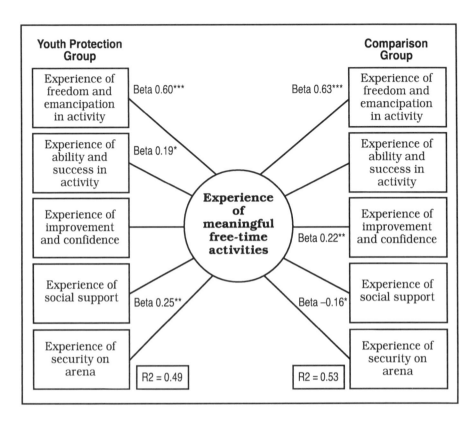

Figure 5   Meaningful free time activities: experiential determinants – comparisons

	Experience of social support	
	HIGH	LOW
Experience of freedom and emancipation in activity — HIGH	Physical activity and sports; other hobbies	Passive receptive activities: watching TV and listening to music
Experience of freedom and emancipation in activity — LOW	Productive activities: homework; part-time jobs	Socialising, game playing, obligatory tasks and TV

Figure 6   The freedom in activity–social support model

identified in sports and intentional physical activity. In more than four out of ten reports (across groups) when both high perception of *freedom/ emancipation* and high perception of *social support* was reported, intentional physical activity or sports were reported as the main activities. This indicates that these variables represent significant meaning-bearing dimensions in sports and physical activity and that they represent the basic motivation for young people to stay in the activity.

Discussion

In some research environments the search for mastery and competence has been characterised as *the* basic motivation for behaviour (Nicholls, 1989; Sternberg and Kolligan, 1990). Results presented from this study, however, give reason to question an unduly strong focus on these concepts. The analyses emphasise the fact that neither perception of success/ability nor perception of improvement had any effect on the experience of meaningful free time activity. These results strengthen the view of free time as a significant part of peoples' lives, with complementary functions that go beyond the activity itself. The results indicate that 'flow', as used in the psychology literature (Csikszentmihalyi, 1975), is not based on a high match between challenge and skills but perhaps on the mismatch which itself contributes to increase the perception of freedom and emancipation.

It should be emphasised that the category of sports and physical activity as used in this paper includes every kind of intentional physical activity, organised as well as unorganised activities and competitive sport as well as play or health-oriented activities. Nonetheless, it is interesting that a high match between perception of freedom in activity and perception of social support (high/high) was primarily identified in sports and intentional physical activity. This indicates a significant experiential potential within the physical activity context yet, according to the drop out rate, it also questions sport federations' ability to consider and respond to the advantages of this potential.

Implications

The results indicate that adolescents in the capital of Norway struggle to elude a productive, instrumental, and achievement-oriented everyday life during their free time activities. This might indicate that the sense of an academic ghost which hangs over the adolescents' present, as well as their future, is perceived as rather oppressive and that free time is perceived as a most significant context compensating for the highly achievement-oriented part of the day. Based on the analyses here, it may be concluded that neither success, mastery, nor competence enhancement should dominate the focus of youth sports. On the contrary, focus should be on the relationship between *freedom from* constraining forces and *freedom to* become involved on one's own premises.

If we are able to make the experience of sports and physical activity open-ended and independent of performance accuracy and inaccuracy, we may increase the experience of sports and physical activity as a meaningful interaction that expands people's quality of life and thus also increases their motivation for further participation. If the Norwegian Sport Federation decides to retain its *Sport for All* perspective, it should align with an interactionist perspective and the world view of contextualism. As a consequence of this choice we should probably look more in the direction of sports sociology and philosophy and perhaps less in the direction of sport psychology when planning physical activity programs for adolescents.

References

Alvim, M. (1998) *Rydd veien for en vinner*. University of Bergen: Hovedfagsopp-
gave.

Bronfenbrenner, U. (1979) *The ecology of human development. Experiments by
nature and design*. Cambridge, MA: Harvard University Press.

Breivik, G. Vaagbø, O. (1998) *Utviklingen i fysisk aktivitet i den norske
befolkningen, 1985–1997*. Report from The Norwegian Federation of Sport
and Olympic Committee. Oslo: Norwegian Federation of Sport.

Csikszentmihalyi, M. (1975) *Beyond boredom and anxiety*. San Francisco, CA:
Jossey Bass.

Csikszentmihalyi, M., Larson, R. and Prescott, S. (1977) 'The ecology of
adolescent activity and experience', *Journal of Youth and Adolescence*
No. 6: pp. 281–294.

Garbarino, J. (1993) 'Childhood: What do we need to know', *Childhood* No. 1:
pp. 3–10.

Houts, A. C. (1991) 'The contextualist turn in empirical social science: Epistemo-
logical issues, methodological implications and adjusted expectations',
in R. Cohen and A. W. Siegel (eds) *Context and development*. New Jersey:
Lawrence Erlbaum Associates, pp. 25–55.

Jessor, R. and Jessor, S. L. (1977) *Problem behaviour and psychosocial
development. A longitudinal study of youth*. New York: Academic Press.

Lerner, R. (1982) 'Children and adolescents as producers of their own
development', *Developmental Review* Vol. 2: pp. 342–370.

Lerner, R. and Tubman, J. G. (1991) 'Developmental contextualism and the study
of early adolescent development', in R. Cohen and A. W. Siegel (eds)
Context and development. New Jersey: Lawrence Erlbaum Associates,
pp. 183–210.

Nicholls, J. G. (1989) *The competitive ethos and democratic education.* Cambridge, Massachusetts: Harvard University Press.

Pepper, S. C. (1942) *World hypotheses. A study in evidence.* Berkeley, CA: University of California Press.

Säfvenbom, R. (1998) *Four thousand hours a year. Leisure time and its developmental potential for adolescents at youth protection institutions.* Unpublished Ph. D thesis, Norwegian University of Sport and Physical Education.

Säfvenbom, R. and Samdahl, D. M. (1998) 'Involvement in and perception of the free-time context for adolescents in youth protection institutions', *Leisure Studies* Vol. 17, No. 3: pp. 207–226.

Säfvenbom, R. and Samdahl, D. M. (2000) 'Leisure for youth in residential care: an important context for intervention', *International Journal of Social Welfare* Vol. 9: pp. 120–127.

Silbereisen, R. K. and Todt, E. (eds) (1994) *Adolescence in context. The interplay of family, school, peers and work in adjustment.* New York: Springer Verlag.

Sternberg, R. J. and Kolligian, J. (1990) *Competence considered.* Hew Haven, CONN: Yale University Press.

Veenhoven, R. (1991) 'Questions on happiness: Classical topics, modern answers, blind spots', in F. Strack, M. Argyle, and N. Schwartz (eds) *Subjective well-being: An interdisciplinary perspective.* Oxford: Pergamon Press, pp. 7–27.

Wichstrøm, L. (1995) *Hvem? Hva? Hvor? Om ungdom og idrett.* Oslo: Ungforsk.

Wozniak, R. H. and Fischer, K. W. (eds) (1993) *Development in context. Acting and thinking in specific environments.* New Jersey: Lawrence Erlbaum Associates.

Identities and Subculture in Relation to Sport: An Analysis of Teenage Girls' Magazines

Claudia Cockburn

Research and Graduate School of Education,
University of Southampton (UK)

Introduction

Traditional sporting structures in the UK, including school physical education, have been criticised as inappropriate for the needs of many girls and young women (Mason, 1995; Scraton, 1992; Sports Council, 1993; Talbot, 1986). Further, it has been argued that girls become alienated by and demotivated towards sport and physical activity in general and physical education in particular (see for example, Leaman, 1986). Yet most research in this field is conducted from the dominant perspective of physical educators: it rarely describes what it is like to be a girl (or a boy) within the physical education process. This paper attempts to adopt the often marginalised perspective of teenage girls and young women themselves (to the extent to that this is possible as an 'aged' researcher). The theme of contradiction is traced throughout the paper in examining how teenage girls and young women perceive their worlds and the tensions and conflicts that they face in relation to sport.

Using the findings of a survey of four current magazines for young adolescent females, some of the prevailing images of sport are revealed that are offered to teenage girls and young women in current discourse. This illustrative material is discussed in relation to the conclusions of other researchers and writers in this field. In the second section of the paper, the nature of teenage girls' subcultures is examined. The portrayal of sport in the discursive practice of teenage girls' magazines is examined for its effects on the readers' identity formation. Finally, some proposals are offered for enhancing girls' involvement in sport through different representations of sport in their magazines.

The study

Writers such as Gill Lines (1993), Angela McRobbie (1991) and Janice Winship (1987) regard the study of the discourse of magazines as a way of accessing and exploring subcultures. Magazines were chosen for this study because:

- they offer teenage girls a relatively affordable, frequently produced and readily available item that they can buy in the high street autonomously, with their own money, without the involvement or permission of others, particularly family members;

- they can be read unobserved, in the private world of the bedroom (a space so important to teenage girls: see McRobbie and Garber, 1976), or other spaces, such as at school or in the park;

- the buying, reading, sharing and discussing of these magazines furnishes readers with a group culture, with its own shared identities. The shared understanding and sense of belonging derived from common readership make a great contribution to a young person's sense of security in an otherwise often confusing and lonely world (Rutherford, 1990).

The four magazines chosen for the study were *Just Seventeen*, *Live and Kicking*, *My Guy* and *Sugar*. The selection of issues was randomised by adopting the current edition (December 1998 in the first three cases, January 1999 in the case of *Sugar*). These four publications were chosen because of their large circulation amongst 12, 13 and 14 year old girls (see Table 1 for sales figures). Their market profile was confirmed by the findings of other researchers (for example, Lines, 1993 and McRobbie, 1991), by high street retailers, and by the ages of the readers who had letters published in the magazines.

Table 1   Monthly sales figures for January to June 1998
              for each magazine

Magazine	Sales per month
Just Seventeen	250,306
Live and Kicking	215,205
My Guy	42,211
Sugar	459,984

(Source: Telephone conversations with each magazine's sales department)

The first stage of analysis involved a reading in its entirety of the selected issue of each of the magazines in order to establish the major themes covered. These emerged as: romance, fashion, beauty/the body, celebrities and music. In this first reading, criteria for coverage of 'sport' were relatively narrow, leading to very few references to formal sports or physical education being found. The search criteria were therefore extended to include a broader range of physical activities such as skate-boarding, dancing and bathing (not necessarily swimming).

All written and visual references to 'sport' and to physical education, using this more inclusive definition, were listed, analysed, interpreted and evaluated. Major themes were identified in a search for patterns in the portrayal of dominant cultural assumptions about teenage girls and young women and sport. The emerging themes were: reconfirmation of stereotypes; the risks girls face on entering the sporting domain; the trivialization of both female and male involvement in sporting activity; and, conflict and tension created by dichotomous images.

Discussion of findings

Over several decades of feminist research, magazines for teenage girls and young women have been criticised for contributing to the perpetuation of patriarchal relations through their "... promotion of a restrictive beauty standard" (Budgeon and Currie, 1995: p. 173). Indeed, studies of magazines from the 1940s to the present have found that 'love always triumphs' and that messages about broader, alternative identities for women, such as those associated with active sport, are rare (Budgeon and Currie, 1995; Lees, 1993; Sharpe, 1976). In comparison with bodies, beauty and relationships with boys/men, references to sport were scant in the magazines analysed for this paper. The few references to sport that were found revealed, through striking imagery, an important set of messages to teenage girls and young women about sport, physical activity in general, and physical education in particular.

'Sport is for boys, not for girls': the reconfirmation of stereotypes

Many of the references to sport concerned boys and young men, portrayed as pop stars for whom typical Christmas presents included "... bikes and ... footballs ... you know, normal kid stuff" (*Sugar*: p. 19), or fishing tackle (*Live and Kicking*), or hockey socks and rollerskates (*Sugar*). There were no mentions of girls/women receiving sporting commodities. Sharpe (1976: p. 196) argues that a magazine is "... important for what it omits from its content ... [as it] ... endorses the status quo by leaving out any suggestions for the possibility or desirability of change".

In this way, the spheres of acceptable masculine and feminine relations to sport are clearly established; that is, sport is for boys but not for girls.

Risks that girls face on entering the sporting domain

Definition of what is for whom was further confirmed by the attention drawn by the magazines to the 'risks' girls face when they enter the domain of sport. Many references warned girls that their femininity, their happiness and confidence, their social acceptance, and even their health and safety, could be at risk in sporting scenarios.

First, a young woman's femininity might be jeopardised simply by association with sport. For example, an advertisement in *Sugar* (p. 21) for Boots the Chemist displayed six types of body spray with trade names such as 'Hot' and 'Streetwear Fling.' The cans in the advertisement were brightly coloured or displayed stereotypical feminine imagery, for example a pink heart. However, the spray called 'Adidas – Woman Sport' was in a white, grey and blue can with no stereotypical hints of the heterosexual, feminine, romance or desirability. The choice portrayed to girl readers was either to be feminine, and therefore desirable, or to associate themselves with sport and to risk forfeiting that (stereotypical) feminine desirability.

The second type of risk found was to girls' happiness, confidence and social acceptability in relation to their bodies. Examples were numerous ranging from "I hate my legs" (*Sugar:* p. 110), to "I couldn't face school for days" (*My Guy*: p. 45). Readers' 'problem' letters illustrated and normalised girls' embarrassment, shame and lack of confidence in their own bodies. One reader expressed concern over going swimming: "I'm afraid my pubic hairs will stick out of my costume" (*Live and Kicking:* p. 28). Another girl had been bullied in a hockey lesson because she was overweight (*My Guy*). Again, the normative messages were clear concerning girls' bodies in sporting scenarios; they were sources of embarrassment, prompted lack of confidence and caused unhappiness.

The third type of risk implied in these magazines was to girls' physical health and safety. One of the very few uses of the word 'exercise' described compulsive exercise as harmful in connection with anorexia (*Sugar*). In another instance, a reader's letter printed in *Sugar* expressed concern over a man who followed her and a friend and who took photographs of them on a local playing field. Notwithstanding the potential physical risks connected with sport, these were not set against the many benefits of active participation in sport (such as weight control, health, self-confidence and so forth). Powerful hegemonic messages in the magazines continually stressed the risks that females faced and appeared to admonish and discourage potentially physically active girls. Even playing fields became associated with outdoor public spaces and represented as a male domain, unsuitable and even unsafe for females.

It is not only in magazines that girls hear warnings that to be 'sporty' jeopardizes their femininity. Thorne (1993) points out that girls who are 'tomboys' are generally acceptable in social terms until the age of about eleven. Indeed, they may even be commended insofar as they portray attributes and qualities, such as strength and vigour, that gain generalised approval from their association with men. However, on entering adolescence, girls become 'the other sex' and are expected to succumb to the dictates of 'emphasised femininity' and its traits and activities (Connell, 1987). Talbot (1986: p. 122) describes how this alienation of teenage girls and young women from sport increases as adulthood approaches, such that "female participation in physical activities is seen as legitimate for *girls*, but only tolerated, at best, for *women*" (emphases added). As a consequence, young women face discontinuity as they find that what has been acceptable behaviour is then abruptly restricted in adolescence. Because adolescence is such a crucial time for identity formation this is can be unsatisfactory and soul-destroying for girls. It becomes clear why "girls tend to reject physical education [and sport in general] as an aspect of the curriculum [and life in general] which is unfeminine, irrelevant and childish." (Leaman, 1986: p. 123).

The trivialisation of female involvement in sporting activity

Even if a girl involved in sport was to overcome the potential risks described above, she could expect, according to the magazines in this research, to find her involvement trivialised or reduced in its importance. In various ways, but without fail, girls' sporting actions and achievements were reduced in the magazines to girls' desirability for, and relationships with, boys and men. Swimming, a sport relatively popular with, and culturally acceptable for, most teenage girls and young women, was referred to several times in the magazines. A photo-story in *My Guy* (p. 42) portrayed a swimming pool as a site not for swimming, but for " teaching him the breaststroke". The magazine images focused on the swimming pool as a site for romance (and the costume as functioning to "get boys interested"), rather than for the sport of swimming.

Another relatively popular and 'acceptable' sport for teenage girls is rollerblading/rollerskating. However, only one image of a girl rollerskating was found (*Just Seventeen*: p. 30–33). This took the form of a photo sequence portraying a "rollergirl in nasty fall". The girl wore pink glittery tights, a short skirt and showed a bare midriff. Boyband members, "our heroes" came "to the rescue" dressed in dark glasses, gold chains and doctors' uniforms. The girl has a "slightly grazed knee" but recovered, thanks to "one elastoplast and plenty of TLC from the boys". The message here was that, when girls do venture into the sporting domain, first they are likely to fail and secondly they are likely to depend for 'rescue' on responsible males in the form of 'sexy' heroes.

Images of girls in sporting action were routinely trivialised or reduced, either directly or indirectly, to (heterosexual) romantic relationships, real or fantasy, with boys/men. Such imagery presents the readers of these magazines with strong messages concerning the inappropriateness of girls' participation in sport which is presented as neither socially important nor valued.

The trivialization of male sporting skill

As with female skill, respect for male sporting skill and achievement was diminished in the magazines. Michael Owen, the young football star, was the most featured celebrity in these issues. Only one image, however, showed him in sporting action. Rather, he was referred to as "poster boy" (*Sugar*: p. 100), "eye candy" (*Just Seventeen*: p. 58) and "totty-tastic" (*Live and Kicking*: p. 1). Other examples included references to an American football team as "hunky" (*Live and Kicking*: p. 43) and to David Beckham, another international footballer, as "gorgeous" (*Sugar*: p. 96).

This kind of imagery (hetero-)sexualises male sporting achievement for the reader by objectifying highly skilled professional sportsmen, reducing them to 'hunks' who 'score' with the girls. The emphasis that the magazines placed on heterosexuality in male physical activity was exemplified in *Just Seventeen*'s article on 'Dumb things boy bands do'. Here, dancing was put firmly in its feminine place: boy bands with dance routines were called upon by the magazines' writers to set a masculine example. "Get real – we don't expect the spunky lads we know to leap around like that, so why should pop stars make complete fools of themselves?" (*Just Seventeen:* p. 122).

Diverse companies profit from the current popularity of football. For example, Fruitella's quiz in *Just Seventeen* offered its girl readers football shirts as prizes. But any transgressive implication in this was immediately countered by Fruitella's suggestion that a girl might be found "reapplying her mascara" or "swooning over – sorry, supporting Michael Owen and his fit footie mates on a Saturday afternoon..." (*Just Seventeen:* p. 107). Not even girls' sporting knowledge was expected to be of any depth as it was deemed "dead easy" to enter the quiz; indeed all that was required was to know which football club Owen played for.

Contradictions

In the magazines surveyed there were several instances where traditional stereotypical messages were presented in parallel with, or encapsulated within, non-traditional, contradictory images of femininity. Indeed, studies from the 1980s describe the emergence of a 'new femininity' reflected in radical changes in magazines' content and style (Lees, 1993). McRobbie's (1994) study on the replacement of *Jackie* by the less 'romanticised' *Just Seventeen* as the UK's top selling magazine, emphasised the decline in the cultural importance placed on romance. Although love, sex and boys have remained foregrounded in the magazines, feminist researchers have noted the decline of female passivity and traditional sex-role stereotyping and have been encouraged to analyse and interpret the magazines in a more 'open-ended way' (McRobbie, 1994). Similarly, Budgeon and Currie (1995) argued that we should not "anticipate oppressive interpretations" of these texts but should recognise their construction of femininity as open to change. However, it is clear that offering alternative images of femininity is bound to give rise to contradictions and tensions. Indeed, McRobbie (1994: p. 163) recognised "...the disruptions and inconsistencies and space for negotiation within the magazines".

Conflicts and tensions created by dichotomous images

Conflict is apparent between the polarised stereotypes of the dominant, traditional ideology of females' beauty-dependent-man-hunting approach to life and the 'new femininity' described above. The two counterposed concepts are:

• traditionally prescribed standards of femininity with a "... timeless, hence essentialist, notion of womanhood' (Budgeon and Currie, 1995: p. 184); and

• bold images of assertive girls and women who use a less rigid feminine identity to overturn dominant cultural assumptions.

Below are described four examples of conflict and tension arising from this polarisation of traditional and alternative images of the place of women in sport and the function of sport for women.

A photograph in *Sugar* (p. 11) of a young female soap opera star playing netball was, at first glance, a positive image. She wore appropriate kit and was in an active pose with the netball in her hand. However, a closer look revealed that, as well as confirming her stereotypical femininity by wearing jewellery and a pink t-shirt, the accompanying comment by the editor placed the image back into the traditional stereotype: "Patsy's heard that the secret to scoring in netball is to imagine you're throwing the ball at someone's head" (*Sugar*: p. 11). The accompanying text foregrounded the character's relationship with her husband (headed "OK Ricky, you've 'ad it!"), rendering ambiguous the positive image of a young woman doing skilful sport for its own sake. The conflicting message was: it is fine to do sport but you should do it in relation to your (heterosexual) relationship and present yourself in a feminine way (Connell, 1995).

A second example of conflict was found in a reader's letter and *Just Seventeen's* reply (p. 42). She wrote "I always wear foundation to the gym because if I didn't I'd end up looking like a tomato". Her make-up melted and she ended up a "blotchy mess". The magazine's reply made a comment on the advisability of wearing too much make-up while exercising but the author, 'Sista Style', contradicted herself by agreeing that the 15 year old reader would want to look her best in case "... some muscle-bound love-god struts his way over". Thus the gym (as with the swimming pool) was not represented as a source of health and fitness but, rather, as a site for heterosexual romance.

A third example of the contradiction was suggested in an article run by *My Guy* (p. 9) on how to "get boys interested". The photograph used was of a girl in a swimming pool — a potentially positive image, but one mediated by that fact that she wore a very brief bikini and jewellery, was dry from the waist up and was being approached by a young man about to embrace her. As in all the magazines' seven photographs of females in swimming pools, the girl was leaning the side of the pool or being embraced by a boy/young man. The image portrayed was not one of intrinsically valuable sporting activity but one of female construction of desirability in relation to boys and young men.

Finally, an advertisement for Sunny Delight drink (*Sugar*: p. 58) exemplified the polarisation of feminine identities and the associated potential costs for teenage girls and young women of making the wrong choice. The advertisement showed a teenage girl skate-boarding in an active and skilful pose. The camera angle was low and the photograph was blurred to portray 'action'. "Freedom for girls" was the message as girls are encouraged to "whenever, wherever, reach for the sun". The onus was placed on the reader to appreciate "the new horizons of possibilities in the field of sexual and social relationships" offered by such images and to act "agentically" with the new-found "girl power" being offered (Davies and Harre, cited in Budgeon and Currie, 1995: p. 180). However, images in the same advertisement portrayed traditional passive femininity, arguably in direct conflict with the image of 'freedom'. The girl had a made-up face, a pretty smile and wore a skimpy top: the colours chosen, of pink, orange and yellow, reinforced traditional femininity. Further, she was a lone girl shown with boys, suggesting the need for girls to 'hang around' with boys (and not with other girls) in order to achieve 'freedom'. This may be an alien notion for many girls, however, whose 'best' friendships, those with other girls (McRobbie, 1978), are threatened by such behaviour.

Although the active images found in this study might be encouraging to advocates of women's sport and physical activity (and to women and girls in general), they also represent ambivalent and contradictory meanings of sport for teenage girls and young women. These may not be easily reconciled by the readers of these magazines. Certainly, the editors and advertisers appeal to as wide an audience as possible, attempting to attract both 'sporty' and 'non-sporty' girls. Tension is caused by a "curiously unresolved blend of conflicting meanings" amongst the images and texts (McRobbie, 1991: p. 184). In summary, the coverage of sport and exercise in these magazines is confusing and contradictory.

As Jonathan Rutherford (1990) explains, dichotomies such as male/female or masculine/feminine force the polarisation of images and the creation of hierarchies (better than/worse than). As a consequence, these dichotomies provide a basis for inequality, discrimination and oppression. This leaves the teenage girls and young women readers with a choice between two unsatisfactory alternatives. The new femininity of 'girl power' may appear to be liberating in comparison with traditional images but it is actually unreal power, commercially constructed. This is exemplified by the girl-band 'The Spice Girls,' who arguably provide a strong positive image for teenage girls and young women to identify with. However, their power lies in commercial viability and skilful marketing, not in any real or sustainable empowerment of females in western society.

The role of advertising in reinforcing or breaking down dichotomies

The prevailing influential powers in magazines are the advertisers rather than the editors since advertising revenue contributes more to profitability than does revenue from sales (Hart, 1991). Whilst school-aged girls do not necessarily have the material means to spend much money on products, advertisers place great importance on winning custom by building 'brand loyalties' for later in life (Winship, 1985: p. 30). They do this through, for example, giving free gifts such as the 'hair mascara' included the analysed issue of *Live and Kicking*.

Clearly, creating submarkets or widening current markets, is of interest to advertisers, therefore developing, offering and exploiting newly adapted subcultural images and identities is highly attractive to them. In this vein, Sunny Delight ran another advertisement (*Live and Kicking*: pp. 39–41) using a cartoon of a female running. The colours were stereotypically feminine, the runner had long hair, wore bracelets and had a 'desirable' body shape with recognisable conformity to traditional femininity. However, the image was also one of the very few in the sample that showed a female in sports clothing, actively doing sport (and sweating).

Advertising like this can offer young people more diverse, fluid or even temporary ways in which to choose *from*, and not *between*, the many activities and identities available to them. Advertisers can thus demonstrate that a redefinition of femininity *is* possible and that the female self can be "... endlessly constructed, reconstructed and customised" (McRobbie, 1994: p.

165). In this way, advertisers can both create a substantial market of independently-minded teenage girls and young women and also encourage other advertisers to produce positive sporting images of and for girls. This, in turn, could help to provide wider choices needed to counter the restrictive and oppressive atmosphere for those teenage girls and young women who are interested in sport.

Advertisers' motives will always be financial, proposing "... to each of us that we *transform* ourselves and our lives by buying something more" (Berger, cited in Sharpe, 1976: p. 109) (emphasis added) but they can also offer choices within this 'transformation'. For instance, Nike UK (1998) produced a booklet, *Girls in Sport*, which shows many positive images suggesting not only that girls can do sport but that they can simultaneously have a recognisable and personally-determined femininity. The booklet's diverse, non-dichotomous images offer the reader a momentary opportunity to define herself autonomously and to resist both of the traditional, stereotyped images discussed above (sporty versus non-sporty).

Magazine editors remain cautious, however, because of their concern not to alienate any advertiser (or reader) and thereby undermine their commercial success. A pertinent example appeared in *Just Seventeen* (p. 59) where their award for the "best sports label" was announced. Adidas received the award with a positive and supportive statement: "We've always encouraged girls to lead active lifestyles'". Meanwhile, the editor's message was contradictory and frivolous: "Looks like you've stripped off those Man U kits (wish David Beckham would!)".

Advertisers motives will always be based on profit-making. Thus, if it is felt that a product needs to be re-marketed to readers who disassociate themselves with a particular image then the advertisers will disassociate themselves from that image. One pertinent example in the data was an advertisement for Tampax tampons (*Just Seventeen*: p. 60), which reversed previous advertising campaigns that had appealed to 'sporty' girls (see Clarke and Gilroy, 1993). The advertisement talked of "*those* sporty types" (emphasis added) in the third person, placing a symbolic distance between the reader and sport and 'othering' female athletes. It continued by ridiculing sporting women in a sarcastic tone. Using the second person, the advertisement invited the reader to be "inclined more towards a certain sprinter's shorts than his sports" (p. 60). Finally, it suggested kissing, cuddling and going to parties as an alternative to being sporty. According to this, then, girls do not do both.

This type of representation is potentially damaging because it reinforces the dichotomous relationship between femininity and sport by celebrating light-heartedly the passive, even lazy, female. Clearly, there exist possibilities for change in the representation of young women's and girls' sport through adolescent females' magazines. However, the contradictions uncovered in this study, fuelled by commercial/capitalist motives, cause "... simultaneous attraction and rejection ... " of the dichotomous images (Winship, 1987: p. 80), creating difficulties for the teenage girl in her negotiation of her world and her search for her sense of self.

Teenage girls' subcultures and identities

The study of subcultures

Ethnographic studies in the 1970s (for example, Willis, 1977) developed an interest in working class male youth subcultures by exploring the "Meanings, values and ideas embodied in institutions, in social relations, in systems of beliefs in mores and customs, in the use of objects and material life." (Hall and Jefferson, cited in McRobbie, 1978: p. 98). The (mainly male) ethnographers were criticised, however, by feminist researchers for being uncritical and for reinforcing stereotyped images of girls as they were represented through the eyes of 'the lads' in their studies. Girls were "fleetingly and marginally represented" (McRobbie and Garber, 1991: p. 1). Nevertheless, writers such as Griffin (1982) and McRobbie (1978) adopted and made use of some aspects of this work, such as 'cultural analysis' which stresses the importance of 'lived experience.' This allowed them to take teenage girls and young women seriously in their research, to recognise the position of girls and to make them visible and vocal (Griffin, 1982).

Who are teenage girls and young women (not)?

Several writers have argued that identities are constructed by a process of exclusions of what a person is not. As Stuart Hall (1996: p. 4) explains,

> It is only through the relation to the Other, the relation to what it is not, to precisely what it lacks, to what has been called its constitutive outside that the 'positive' meaning of any term – and thus identity – can be constructed.

In this way young women's identities are established, for example by teenage girls' magazines, "... in relation to a series of differences that have become socially recognised" (Connolly, 1991: p. 64). In order to consider the distinctive peculiarities of teenage girls' subcultures it is important to establish these differences by first considering their specificities. First, girls are not boys — their subcultures are gender specific. Secondly, teenage girls are not adults – there is also an age specificity. Thirdly, contemporary teenagers are teenagers in 1998, not in 1978 nor in 2008 nor 2018 when my generation's children will be teenagers. There is also a time specificity, which renders culture, and thence subcultures, in a state of continual flux. Finally, teenage girls are also specifically *not* their parents, their teachers, magazine editors, advertisers or researchers – they have experiential and motivational specificity as well. Thus, each particular group of teenage girls shares the common ground of female lived experience.

Collective identities: what is it like to be a contemporary teenage girl/young woman?

The magazines analysed above illustrate how identities are discursively offered to groups, categories or collections of people. Hall (1996: p. 4) describes how,

> Identification is constructed on the back of a recognition of some common origin or shared characteristics with another person or group, or with an ideal, and with the natural closure of solidarity and allegiance established on this foundation.

The magazines need people purchasers to identify with their product, so they 'play into' teenage girls' subcultures and attempt publicly to create for their readers a collective 'teenage girl' identity. Meanwhile, teenage girl consumers of these magazines grasp at the images offered in order to avoid feeling isolated and 'not belonging' (Rutherford, 1990).

Two decades of research on teenage girls' subcultures has demonstrated their recurring, dominant ideological theme of romance. It has been argued (for example, by Cockburn, 1987; Griffin, 1982; McRobbie and Garber, 1976; and McRobbie, 1978) that this dominant notion of romantic love relates to the obligatory and demanding nature of heterosexual culture, compelling teenage girls and young women to devote their time, energies and skills to competing, and succeeding, in a romance 'market'. Alternatives to this ideal for girls, such as lesbianism, are labelled as 'deviant', 'evil', 'abnormal' or simply non-existent (Griffin, 1982: p. 3; Lees, 1986). Thus, the position of 'romantic female' may become positively attractive to teenage girls who are eager to establish a secure place in their world through an unambiguous, feminine, heterosexual image. In this way, "They are both saved by and locked within the culture of femininity" (McRobbie, 1978).

The freedom of consumer choice may seem to offer a partial escape from the "enslavement of romance" (McRobbie, 1994: p. 166) but, paradoxically, the 'commercialisation of culture' is, in itself, a form of enslavement for teenage girls and young women as "none of the choices is absolutely free. They are constrained and limited by relations of power, by structures of domination and subordination" (Weeks cited in Clarke, 1996: p. 196). These hegemonic power relations depend upon the labelling of groups of people and these labels or categories often emerge through official discourse to become collective identities. Whilst teenage girls do have much in common, it is important to realise that they are not a homogenous group.

Teenage girls / young women as a heterogeneous group

There is no generic teenage girl. A previous study of 75 girls, based on a questionnaire administered by the author to Year 9 girls (13–14 years of age) (Cockburn, under review) showed the impossibility of simplifying girls' attitudes to sport and physical education (PE). Their attitudes were seldom wholly negative or positive. Each girl had an individual array of experiences, strengths, weaknesses, likes and dislikes in relation to sport and PE. The 'sporty'/'non-sporty' dichotomy was thus demonstrated to be false with individual girls adopting very diverse views. They also experienced a plurality of subcultures and located themselves very differently within the broad category of 'girl' depending on a range of factors. These factors included social class, race, ethnicity, age, sexuality, physical ability, body shape, geographical location, type of school attended, and experience of family life (see Dewar, 1993). It appears, therefore, that there is reason to challenge McRobbie and Garber's claim that teenage girls form "... a distinct culture of their own; *one* which is recognised by and catered to in girls' weekly comics and magazines" (1991: p. 11) (emphasis added). Rather, the magazines, in the main, cater to a dominant discourse of middle class, heterosexual, physically able, usually slim and pretty teenage girls.

There are occasional exceptions to this, however (Winship, 1987). For example, in McRobbie's (1994) analysis of *Just Seventeen* magazine she found that, in keeping with the postmodern world, "... there is more of the self in this new vocabulary of femininity, much more on self-esteem, more autonomy" (p. 165). In the sample under investigation here there was also occasional ideological encouragement for girls to identify themselves as individuals. One example was a L'Oreal advertisement in *Just Seventeen* (p. 66) for 'UP 2 U' make-up, enabling you to "change your ID". As Rutherford (1990: p. 11) points out, advertising (and consequently the discourse of these magazines) "... thrives on selling us things that will enhance our uniqueness and individuality". Again, it appears that girls are obliged to deal with contradictions and apparently unresolvable conflicts as they strive to adopt an individual identity out of the dominant and oppressive collective identities being offered them. This is not unproblematic, as is discussed below.

'Belonging' as problematic

Certain problematic factors must be acknowledged here with reference to teenage girls and young women. Not everyone 'fits' into the ready-made collective identities (or categories) on offer. Hall (1996: p. 3) cites Laplanche and Pontalis (1985) who propose that "the ego-ideal is composed of identifications with cultural ideals that are not necessarily harmonious".

This was confirmed in another qualitative study (Cockburn, 1999) of six Year 9 girls, designed to explore girls' relationships to school physical education. Each girl wanted, in different ways and to differing extents, to resist the commonly proffered identities, including the 'emphasized femininity' of teenage girls' magazines. They showed signs of wanting to live their femininity in many different and changeable ways. Yet these four magazines, and many others like them, offer extraordinarily little diversity, offering only one model identity for these young readers to measure themselves against. It is not surprising, therefore, that girls in the study often encountered the loneliness of 'not belonging' (Cockburn, 1999).

During the process of striving to be 'individual', teenage girls face powerful cultural limitations and take social risks regarding their perceived femininity and, consequently, their confidence and happiness. They run a high risk of experiencing conflict, tension and confusion about their sense of self, as the process of identification and the identities on offer, are never simplistic, usually contradictory and always problematic. Cynthia Cockburn (1998: p. 216) describes these tensions well:

> Many (sometimes it seems most) identity processes are coercive. We are labelled, named, known by identities that confine us, regulate us and reduce our complexity. The subtleties in our sense of self are difficult to convey in the terms available to us. We often feel misunderstood and misrepresented. And these processes are the more painful because they exploit our irreducible need to belong, our happiness in belonging.

Conclusion

The magazines surveyed here provide clear examples of identities being constructed 'discursively' (Foucault, 1970), and of how discourse coercively "... invites certain behaviours" (Moore, cited in Cockburn, 1998: p. 213). As Hudson (1984: p. 51) comments, this reinforcement helps to "... keep in circulation established stereotypes and uncontroversial notions of what it is to be feminine and teenaged". It also ensures that the "... centrality and privileging of heterosexuality is always assumed" (Winship, 1985: p. 41). The paper has demonstrated how inconsistent and unsatisfactory are the polarised and conflicting stereotypes on offer to young female readers. The discursive construction and marketing of femininity to teenage girls and young women precludes their serious participation in sport. As Oliver Leaman (1986: p. 123) claims,

> It is hardly surprising, then, that girls tend to reject physical education [and sport in general] as an aspect of the curriculum [and life in general] which is unfeminine, irrelevant and childish.

The way forward for many is to refuse the choice (Theberge and Birrell, 1994). The contradictions need to be challenged and transcended, both in theory and in practice, in the search for a satisfactory conclusion. The latter surely lies in allowing and encouraging teenage girls and young women to define a stronger sense of self, to empower themselves and to define themselves autonomously but not at the price of their sense of belonging. Magazines, and other discursive practices, such as school physical education, need:

- to begin to respect females as heterogeneous individuals rather than generic stereotypes; to recognise how, in crucial ways they are the same and in crucial ways they are different, "... breaking these hierarchies and dismantling this language of polarity and its material structures of inequality and discrimination" (Rutherford, 1990: p. 10); and,

- to develop and nurture a genuinely skilled and fit sporting female subculture.

There are currently efforts being made to do this, for example by the *Girls In Sport Campaign* which is carrying out research on girls' PE and by the Women's Sports Foundation who produce a sports magazine for girls which is distributed nationally to school physical education departments. Clearly, there is a need for liberating, and less contradictory discursive material like this to be more readily available in the high street, alongside other magazines. In this way teenage girls and young women could autonomously and privately choose, read about and identify with a less restrictive and oppressive range of images and identities.

Acknowledgement

Many thanks to Dr. Gill Clarke from the University of Southampton for her support and guidance throughout the study.

References

Budgeon, S. and Currie, D. H. (1995) 'From feminism to postfeminism: Women's liberation in fashion magazines', *Women's Studies International Forum* Vol. 18, No. 2: pp. 173–186.

Clarke, G. (1996) 'Conforming and contesting with (a) difference: How lesbian students and teachers manage their identities', *International Studies in Sociology of Education* Vol. 6, No. 2: pp. 191–209.

Clarke, G. and Gilroy, S. (1993) 'This bloody business: Menstrual myths and periodic leisure', in C. Brackenridge (ed) *Body Matters: Leisure images and lifestyles.* (LSA Publication No. 47). Eastbourne: Leisure Studies Association.

Cockburn, Claudia (1999) '"Everybody's looking at you!": Girls negotiating the "Femininity Deficit" they incur in physical education', unpublished undergraduate thesis, University of Southampton.

——— (under review) 'Year 9 girls' opinions of physical education: A questionnaire wurvey', *Bulletin of Physical Education.*

Cockburn, Cynthia (1987) *Two-track training: Sex inequalities and the YTS.* London: Macmillan.

——— (1998) *The space between us: Negotiating gender and national identities in Conflict.* London: Zed Books.

Connell, R. W. (1987) *Gender and power.* Cambridge: Polity Press.

——— (1995) *Masculinities.* London: Polity Press.

Connolly, W. E. (1991) *Identity/difference: Democratic negotiations of political paradox.* London: Cornell University Press.

Dewar, A. (1993) 'Would all the generic women in sport please stand up? Challenges facing feminist sport sociology', *Quest* Vol. 45: pp. 211–229.

Foucault, M. (1981) *The history of sexuality: An introduction.* Harmondsworth: Penguin.

Griffin, C. (1982) 'Cultures of femininity: Romance revisited', *Centre for Contemporary Cultural Studies Occasional Paper*, Women Series (Spring) No. 69.

Hall, S. (1996) 'Who needs "identity"?', in S. Hall and P. Du Gay (eds) *Questions of cultural identity.* London: Sage Publications.

Hart, A. (1991) *Understanding the media: A practical guide.* London: Routledge.

Hudson, B. (1984) 'Femininity and adolescence', in A. McRobbie and M. Nava (eds) *Gender and generation.* London: Macmillan.

Leaman, O. (1986) 'Physical education and sex differentiation', *British Journal of Physical Education*, Vol. 17, No. 4: pp. 123–124.

Lees, S. (1993) *Sugar and spice: Sexuality and adolescent girls.* London: Penguin Books.

Lines, G. (1993) 'Media and Sporting Interests of Young People', in G. McFee and A. Tomlinson (eds) *Education, sport and leisure: Connections and controversies*. Chelsea School Research Centre: University of Brighton, pp. 167–177.

McRobbie, A. (1978) 'Working class girls and the culture of femininity', in Centre for Contemporary Cultural Studies (eds) *Women take issue*. London: Hutchinson.

McRobbie, A. (1991) *Feminism and youth culture: From 'Jackie' to 'Just Seventeen'* London: Macmillan.

McRobbie, A. (1994) *Postmodernism and popular culture*. London: Routledge.

McRobbie, A. and Garber, J. (1976) 'Girls and subcultures', in S. Hall and T. Jefferson (eds) *Resistance through rituals: Youth subcultures in post-war Britain*. Centre for Contemporary Cultural Studies, London: Hutchinson.

Mason, V. (1995) *Young people and sport in England, 1994*. London: Sports Council.

Nike (1998) *Girls in sport*, unpublished report.

Rutherford, J. (ed) (1990) *Identity: Community, culture, difference*. London: Lawrence and Wishart.

Scraton, S. (1986) 'Images of Femininity and the Teaching of Girls' Physical Education', in J. Evans (ed) *Physical education, sport and schooling*. London: Falmer Press.

—— (1987) '"Boys muscle in where angels fear to tread" – Girls' subcultures and physical activities', in J. Horne, D. Jary, A. Tomlinson (eds) *Sport, leisure and social relations*. London: Routledge and Kegan Paul.

—— (1992) *Shaping up to womanhood: Gender and girls' physical education*. Milton Keynes: Open University Press.

Sharpe, S. (1976) *"Just Like a girl": How girls learn to be women*. Harmondsworth: Penguin Books.

Sports Council (1993) *Women and sport: Policy and frameworks for action*. London: Sports Council.

Talbot, M. (1986) 'Gender and physical education', *British Journal of Physical Education* Vol. 4, No. 1: pp. 120–122.

Theberge, N. and Birrell, S. (1994) 'Feminist resistance and transformation in sport', in M. Costa and S. R. Guthrie (eds) *Women and sport: Interdisciplinary perspectives*. Champaign: Human Kinetics.

Willis, P. (1977) *Learning to labour*. Farnborough: Saxon House.

Winship, J. (1985) 'A girl needs to get streetwise: Magazines for the 1980s', *Feminist Review* Vol. 21, Winter: pp. 25–46.

Winship, J. (1987) *Inside women's magazines*. London: Routledge and Kegan Paul.

Glencoe: A Case Study in Interpretation

Judith E. Brown

School of Leisure, Tourism and Hospitality Management,
Cheltenham and Gloucester College of Higher Education (UK)

Introduction

This paper seeks to explore the language used in representations of the area
of Highland Scotland called Glencoe. Glencoe is situated about 100 miles
north of Glasgow, about 15 miles south of Fort William towards the west of
the Highlands of Scotland. The representations are widely available to tourists
and leisure visitors to the area and take the form of books, web sites and
videos. From a wide range of these sources, six texts, which appear typical
of what is available either on the subject of Glencoe or Scotland in general,
have been selected for analysis and discussion. This discussion is based on
the textual analysis of these examples, and is set in the context of the current
literature on heritage tourism and interpretation.

This paper, using the texts mentioned above, seeks to identify the ways
in which language is used in some of these representations of Glencoe to create
or reinforce perceptions of Scottish identity: that is, 'Scottishness'. The
language used, while discussing Glencoe in these texts, also draws meaning
from many of the cultural codes of Scottish society. At the same time, it
appears that many Scots draw some of their identity directly from the
mythology surrounding Glencoe.

It can be argued that Glencoe, and the massacre which took place there
in 1692, has become used by many Scots as one of the touchstones of their
identity. Glencoe offers a number of symbols of a version of Scottish ethnicity
and nationhood. Visitors to the Highlands of Scotland are encouraged, through
a variety of forms of representation such as leaflets, books, video, and web
sites, to accept these symbols as the 'authentic' images of Scotland. These
symbols are of a nation which is proud, noble, hardy, independent and brave

in the face of subjection to what is perceived by some Scots and visitors to Scotland to be English rule (Beveridge and Turnbull, 1989). Furthermore, the scenery of Glencoe, which can be described as bleak and grey, frightening, threatening, gaunt and unfriendly, can also be seen to support the feeling that the people who live there (and by implication those who live in the rest of Scotland) are hardy, tough and independent. Thus, as McCrone, Morris and Kiely (1995) suggest, cultural forms not only reflect a national identity but also help to construct and shape that identity. In the case of Glencoe, representations of the place, including the mythology surrounding the massacre, have to an extent been manufactured as a reflection of these ideas of 'Scottishness' by some Scots, including those authors of the various texts considered here. Alternatively, ideas of 'Scottishness' can be seen to be derived by many Scots from the various representations of Glencoe (McCrone, Morris and Kiely, 1995).

An estimated 300,000 people used the Glencoe National Trust Visitor Centre car park in 1998 (Smith, 1999). It is one of the most visited locations in the Scottish Highlands (Smith, 1999). People visit the area to experience the extraordinarily bleak and grey scenery, and because it is the site of a notorious massacre. These two factors (scenery and history) have caused Glencoe to develop a mythology of its own; but that mythology has been shaped, in turn, by texts on Glencoe as a Scottish site.

The history of the Massacre of Glencoe

It is difficult to overstate the importance of the Massacre of Glencoe in the Scottish imagination. A recent article in a Scottish tabloid newspaper carries the headline "Glencoe killings weren't our fault" and carries on to state "The Campbell clan are trying to claim they were not to blame for the Glencoe massacre" and that "lowland troops and not Campbells carried out the 1692 slaughter." However, " ... the MacDonalds insist [that] the account is a futile cover up" (*The Daily Record*, 13th March 2000: p. 15).

In the massacre of February 1692, an estimated 36 of the residents of the village of Glencoe were killed (no completely accurate number could be established at the time), while the rest of the population hid in the hills where more died of exposure. All the houses in the village were burned (Prebble, 1968; Buchan, 1938; Morton, 1991). There are many anecdotal tales of Fairy pipers leading the residents away from the village to safety in the hills, and of Campbell soldiers refusing to kill the MacDonalds who had lately been their hosts (Fairweather, 1984). The massacre has become, in mythology, a longstanding clan feud ending in the bloody events of 1692, with the evil Campbells murdering an indeterminate number (anything between 2 and 200) of the heroic MacDonalds.

Representations of 'Scottishness'

Many ordinary Scots can be said to claim proudly characteristics such as honesty, patriotism, individuality, independence, bravery, kindness, toughness, hospitality and a dislike of the English (McCrone, Morris and Kiely, 1995; Beveridge and Turnbull, 1985). Many of these characteristics link closely with ideas of the Romantic and the Romantic Hero. Indeed, many of the texts about Scotland, including those about Glencoe, promote what is arguably a Romantic view of 'Scottishness', not just for the tourist industry but also for the Scots themselves. It is largely due to the work of Sir Walter Scott that many of the Romantic attributes of 'Scottishness', such as Scottish tradition, noble behaviour and tartanry, have been adopted (Gold and Gold, 1995). Scott's version of clanship and clan conflict present what has been termed a false and sanitised version of Gaeldom (Clyde, 1996). Indeed, Clyde argues that Scott created a plaided panorama, representing Scotland as a picturesque, homogeneous place draped in tartan (Clyde, 1996). This view of Scotland can be said to justify the notion of it being a nation not quite independent (Beveridge and Turnbull, 1989).

These characteristics, claimed by many Scots, have been explored in a variety of ways. McCrone *et al.* (1995), for example, discuss research into Scots' own views of their national characteristics, using interviews with members of the National Trust for Scotland. The members' responses (pp. 167–8) indicated that:

> Scotland is a family orientated society, with close knit communities unlike England.

> I think in terms of the toughness and resilience of the Scots. Scots are very enterprising.

> Scotland's character and its people. The country is less populous and more rugged. This appears in the character of the people – tough and down to earth.

> There's a distinct hardy feeling to the buildings and the people.

These descriptions of the idea of Scottishness by some Scottish people can be seen as a product not just of their past but also of the geography of the area, particularly in relation to the difficulties they are commonly believed to have endured. The quotations mention a sense of perseverance, hardiness and a struggle to survive.

Clyde (1996) sees the idea of a Scottish national character, where the people display common qualities, as springing from the Union of Scotland and England in the seventeenth century. He argues that these political events have provided a framework of nationhood which has enhanced and given reality to Scottish identity. This framework includes what has been described as a sense of loss for the romantic past of kilt and Highland Dress, which was Scott's representation of Scottishness and which has since become even more strongly attributed to Scottish people because of the historical distance from events (Morton, 1993). According to Morton (1993), the difficulties of life in the past can be safely forgotten with that historical distance. On the other hand, Beveridge and Turnbull (1989) describe the perceived characteristics of the Scots as 'Scottish Inferiorism' where Scotland is described as dark, backward, fanatical, violent, barbaric, savage, harsh and primitive.

These politics of identity can be seen to contribute to the creation of what Palmer (1999) terms a nationalistic rhetoric. This rhetoric, she claims, conveys images and meanings about what is considered to be the nation's communal heritage. Part of this nationalistic rhetoric can be seen in the way that Scots are portrayed as honourable, brave, hardy and so on. Palmer discusses the way in which images create ideas in the mind: Glencoe can be seen as one such image, promoting the image of the Scot as described earlier by Gold and Gold (1995) and Beveridge and Turnbull (1989).

Heritage and tourism

Lowenthal (1998) analyses the construction of a representation, stating that the past is changed to suit the representation. He also discusses the notion that memory forms identity but that memory is revised over time and that heritage is the story of the victims of history. MacCannell (1989) explores the ways in which texts can be seen to use a mixture of natural, historical, social and cultural representations, combined into a stream of impressions. When discussing representations of heritage, Timothy (1997) examines the way in which national monuments often represent not only an event but also a set of "durable national ideals" (p. 252). Glencoe, and the way it is portrayed in the six texts analysed in this study, can be seen to be a representation of a defined set of national ideals, as described above.

It might be argued that, as a result of such representations, our actual knowledge and understanding of the past is weakening (Prentice, 1993). This would appear to be the case with representations of Glencoe and the history surrounding it. The history of Glencoe is adapted to suit a perception of 'Scottishness' and one which is revised over time in order to include both the icons of Scotland, such as the tartan and the village communities, and the characteristics the Scots ascribe to themselves – honesty, bravery, self reliance and a sense of being forced into second place by the English. These are the national, social, cultural and historical features of MacCannell's (1989) stream of impressions. It appears, however, that it is the way these representations are put together in texts that make them convincing to many Scots and also to the visitor.

Hitchcock's (1999) discussion of anachronistic representation of an area and its people can equally be applied to Glencoe and the Scots. The historic attitude of the Scots to the English — the old enemy — can be seen as an anachronistic element of the representation of the Scots in history, and in Glencoe, emphasised by the language used.

The analysis

A variety of texts (books, leaflets, videos and web sites) available to visitors to Glencoe and to tourists to Scotland, were analysed: six of these are discussed here. They include the video, entitled *The Massacre of Glencoe*, shown in the National Trust Visitor Centre at Glencoe and widely available books such as *Glencoe* by John Prebble (1968). A number of brightly illustrated 'coffee table' books were also studied. Most of these books are available in Tourist Information centres, Visitor Centres and book shops throughout Scotland. Of these, three are selected for discussion in this paper as typical of the range available. These are: *The Scottish Highlands* (Dunnet, 1988); The *Highlands and Islands of Scotland* (Maclean, 1976); and *The Nature of Scotland, Landscape, Wildlife and People* (Magnusson and White, 1997). Additionally, web sites advertising local hotels, providing information for the visitor about Glencoe, were studied. One example of these is that of the Clachaig Inn, situated in Glencoe. Many of the texts provide similar accounts of events and the scenery, using a form of wording which can be described as old fashioned and flowery.

Findings

Throughout the day, the National Trust for Scotland Visitor Centre in Glencoe runs a 15 minute video, titled *The Massacre of Glencoe*. This tells the story of the massacre in a way designed to be suitable for a wide range of viewers. The video attempts to evoke the atmosphere of the glen and the hardness of the life led by the inhabitants. Drawings of the bearded but benevolent clansmen battling through the winter weather in their plaids, on their hardy Highland ponies, are just some of many similar images of the tough Highland Scot. Phrases such as "history hangs heavy", "seeking shelter" and "echoing down the years" are used. It would appear that this use of language contributes to an atmospheric representation of Scotland. It is made clear that the events in question took place a long time ago, giving the impression that this was how people would have spoken then. This wording also reflects the sense of nostalgia felt by the Scots for the turbulent past, as described by Lowenthal (1998: p. 74) in his discussion of "the cult of victims" and by McCrone *et al.* (1995) in their discussion of Scottish characteristics.

Lowenthal's (1998) notion of heritage as the story of the victims of history can be seen to be reflected in the idea that the heroes of the massacre were the 'ill fated' MacDonalds rather than the 'victorious' Campbells. This characteristic representation of the MacDonald-as-victim can be related to the wider perception of Scotland being a victim of English subjugation (the Campbells were in the pay of the English king). Other major tourist sites in Scotland include the battle site of Culloden, where the English defeated the Scots in the final battle for Scottish independence. This reflects a similar idea of the 'cult of the victim'. Research by McCrone *et al.* (1995: p. 168) showed that members of the National Trust surveyed displayed similar feelings to those found in the previous study:

> ... highly influenced by its geography, by the sense of persecution, the covenanters and the highland clearances for example ...

> Scotland is fascinating – it has always been on the margins and we have had to struggle to survive, so that has made us keener to leave our mark and conquer the natural elements.

The spirit of perseverance over hardship

In the video, *The Massacre of Glencoe*, the MacDonalds are described as carrying out 'raids hallowed by custom'. This is not only an example of old fashioned language but also of the use of *quasi* religious wording. The MacDonald clan has developed in popular myth as the epitome of all good things Scottish and the use of this *quasi* religious terminology appears to transform their illegal cattle raids, as described in the video, into righteous acts. The clan chief is described as an 'impressive patriarch'. Adjectives such as 'stubborn' and 'proud' are used to describe the MacDonald clan. The Campbells, 'the avaricious Lowlanders', are clearly portrayed as the villains and the MacDonalds seem to have been ascribed hero status. This recreates Sir Walter Scott's idea of the 'Romantic Hero' and the notion of the Highland Scot being persecuted by the followers of the English, in this case, the Campbell Lowlanders (Gold and Gold, 1995; McCrone *et al.*, 1995). The video also describes the 'rigid code of Highland hospitality' where any traveller is given food and a bed, no matter who he is. There are parallels here with McCrone *et al.*'s (1995) interviews with members of the National Trust, described earlier, which indicate that many Scots see themselves as hospitable, close-knit and family-orientated.

John Prebble's *Glencoe* (1968) is an historical account for a popular market and is on sale in many book shops, Visitor Centres and Tourist Information Centres throughout Scotland. Prebble uses the landscape of Glencoe to evoke many of the Scottish characteristics mentioned above. For example, he describes the glen (p. 20):

> On the south is a loosely clenched fist of mountains, five ridges joined to the great knuckle of Bidean nam Bian, the Pinnacle of the Peaks.

The idea of a fist indicates toughness, hardiness and courage in fighting, as well as a sense of surliness. The idea that this mountain is a fist loosely clenched can be seen as a constant willingness to fight and to defend.

Prebble (1968: p. 26) also writes about the men of the Highlands being "large bodied, stout, subtle, active, patient of cold and hunger". These descriptions evoke both the notions of the Scot as Romantic Hero and the toughness and resilience of the Scots, as described by McCrone *et al.* (1995) and Beveridge and Turnbull (1989).

'Coffee table' books describing Scotland, such as *The Highlands and Islands of Scotland* (Maclean, 1976), *The Scottish Highlands* (Dunnett and Dunnett, 1988) and *The Nature of Scotland* (Magnusson and Whyte, 1997), emphasise the beauty of the landscape and give only a limited explanation of its history. Most of these books have a section on Glencoe, one describing the area as a:

> ... wild army of gaunt peaks, savaged by bleak ravines – heavy with brooding melancholy in rain and mist, towering in fearsome sombre majesty under snow. (Maclean, 1976: p. 40)

Dunnett and Dunnett (1988) depict the rocks of Glencoe, and Magnusson and White (1997) describe the rough climbing country of Glencoe and mention the wild quality of the area. These accounts are typical of such books. The adjectives used, such as 'gaunt', 'bleak', 'brooding', 'melancholic', 'fearsome' and 'sombre', are similar to those used to describe the Scottish people (McCrone *et al.*, 1995; Beveridge and Turnbull, 1985; Morton, 1991). It is probably no coincidence that Maclean uses warlike metaphors, such as 'an army of gaunt peaks', in his description of an area where the army (the Campbells) was blamed for the massacre. 'Gaunt', an adjective more often descriptive of persons, also gives a human face to the area. The elements, rain, mist and snow, not only give an air of melancholy appropriate to an area where a massacre occurred, but also give the impression that anyone from the area has to be resilient to these weather conditions, as the 'tough', 'hardy' Scot is portrayed. These descriptions also create an impression of the historic value of the area, implying a link between the modern scenery and its history. These texts also relate to Clyde's (1996) version of Scotland as a picturesque and homogenous place.

Maclean (1976: p. 40) describes Glencoe as "doom laden" and comments that "tragedy had to happen here". The portrayal of scenery in this way creates the perfect backdrop for an 'inevitable' historical tragedy to unfold. This is Glencoe as victim heritage, and it provides an illustration of the alteration of the past to suit the representation, as suggested by Lowenthal (1998). Maclean (1976: p. 40) calls the landscape "prophetic", capturing both the religious and historic inevitability. The "MacDonald men, women and children" who had "billeted the soldier assassins in their homes", were:

> ... done to death by a company of Argyll's regiment under the command of Captain Robert Campbell, talking of murder under trust, universally regarded even by the seventeenth century brigands weaned on the blood feud, as the foulest act of treachery. (Maclean, 1976: p. 40)

The emotional blaming of the massacre of the 'innocent' MacDonalds on the 'assassin' Campbells sets the tragedy in black and white terms. The ideas of the Highland Scots as the 'Romantic Heroes' and the Lowland (that is, English) Campbells as the evil enemy are set out by Maclean (1976), notions also supported by other writers (Buchan, 1938; Prebble, 1966). Maclean indicates that the MacDonalds were innocent victims of persecution, again the view held by some Scots (Beveridge and Turnbull, 1989; McCrone *et al.*, 1995). The true Scot appears to be prey to English victimisation and certainly not an ally to the English.

Websites are now available which have the power to project similar images to a wider community than can be reached through printed texts. One example, written by the Clachaig Inn, a local hotel, gives a description of the massacre. It emphasises that the MacDonalds were rebels and that the Campbells were involved with the authority of the ruthless English central government (Clachaig Inn, 1998). Here, again, the MacDonald is portrayed as the Romantic rebel hero, living a "carefree and lawless" life (Clachaig Inn, 1998: p. 2). The sense of nostalgia for this way of life is evident, as is the Romantic view of the Highlander. As might be expected from a website, the view of Glencoe and its past is sanitised through the use of the terms mentioned above (Clyde, 1996).

Conclusions

Lowenthal (1998) discusses the construction of a representation, noting how the past can be 'rewritten' to suit the 'user'. This is undoubtedly the case with texts about Glencoe, where the 'facts' have become all but indistinguishable from the stories used to promote the area to leisure visitors and tourists. The language used in the representations of Glencoe discussed here, clearly aimed at tourists and other visitors, has helped to give shape to notions of Scottish national identity, just as the notions of Scottishness have shaped representations of Glencoe. The way in which the texts are written shows the range of images of 'Scottishness', from the Romantic as described by Clyde (1996), through the 'quasi religious' wording of Scottish myth, to the Scottish version of a 'culture of victims' (Lowenthal, 1998).

The various ways in which the landscape and the events are represented in different texts support the view that many Scots hold themselves to be historically struggling for survival, thus creating a nation of independent, honest, tough, rebellious people. It is because of these images that Glencoe and the site of the massacre has become a popular site for visitors. The history of the massacre has been adapted to encourage the view that the Campbells were 'bad' and the MacDonalds 'good' – in other words the Scots are 'good' and the English are 'bad'. These images of the Scot as a 'Romantic Hero', acceptable to many, have made possible the view of the MacDonalds as honourable rebels. This encourages 'the stream of impressions', specifically impressions of nationalism and 'Scottishness', described by MacCannell (1989). The texts create a view of the massacre, and of the two clans, which in turn sustains Timothy's (1997) notion of a set of durable ideals that includes the Scot as 'Romantic Hero'.

Glencoe has many characteristics which have made it ripe for moulding memory to shape national identity. Because of its geography and history, Glencoe has become representative of, and has added to, the ideas many Scots have about their own identity. Glencoe has become a focus for a shared recollection of Scotland. It is a tangible feature which appears to symbolise much of Scotland's history and, as such, supports this sense of Scottish identity (Timothy, 1997). However, in order to ensure that this identity is convincing for visitors to Glencoe, the language in the representations offered to these visitors appears to be almost as important in conveying the ideas of Scottish identity and the history of the area as the representations themselves. Edensor and Kothari (1994) discuss the advertising of place images and the propagation of symbolic metaphors which construct 'imagined communities'. Glencoe can be seen as one of these 'imagined communities'; the metaphors used to construct it are in terms which are useful to the groups who wish to promote the area.

References

Aitchison, C., (1999) 'Heritage and nationalism: Gender and the performance of power', in D. Crouch (ed) *Leisure / Tourism geographies; Practices and geographical knowledge*. London: Routledge, pp. 59–73.

Beveridge, C. and Turnbull, R. (1989) *The eclipse of Scottish culture*. Edinburgh: Polygon.

Buchan, J. (1938) *The massacre of Glencoe*. Edinburgh: Peter Davies.

Clyde, R. (1996) *From rebel to hero: The image of the highlander 1745–1830*. East Linton: Tuckwell.

Dunnett, D. (1988) *The Scottish Highlands*. Edinburgh: Mainstream.

Edensor, T. and Kothari, U. (1994) 'The masculinisation of Stirling's heritage', in V. Kinnaird and D. Hall (eds) *Tourism: A gender analysis*. Chichester: John Wiley and Sons, pp. 164–187.

Fairweather, B. (1984) *Highland heritage*. Fort William: Glencoe and North Lorne Folk Museum.

Hewison, R. (1987) *The heritage industry: Britain in a climate of decline*. London: Methuen.

Hitchcock, M. (1999) 'Tourism and ethnicity: Situational standards', *International Journal of Tourism Research* Vol. 1: pp. 17–32.

Gold, J. R. and Gold, M. M. (1995) *Imagining Scotland, tradition representation and promotion in Scottish tourism since 1750*. Aldershot: Scolar Press.

Lowenthal, D.(1998) *The heritage crusade and the spoils of history*. Harmondsworth: Viking

MacCannell, D. (1989) *The tourist – a new theory of the leisure class*. London: Schocken.

Maclean, A. C. (1976) *The Highlands and Islands of Scotland*. Glasgow: Collins.

McCrone, D. Morris, A. and Kiely, R. (1995) *Scotland the brand: The making of Scottish heritage*. Edinburgh: Edinburgh University Press.

Magnusson, M. and White, G. (1997) *The nature of Scotland: Landscape, wildlife and people*. Edinburgh: Canongate.

Morton, G. (1991) *The massacre of Glencoe*. National Trust for Scotland (video).

Morton, G. (1993) *Unionist nationalism: The historical construction of Scottish national identity Edinburgh 1830–1860*. Unpublished PhD thesis, University of Edinburgh.

Palmer, C. (1999) 'Tourism and the symbols of identity', *Tourism Management* Vol. 20: pp. 313–321.

Prebble, J. (1968) *Glencoe*. Harmondsworth: Penguin.

Prentice, R. (1993) *Tourism and heritage attractions*. London: Routledge.

Smith, R. (1999) *Glencoe 2000, The Millennium appeal*. Edinburgh: The National Trust for Scotland.

Timothy, D. J. (1997) 'Tourism and the personal heritage experience', *Annals of Tourism Research* Vol. 24, No. 3: pp. 751–754.

The Clachaig Inn About Glencoe (1998) *http://www.glencoescotland.co.uk/zaboutgc.htm*

The Daily Record (Glasgow) (2000) 'Glencoe killings weren't our fault', March 13th: p. 15.

Who Are These People?
And What on Earth Are They Doing?![1]

Lesley Lawrence

Department of Tourism and Leisure, University of Luton (UK)

People think *Star Trek* fans are weird — sad people. (*Star Trek* convention Interviewee 18)

I don't tell many people that I'm off for the weekend to a *Star Trek* convention. (*Star Trek* convention Interviewee 24)

Introduction

The opening quotes suggest that, in much media fandom, fans are very likely to 'deny their own fandom' and carry on 'secret lives as fans' (Lewis, 1992: p. 1). Traditionally associated with train spotters and internet/computer buffs, disparaging terms such as anoraks, geeks and nerds are also common utterances levelled at *Star Trek* fans. They have been "characterized as 'kooks' obsessed with trivia, celebrities, and collectibles" or as "misfits and crazies "(Jenkins, 1992a: p. 11), with *Star Trek*'s hard core audience portrayed as "unknowable and irrational" (Tulloch and Jenkins, 1995: p. 3). Many forms of media fandom are perceived as such by 'outsiders', contrasting with the views of 'insiders' who see their fandom as acceptable leisure practice and, in many cases, as 'serious leisure'.

The work of Robert Stebbins (1992, 1997) on 'serious leisure and marginality' informs the paper. Serious leisure is perceived as "marginal to the main problems around which the social institutions of work, family and leisure have developed" (Stebbins, 1997: p. 125). Where *Star Trek* fans are concerned, their leisure practice is not only marginalised but also trivialised and often ridiculed by 'outsiders'. This raises issues of leisure inequity, leading us to the thorny question of 'what is leisure'? The advertisement for the 1999 Leisure Studies Association conference (LSA 1998: p. 5) refers to a central issue within Leisure Studies in asking whether leisure itself is "normatively rooted only in certain socially approved practices"? This paper uses findings from research conducted to elicit *Star Trek* fan perceptions to discuss two inter-related issues: first, the acceptability and unacceptability of certain leisure forms; and secondly, the apparent mismatch in 'insider' and 'outsider' perceptions from the perspective of the fans themselves.

Why is it generally accepted to walk around town wearing a football shirt that shows an identification with a favoured football team (or being used simply as a leisure/fashion top) but unacceptable to do so wearing *Star Trek* gear? Moreover, why is going to a football match more acceptable than attending a *Star Trek* convention? As an active football fan and *Star Trek* fan I would suggest that there should not be any difference in acceptability. Yet, the comment 'sad people' has often been heard about *Star Trek* fans, hence the questions which form the title for the paper.

Why choose *Star Trek*? Why not examine Dr Who or soap opera fans? Although the original motives for conducting the research on *Star Trek* fans can be viewed as personal, other justifications for such a focus soon emerged. For example, I had already been accepted within the *Star Trek* fan community, and therefore had ready access to a fan community. The significance of *Star Trek* was another reason. Much media fandom has been seen as growing out of *Star Trek* fandom, with *Star Trek* conventions setting the model for subsequent conventions (Harrison, 1996). The size of the fan base is vast and *Star Trek* itself has been recently described by Bernardi as "an enduring icon in United States popular culture" (Bernardi, 1998: p. 5). Although this is certainly not the case in the UK, the UK is identified as being one of "Trek's most fertile international markets" (Bernardi, 1998: p. 11).

This is a study of the perceptions and behaviour of one fan community. Although many similarities exist between different fan communities, care should be taken when generalising from the findings reported in this paper. Concepts can be broadened and used to talk about other kinds of fandom but these need to be tested through fieldwork (Henry Jenkins, cited in Harrison, 1996).

The context: preconceptions and portrayal

Fans of a range of media products tend to be described in derogatory terms. For example, daytime soap opera fans are often described as "abnormal" (Harrington and Bielby, 1995: p. 112). "The myth of the 'orgiastic' fan, the groupie, survives as a staple fantasy of rock music reporting and criticism" (Jenkins, 1992a: p. 15). Several internet sites are aimed at anoraks, for example 'anorak's archive — the world of pirate radio' and 'anorak' (referring to radio rallies). Zine[2] editors have been summed up as being "freaks, geeks, nerds, and losers — that's who zines are made by" (Duncombe, 1997:p. 17). Comparing the writers of zines and science fiction, the fans is considered by both to be:

> something of a nerd, rather above average in intelligence and below it in social skills ... alienated from his peers and finding in *ST* and fandom a means of escaping some of the unpleasantness and stress of the Real World. (Fitch, 1994, cited in Duncombe, 1997: p. 17)

With respect to the science fiction audience, a long history of negative images exist which construct "the fan as extraterrestrial; the fan as excessive consumer; the fan as cultist; the fan as dangerous fanatic" (Tulloch and Jenkins, 1995: p. 4). A notorious sketch on prime-time US television in 1986 (*Saturday Night Live*) has been held responsible for the perceptions that many people have of *Star Trek* fans. As Hertenstein (1998: p. 5) reported, "The Trekkies in the *Saturday Night Live* sketch were depicted as stereotypical sci-fi nerds, outsiders, aliens". Journalists' perceptions and associations of fandom with "immaturity and mindlessness" (McQuail, 1997: p. 36) are also held by many academics. As a reaction to this, some authors have argued instead that media fandom, such as that associated with *Star Trek*, is normal (for example, Fiske, 1992; Jenkins, 1992b; Jenson, 1992; Abercrombie and Longhurst, 1998; and Jones and Lawrence, 2000). On the whole, however, Jenkins (1992a: p. 7) considers "academic accounts of fan culture as being sensationalistic and [that they] foster misunderstandings about this subculture". Academic writers are accused of being "influenced by constructs mapped by popular journalism and preconceived by the reading public" (Tulloch and Jenkins, 1995: p. 5). This may be a contributory factor in the suspicion and distrust of fans towards media and/or researcher presence at *Star Trek* conventions.

Another illustration of the labelling of fans is in the distinction between the use of the terms 'trekk*ies*' (often used by 'outsiders'), and 'trekk*ers*' (the fans' own preferred term for themselves). 'Trekkie' is viewed by fans as a derogatory label with connotations of abnormality. The term 'Trekkie' has increasingly come to refer to what Jenkins (1992a: p. 21) calls the "media constructed stereotype". Thus, many fans and/or Trekkers are sensitive to, and resist the term 'Trekkie' which represents:

> an identity imposed upon the group from the outside while 'Trekker' came to refer to the group's self-constructed and more affirmative identity. (Tulloch and Jenkins, 1995: p. 15)

As noted above, many forms of media fandom are open to ridicule and, in some cases, border on unacceptability to 'outsiders' or 'them'. "Fandom is typically associated with cultural forms that the dominant value system denigrates" (Fiske, 1992: p. 30). However, as will be shown in this study of *Star Trek* fans, such fandom to 'insiders' or 'us' can be perceived as leisure practice that certainly is not illegal or harmful, and that makes a positive contribution to the lifestyle of fans. It could be surmised that we are dealing here with what Tulloch and Jenkins (1995: p. 14) describe as:

> the thinly drawn yet sharply policed boundaries between normal and abnormal audience behaviour, appropriate and inappropriate ways of relating to mass culture (both within fandom and in the culture at large).

Similarly, Jenson (1992: p. 20) interprets fandom and affinity as distinct elements of a cultural hierarchy:

> ... it is normal and therefore safe to be attached to elite, prestige-conferring objects (aficionadohood), but it can be abnormal, and therefore dangerous to be attached to popular, mass-mediated objects (fandom).

Star Trek, it is believed, courts controversy because it exists in "the liminal area between entertainment and seriousness" (Jindra, 1994: p. 48). As Jindra goes on to explain:

> Nonfans sense the 'seriousness' of *Star Trek* when they witness fandom activities and react against it because they believe it should remain totally in the realm of entertainment. That people take it seriously offends them. *ST* fans, on the other hand, want to be respected and understood, and want their devotion to be recognized as legitimate. (Jindra, 1994: p. 48)

Despite challenges from some colleagues like "why on earth study something as frivolous and non-serious as *Star Trek* subcultures?" or, indeed, other simi-lar media subcultures, it is argued here that researching of *Star Trek* subcul-tures is a legitimate academic activity. Jenkins (1991: p. 174) provides one possible answer to such challenges when he points out that "behind the exotic stereotypes fostered by the media lies a largely unexplored terrain of cultural activity". Little seems to have changed since Jenson's comment in 1992 that very little literature exists that "explores fandom as a normal, everyday cultural or social phenomenon" (Jenson, 1992: p. 13). She believes that:

To the extent that we stigmatize fandom as deviant, we cut ourselves off from understanding how value and meaning are enacted and shared in contemporary life. (Jenson, 1992: p. 26).

Jones and Lawrence (2000: p. 4), in their comparison of football and *Star Trek* fan identification, drew attention to the motivations and sentiments of Henry Jenkins:

Fans are often represented as antisocial, simple-minded, and obsessive. I wanted to show the complexity and diversity of fandom as subcultural community. (Jenkins, 1992b: p. 277)

An interesting reaction was caused by a newspaper report announcing Economic and Social Research Council-funded research on the audiences of the film version of *Judge Dredd*: for example, "is this trivia really worth studying" was a newspaper comment in *The Times* (Lawson, 1995 cited in Barker and Brooks, 1998: p. 2). The authors of the research, however, considered their research to be ground-breaking: " ... until now, no one has had the common decency to ask the views and explore the understandings of the film-users themselves" (Barker and Brooks, 1998: p. 298). Other authors have made similar observations, such as Jindra (1994: p. 29) who said: "It is in the practice of the fans that an understanding of the nature of any social group can be gained". This debate is, of course, not unique to the study of media fandom, as highlighted by Jenson:

Social inquiry can and should be a form of respectful engagement. It can and should illuminate the experiences of others in *their own terms*, because these 'others' are us, and human experiences intrinsically and inherently matter. (Jenson, 1992: p. 26)

Researching Star Trek fans

For this research project, data were collected at three *Star Trek* conventions. Excluded from the research were casual viewers of an episode on television as the focus was upon *Star Trek* fans. Although *Star Trek*, in its various forms, is estimated to have a television audience of millions, not everyone who watches is labelled a fan. An audience is not a "singular homogeneous entity" (Grossberg, 1992: p. 53) and this particular research falls into Barker and Brooks' (1998: p. 8) category of "studies of audience activities in fan groups and subcultures". As is suggested, media experience has the potential:

to form the basis of distinctive subcultures and identifications. Not only are fans often organised social groups, but they interact very actively with their object of attention and affection. (McQuail, 1997: p. 36)

Research interest thus focused on those fans who could be viewed as constituting "an elite fraction of the larger audience of passive consumers" (Grossberg, 1992: p. 52). It seemed appropriate to examine this 'elite fraction', namely the participant or the 'active' fan, and particularly those 'active' fans of *Star Trek* who actually *attended Star Trek* conventions and who fell into the third of the following categories: "Media fans are consumers who also produce, readers who also write, spectators who also participate" (Jenkins, 1992b: p. 208). Unlike early research on *Star Trek*, which examined fans and the relationship between audience and text (such as Bacon-Smith, 1992; Jenkins, 1992a), interest here was not with the conventional 'active audience'. The latter was popularised within Cultural Studies during the 1980s and used in 'new audience studies' to convey how the audience are "active in their pursuit of pleasure from watching TV — making their own choices and meanings" (Ang, 1996: p. 8). 'Active', in the context of this research, placed the meaning of the text at the forefront where "the relationship between the audience and popular texts is an active and productive one" (Grossberg, 1992: p. 52). Applied to *Star Trek*, this meaning of active suggests that fans "actively rework the givens of the *Star Trek* universe to make their own cultural meanings" (Penley, 1991: p. x). Also excluded from this research were fans who did not attend conventions. Many of these fans, however, may be active in other capacities, for example as collectors of memorabilia, traders of cards, contributors to fanzines, involved in artistic enterprises such as costume art, or as fan club members. Bacon-Smith believes that 'outsiders' associate fans with clubs, yet this "image tends to be wrong on all counts ... while many fans do belong to formal clubs, the majority do not, and organize more informally" (Bacon-Smith, 1992: p. 9), often via the convention.

The first Science Fiction convention has been reported as being held in 1936 (Bacon-Smith, 1992). The first convention in the US was believed to have been held in New York in 1972 with an attendance exceeding 3000, when only a few hundred were expected by the organisers (Tulloch and Jenkins, 1995: pp. 1011). Wagner and Lundon (1998: p.2) contend that "every weekend a *Trek* convention is held somewhere on the globe". *Star Trek* conventions are classified as either professionally-run (commercial)[3] or fan-run (not-for profit/charitable). The research discussed here was conducted at the latter type of event. Not-for-profit events are run by a committee, with any income going towards the cost of running the event and to one or two main charities. Jindra (1994: p. 39) suggests that conventions can afford:

a unique opportunity to observe fandom, for they can be a direct expression of the fervency of fandom and of its relationships with the general public.

Conventions, he believes, gives *Star Trek* 'public visibility' due to local media coverage and attendance by those fans who are new to fandom. Importantly, as Jenkins (1991) suggests with regard to media fandom in general,

> the ability to transform personal reaction into social interaction, spectatorial culture into participatory culture, is one of the central characteristics of fandom. (Jenkins, 1991: p. 175)

The chance of finding fans who might perceive their involvement as 'serious leisure' (a concept named by Stebbins, 1992) is much greater at conventions than through other avenues. Stebbins argues that, of six qualities associated with participating in serious leisure, the most relevant is the tendency to "identify strongly with their chosen pursuits" (Stebbins, 1997: p. 119)[4]. Fans attending *Star Trek* conventions or football matches are generally likely to be classed as highly identified and, additionally, participants in serious rather than casual leisure (Jones and Lawrence, 1998).

   The convention for *Star Trek* fans, and for many science-fiction fans in general, has been described as acting as one means of 'engaging with the community' (Bacon-Smith, 1992). Indeed, media fans become fans by translating the viewing of a programme into some kind of cultural activity and by "joining a 'community' of other fans who share common interests and a sense of identity" (Jenkins, 1991: p. 175). Fandom offers:

> a community [that is] not defined in traditional terms of race, religion, gender, region, politics, or profession, but rather a community of consumers defined through their common relationship with shared texts. (Jenkins, 1992b: p. 213)

One of the more obvious ways of engaging with the community is to attend a convention. These normally take place over two to three days, many with 24 hour daily programmes. Late night themed discos and continuous video are the norm for the early morning slots. Usually, there are guest talks (from actors from the various series), autograph sessions, panel discussions, fancy dress and art competitions, charity auctions, a dealers' room and, importantly, space available for informal sitting around and chatting. Unlike fan clubs, the community in this case is not geographically fixed, but "the fan world structures itself around a series of conventions, held in a 'mobile geography' of hotels all over the world" (Bacon-Smith, 1992: p. 9).

The importance of conventions as meeting places for both new and existing members, and for social interaction, has been noted (Bacon-Smith, 1992; Joseph-Witham, 1996). Conventions act to:

> spatially and temporally organise the interaction between the community and potential new members, and serve as formal meeting places for the various smaller groups of fans who follow a convention circuit. (Bacon-Smith, 1992: p. 9)

Methods

It was in the 1990s that a significant amount of work on *Star Trek* began to be published. This resulted in a certain degree of credence being given to the study of *Star Trek* from a feminist perspective within media and cultural studies (for example, Bacon-Smith, 1992; Helford, 1996; Projansky, 1996; and Penley, 1997). Arguably, the most prominent study of *Star Trek* fandom is Camille Bacon-Smith's ethnography based on the sub-community of fans (largely women) who create and distribute fiction and art. Any substantial non-feminist work also tends to be ethnographic in nature (for example, Jenkins, 1988, 1992b; Jindra, 1994), with the odd exception. For example, Bernardi's doctoral work in critical and cultural studies employed a historiographic approach in addressing the way in which race is articulated in *Star Trek* (Bernardi, 1998). When trying to "understand any group phenomenon, especially a rather diffuse one like ST fandom", an ethnographic approach is regarded as ideal (Jindra, 1994: p. 29).

In Phase One of this two-phased study, data were collected through covert participant observation at two 3-day *Star Trek* conventions early in 1998: the 'Starfleet Academy Ball' in Bournemouth, and at 'Starfury 98' in Leicester. One of the advantages of conventions to someone who has access and is already accepted as part of the community is the friendly social atmosphere where people are very willing to chat. Consequently, invaluable data were collected in Phase One. However, the act of collecting data covertly caused the researcher great unease. In such an open, trusting environment it was difficult to ignore feelings of guilt and deception when seemingly taking advantage of the friendliness of many attendees for the purposes of 'secret' data collection. These feelings were particularly noticeable when collecting data from interactions with friends.

Phase Two of the data collection consisted of observation and 30 semi-structured interviews with attendees at the 3-day Scottish *Star Trek* convention 'Continuum 98' in Glasgow in June (interviews ranged in length from 30 minutes to 90 minutes). Permission to conduct the research was

Table 1   **Characteristics of interviewees (n = 30)**

Gender	50% male, 50% female (77% believed that Star Trek fandom was equally represented in terms of female/males)
Age	mean age 29.0, ranging from 9 to 57 (93.3% believed that Star Trek fandom catered for all ages)
Employment	63% were in paid employment or self-employed; 27% were students at school or in Higher Education

granted by the organising committee, following reassurances on the researcher's part of its non-exploitative nature. Just as the decision to undertake covert research was difficult, 'coming out' as a researcher was also not an easy decision. I was concerned that it might adversely affect relationships in the future, as a non-researcher convention attendee. The convention hotel was ideal for an interviewer due to the many open spaces where attendees socialised, read or waited to enter one of the halls. Convention attendees were primarily interviewed on the basis of availability. Equal numbers of male and female fans were included in the study (see Table 1).

The three events were all fan-run, with between 300–700 people in attendance over the course of each weekend. The Bournemouth and Glasgow conventions were *Star Trek* conventions with largely *Star Trek* guests. Although many *Star Trek* fans attended the Leicester Convention, the focus was on *Babylon 5*. The quantitative data were analysed using SPSS and the open-ended questions were analysed for patterns and trends.

Findings

The following findings are reported here: characteristics of *Star Trek* convention attendance; main reasons for attending conventions; what it means to be a *Star Trek* fan; and external perceptions of *Star Trek* fans. A comparison is made between the acceptability of being a *Star Trek* and football fan. The legitimacy and justification for such a comparison, however, bears further examination. This preliminary comparison enables some interesting insight that might guide further comparative research.

Convention attendance: Some sample characteristics in terms of convention attendance are shown in Table 2.

Table 2   Star Trek convention attendance (n=30)

No. of Star Trek conventions attended in last 12 months	1.76 (SD –1.28)
No. of conventions attended in total	2.60 (SD –1.58)
Length of time attending conventions —	5.5 years (mean)
Attend mainly with: relatives friends alone	36.7% 23.3% 16.7%
Attend conventions: only in the UK also in the US	93.3% 6.7%
Usually stay at the convention hotel	56.7%
Had been Star Trek fans for an average time period of 14.10 years (SD 7.71), ranging from 4 years to 30 years	

Main reasons for attending conventions: Five main reasons for attending *Star Trek* conventions were given:

- Enjoyment of *Star Trek* and Sci-Fi in general: typical responses were "I love *Star Trek*"(Interviewee 19) and "I like Sci-Fi genre" (Interviewee 2).

- Escapism and enjoyment: for example, "I can enjoy myself, it's a good week-end where you can completely overdose [on *Star Trek*]" (Interviewee 25).

- Acceptance: feeling of 'fitting in and being accepted at the convention'.

- Social interaction: the chance to meet new people and renew friendships.

- Guests: the chance to meet the guest actors was also important: for example, "see the characters and the actors as people rather than TV characters" (Interviewee 3).

The importance of spending social time was also shown when attendees were asked (on a scale from 1 [not important] to 8 [very important]), how important certain activities and elements were to their enjoyment of a *Star Trek* convention. Guest-related items ranked highly, but the social/ atmosphere items featured more highly overall (see Table 3). One fan considered that they

Table 3   **Importance of factors contributing to enjoyment of the convention**

Rank order	Average score (1=not important to 8=very important)
1	attending guest talks (6.77)
2	being with Star Trek fans (6.53)
3	friendly atmosphere (6.50)
4	good organisation (6.43)
5	socialising (6.40)
6	dealer's room (5.87)
7	meeting the guests (5.83)
8	charity auction (5.43)
9	getting guest autographs (5.33)

were having a "good time … even if you take away the guests, I'd still have a good time" (Interviewee 14). Other such comments included: "Great convention. Meet lots of people" (Interviewee 18); and

> … it's been very enjoyable for me. I've made new friends and had a great time with old friends. When I leave the convention I'm sad to leave, but happy as I've had a good time. (Interviewee 24).

To some of the older fans, the social side was key. For this group, maintaining old friendships had become more important than their *Star Trek* fandom. As Interviewee 6 observed:

> You see at this type of event, similarities with groups of fans. I went to a folk concert/event with friends and you see similar things — groups of people get together and make friends, get keen and get organised. You see it also in forms of motor cycling. So, my main reason for being here isn't because it's necessarily *Star Trek* — it's where people can get together.

Fitting in and being accepted (the fourth factor), emerged as being a key element of the *Star Trek* convention experience, as indicated in the following comments: "*Star Trek* conventions are 'safe havens' — you're accepted" (Interviewee 18), and:

> If you just go and attend, it doesn't matter what background you come from. Most attendees are unaware of backgrounds ... people take you for what you are with the common factor being the *Star Trek* shared interest. (Interviewee 9)

This reinforces Jenkins' (1992b: p. 213) contention that:

> Fandom is particularly attractive to groups marginalized or sub-ordinated in the dominant culture — women, blacks, gays, lower-middle-class office workers, the handicapped — precisely because its social organization provides types of unconditional acceptance and alternative sources of status lacking in the larger society.

One fan believed that:

> quite a few people come to *Star Trek* conventions, not because they're real fans of *Star Trek*, but because they can be accepted.. there are unwritten rules of conventions — you don't laugh out loud at fancy dress garb, you accept things. You get different groups that come along, for example, disabled, obese people — it's really good in that sense. (Interviewee 23)

This was evident at all three conventions. Such 'unwritten rules' are common to many leisure groups in which social norms are formed:

> these are not only shared but are also, to some extent, enforced, by the disapproval, or eventually by the rejection, of members who fail to conform. (Argyle, 1996: p. 129)

At the Bournemouth convention, as with many conventions, the opening ceremony included a list of 'do's and don'ts' to help fans get the maximum out of the weekend. This included — "no excesses of behaviour ... this is a family event". Also, unofficial codes of conduct were apparent in the more formalised clubs and groups. One informant at Bournemouth talked about how his group tried to 'replicate Starfleet', in which there is no sexism and no ageism. One fan had joined, for example, but was found to be very sexist and was later excluded. An interviewee who had initially been attracted to watch *Star Trek* on the television when the original series came on air, talked enthusiastically about how:

> Baddies were not from outer space — a vulcan first officer was a main character and wasn't a baddie. Vulcans could get on with people like us. There was a communications officer who was female and black and could fix things. It suggested that people can get on and that we can get rid of prejudices, for example, apartheid. (Interviewee 23)

It could be argued that this environment of acceptance at *Star Trek* conventions acts to increase the numbers of people attending a convention who might normally be labelled as 'misfits in society' (one attendee's apologetic label for some *Star Trek* fans) thus helping to perpetuate stereotypes. Equally, the suggestion has been made above that not all convention attendees are necessarily *Star Trek* fans. Some will attend due to the acceptance element and others may now be 'less serious' fans than they once were, but might still enjoy the social element.

Being a Star Trek fan

It cannot be assumed, therefore, that all *Star Trek* convention attendees are fans of *Star Trek*, or that the primary attachment or identity is *Star Trek*. "Media fans can take pleasure in making intertextual connections across a broad range of media texts" (Jenkins, 1992a: p. 36), and they may "drift from one serious commitment to another" (Jenkins, 1992a: p. 41). Three quarters of interviewees (76.6 per cent) identified most closely with one of the *Star Trek* series[5] or with *Star Trek* in general. *Babylon 5* was the next most highly identified (10 per cent). Interviewees were asked to rate how strongly they saw themselves as *Star Trek* fans (from 1 'not at all a fan' to 8 'very much a fan'). Some attendees were fans of several series/programmes and identified more closely with *Babylon 5*, *Alien Nation* or *Red Dwarf*. However, the majority of them were *Star Trek* fans. One attendee (Interviewee 19) admitted, "I like Sci-fi ... I'm more of a *Babylon 5* fan"; nevertheless she still rated herself a *Star Trek* fan (6/8). Indeed, 90 per cent rated themselves between 6–8, with an overall mean score of 6.4, suggesting high degrees of attachment to *Star Trek* (8–23.3 per cent; 7–33.3 per cent; and 6–33.3 per cent).

Of the 30 attendees interviewed, only three did not class themselves as *Star Trek* fans (ratings of 2). A fifty year old male (Interviewee 6) had been attending *Star Trek* conventions for fifteen years and was not a fan of the spin-off series *Deep Space Nine* and *Voyager*. He commented "*Star Trek* fandom has outgrown me really. I was a fan of the original series". His main reason for continuing to attend conventions was "the social events, meeting people, the social side". It was this social element that had also attracted one of the other non-fans. She had been attending *Star Trek* conventions for three years and her friends call her "the world's greatest anti-trek trekker". Although admitting to liking *Deep Space Nine*, she described herself as "not really a *Star Trek* fan as such". She liked being able to meet people in the "open and friendly atmosphere" of fan-run conventions, and treated conventions as a "bit of a holiday". The final non-*Star Trek* fan (Interviewee 18) was at the convention as he had taken his son, who was a keen fan. "I feel I need to be here 100 per cent of the time as son is still only 13 and needs to know I'm around". He believed that "some take fandom too seriously".

The fans themselves described 'a fan' in the following ways:

> Someone who enjoys something so much [the TV series etc.] that they are willing to participate in the events surrounding it. (Interviewee 1)
>
> ... someone who is committed, emotionally committed and feels strongly about it. (Interviewee 15)
>
> ... totally into their hobby — knowledgeable, likes discussing elements of it. Committed. (Interviewee 20)

These explanations reflect Grossberg's (1997: p. 222) definition of fandom:

> Fandom is different from consumption or simply enjoyment (although it may incorporate it) because it involves a certain kind of identification or investment.

'Is being a *Star Trek* fan, perceived as leisure?' was another key question asked. Excluding from the analysis the 10 per cent who deemed themselves to be non-fans, 81.5 per cent perceived being a *Star Trek* fan as leisure. Of those, two thirds considered it to be 'serious' rather than casual leisure. One, who deemed it as non-leisure, went as far as to say that, "it's too serious for that" (Interviewee 25).

Of those interviewed, 76.6 per cent considered themselves to be 'fairly passive' in *Star Trek* fandom, as opposed to 'actively involved'; 56.7 per cent were a member of a *Star Trek* fan club or group, with 23.3 per cent running or organising an associated club or group. The average spend per head on *Star Trek* merchandise in the previous year was £269.47, with a range from £0 to £1500. 25 per cent considered themselves to be serious collectors of *Star Trek* merchandise.

One interviewee rated himself at the top of the scale, that is at 8 (very much a fan) "I'd be kidding myself if try to say otherwise. If not an out-and-out fan, why come here?" Later however, he admitted that he was not a "blinkered fan of *Star Trek* like some.. I'm not an obsessive fan. Some take it too far" (Interviewee 14). Similar views were expressed by another fan

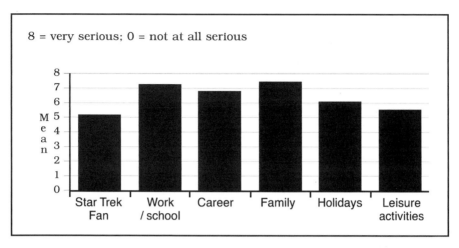

Figure 1   Seriousness of being a Star Trek fan (comparison)

(Interviewee 5) who rated himself 6 /8 — "I really enjoy it, but I'm not a complete anorak. I collect tapes [video], read, but I'm not obsessive ... I like Sci-Fi in general".

There appears to be a general awareness of a minority in the community who 'take it too far', and this minority are normally present at every convention. As one informant at Leicester suggested, "all the fans are marvellous — but you get the one or two odd ones who spoil it". He was at pains to point out that most fans were 'quite normal'. Even within the *Star Trek* community "there is always someone more extreme whose otherness can justify the relative normality of one's own cultural choices and practices" (Jenkins, 1992a: p. 19).

Amongst the 'majority' fans attending conventions, the extent to which they took being a *Star Trek* fan seriously, in comparison with other elements of their lives, varied enormously. Figure 1 (above) shows that, although many of the interviewees saw themselves as definite fans of *Star Trek*, their fandom was taken much less seriously in comparison with, for example, family, work/school, and career.

At the same time, 81.5 per cent of the *Star Trek* fans believed that being a *Star Trek* fan had impacted upon other areas in their life, for example regarding career choice and holidays: "I've made a lot more friends that I would have — thanks to *Star Trek*" (Interviewee 7)

> I tend to spend some of my holidays meeting with friends and going to conventions. Also, I spend a lot of money on *Star Trek* stuff and can't afford to go on holiday! (Interviewee 15)

Two University students, one reading philosophy and logic, the other physics, both believed that their choice of academic programme was influenced by *Star Trek*. Other impacts included 'travel opportunities' and issues related to the text of *Star Trek* such as vision and acceptance.

External perceptions

Fans were asked how strongly friends saw them as fans of *Star Trek* (on a scale from 1 'not at all a fan' to 8 'very much a fan'). Some admitted that the extent of their fandom was not always revealed to friends. A mean score of 6.8 was obtained, with 90 per cent scoring between 5 and 8, and 36.7 per cent considering themselves as being perceived as 'very much a fan'. The manner in which friends described them was revealing. No positive comments were reported. Instead, a range of disparaging terms were frequently used such as 'nutter', 'odd', 'freak', 'obsessed', 'eccentric', 'a bit crazy?', 'a bit funny' and 'mad'. Phrases included: "probably 'a bit of an anorak' " (Interviewee 28), "a fan of *Star Trek* ... and laugh" (Interviewee 20), and "I hate to think" (Interviewee 25). One fan (Interviewee 29) described how a photograph of her in *Star Trek* uniform, taken at a large commercially-run convention in this country in 1995, had appeared in a newspaper and then in PR literature for her company. The reaction at work had caused her to vow "I'm never going to wear uniform again at a convention ... I was made fun of and sensed people were laughing at me behind my back".

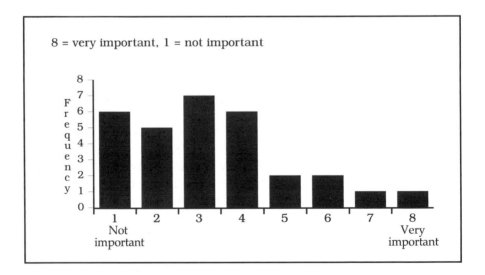

Figure 2   Importance of a favourable reception by other people

At the same time, results would seem to suggest that many fans had got used to these external perceptions. As Figure 2 demonstrates, when asked about 'the importance of a favourable reception by other people e.g. press, media, friends, others', a low mean score of 3.27 was obtained ranging from [(1) 'not important' to (8) 'very important'].

As one fan commented, "you come to expect it"(Interviewee 14), and another responded "I don't care what they think, though I prefer people to realise that some sane people can be fans" (Interviewee 7). Other fans were quite critical, though deeming favourable reception as relatively unimportant, for example "you shouldn't rubbish it if you don't know it"(Interviewee 8), and "if genuine criticism comes from someone who knows about it... OK ... but not if it's from an ignorant person" (Interviewee 17). On the whole, the findings supported the assertion that *Star Trek* fans want respect, under-standing and their "devotion recognised as legitimate" (Jindra, 1994: 48).

Jones (1996) writes how many fans attend conventions "attired in highly creative costumes that identify them as "Trekkers" and arouse a spirit of com-munity" (Jones, cited in Joseph-Witham, 1996). When asked about wearing uniform[6] , 26.7 per cent reported wearing uniform at conventions, with only 6.7 per cent doing so in a non-*Trek* environment: "I wore my *Star Trek* uniform to school one day and people laughed ... yet if I'd worn a football strip, bet they wouldn't have" (Interviewee 12). Likewise, one interviewee related how his brother was changing out of his uniform to go outside (Interviewee 16). As two other fans explained, "if I go out like this [in costume] you get laughter — it's not worth the hassle" (Interviewee 17); and "outside of the convention I get laughed at ... it's up to them ... it's a really silly attitude" (Interviewee 22). Wearing *Star Trek* t-shirts and caps and so on, both in- and outside the convention venue itself, is more common: often a convention will sell a special t-shirt.

The media quite naturally tend to focus on attendees wearing costume at conventions. During a panel debate at the Leicester convention an incident involving the BBC was reported. They had been filming at a large, commercially-run convention in London in 1995 and just as they were about to interview a Klingon, a woman walked by in a costume portraying an episode character. The producer told the camera technicians, "Forget that guy, there's a bigger weirdo over there". This comment was not well received by onlookers. Tulloch and Jenkins (1995: p. 14) tell the story of a cameraman asking fans who were being interviewed: "don't you think it's pretty *abnormal* for grown people to run around in costumes etc.?" One fan asked the cameraman about his own detailed knowledge of baseball statistics. The threatened journalist then retorted "No! Baseball is *normal*; this stuff isn't". But is baseball, or indeed any other sport, more 'normal' than *Star Trek* or other media products? The literature suggests that this is the perception. For example, when discussing the differences in acceptability or non-acceptability of sport and media fans by the non-fan public, Harrington and Bielby (1995: p. 5) contend that:

> media fans particularly are subject to marginalization because their pleasure derives from fictional narratives rather than from something 'real', like a basketball game.

Football v. Star Trek fans and acceptability

In terms of the acceptability of wearing gear which identifies them as *Star Trek* fans, only 16.7 per cent felt that it was acceptable. However, only 3.3 per cent believed it *not* to be acceptable to wear football colours to demonstrate an identity with a particular team (see Figure 3). Common reactions were:

> I'd like it to be acceptable [wearing *Star Trek* gear]. People think you're weird if you wander around wearing *Star Trek* stuff, whereas it's pretty normal to wear football gear. (Interviewee 1)

> Where football's concerned, there's a wider base in society and it's more   acceptable to friends. Friends don't laugh if you're a football fan" (Interviewee 2)

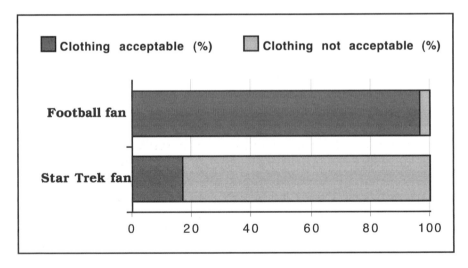

Figure 3   Acceptability comparison — football and Star Trek clothing

43.3 per cent of the sample professed to be football fans. The strength of being a fan averaged out at 4 (8 being the top of the scale). This compared with the *Star Trek* equivalent of 6.4. Only one interviewee, a Leeds United fan for thirty years who attended all home games, considered that he identified more closely with his football team than with *Star Trek*. Generally, the football fans in the sample had been football fans longer than they had been *Star Trek* fans, with the mean scores 12.6 and 5.5 years respectively.

Only one interviewee considered that there was no difference between football and *Star Trek* fans, arguing that "they are both committed" (Inter-viewee 12). Most perceived that the *Star Trek* community was characterised by less rivalry, no violence, less obsession and greater tolerance. For example, "*Star Trek* is a much more social thing and you get this machoness in football and it's tribal" (Interviewee 6). One *Star Trek and* football fan said:

> I like *Star Trek* fans better ... they're nicer, whereas football fans are more antagonist towards each other. Out of any group in society, Sci-Fi fans are less bigoted and prejudiced. (Interviewee 17)

And another said:

> Trek is all about getting together with people who are slightly different ... it's about getting rid of prejudices. Football is all to do with localism, identity, narrowness and finding the differences. Because of my fan-atical following of the Welsh Rugby team and being a nationalist, I can understand why football fans become violent — it's the extreme end of the narrow wedge of nationalism. I see rugby and *Star Trek* fandom as opposites — *Star Trek* as hedonistic and rugby as nation-alistic. (Interviewee 7)

Conclusions

This research into the attendees of *Star Trek* conventions is intended to make a contribution towards satisfying Jenson's (1992: p. 13) call for more literature that "explores fandom as a normal, everyday cultural or social phenomenon". The research aimed not to "distort actual fan behaviour and practices", a criticism levelled in the past at the media and academics by Tulloch and Jenkins (1995: p. 14). Through the perceptions of *Star Trek* fans, the study set out to examine the acceptability and unacceptability of certain leisure forms. From the findings it seems that reality paints a different picture of *Star Trek* fans than that found in the many disparaging public/media descriptions. As Jenkins (1992a: p. 15) suggested:

> The fan still constitutes a scandalous category in contemporary
> culture ... whose interests are fundamentally alien to the realm of
> 'normal' cultural experience and whose mentality is dangerously out
> of touch with reality.

This study provides evidence to the contrary, that is that the majority of fans
are in touch with reality, illustrated through their prioritising of work, careers
and holidays over their *Star Trek* fandom. That many take being a *Star Trek*
fan seriously is not in dispute here. The majority (81.5 per cent) of interviewees
classified their *Star Trek* fandom as leisure and two thirds of them deemed
it serious leisure. Detractors need to recognise that the majority of these people
have *chosen* to attend a *Star Trek* convention and to be a fan of *Star Trek*.
Where leisure is concerned, it is "the *perception* of freedom and being able
to choose between activities" (Ingham, 1987: p. 10) that is important to them.
Significantly, Shaw (1984) found that leisure can best be differentiated from
non-leisure though factors such as freedom of choice, intrinsic motivation,
enjoyment, relaxation, and the lack of evaluation (by self and from others).

Although many interviewees were aware that being a *Star Trek* fan
bordered on unacceptability to 'outsiders', the majority felt that external
evaluation was unimportant. Some, however, bemoaned the 'criticism through
ignorance' that they received. Nonetheless, the question remains: "is leisure
normatively rooted only in certain socially approved practices?"(LSA, 1998:
p. 5). The Leisure Studies academic community itself could be accused of
reinforcing this impression in its publications. *Star Trek* conventions have
similar characteristics to other leisure settings yet media fandom is not
perceived externally as leisure activity that conforms to the norm (Jenson,
1992). Arguably, this leads to marginalisation (Stebbins, 1997: p. 124).
Jenkins could well be correct in his assessment that:

> the stereotypical conception of the fan, while not without a limited
> factual basis, amounts to a projection of anxieties about the violation
> of dominant cultural hierarchies. (Jenkins, 1992a: p. 17)

Negative representations of fandom offer non-fans "extreme versions of the
'Trekkie' stereotype as reassurance of the normality of their own media consumption habits" (Tulloch and Jenkins, 1995: p. 15). Fans have simpler
explanations: "People don't appreciate that peoples' interests differ ... they see
Star Trek as strange, and it and the fans get bad publicity" (Interviewee 15).

It seems ironic that *Star Trek* fans can be ridiculed by the non-fan public/
media for belonging to a subculture which, according to Tulloch and Jenkins
(1995), holds to the idea of a social utopia where there is tolerance and
equality. Within *Star Trek* fandom the view is that "money doesn't matter.

You're rich, black, white, short, tall, heavy, brilliant, dumb" (Josephy-Witham, 1996: p. 10). The phrase 'utopian appeal' is widely used in discussions of *Star Trek* (for example, Boyd, 1996; Harrison *et al.*, 1996; Hertenstein, 1998; and Bernardi, 1998). Bernardi (1998: p. 5) considers for example, that:

> *Star Trek*'s vision of a utopian future, where humans no longer engage in racism, sexism, capitalism, and many other 'isms' is a main reason for fan loyalty.

Doubts have been expressed as to whether this vision is enacted through the various TV series (for example, by Bernardi, 1998; and Wagner and Lundeen, 1998). However, it is apparent that this utopian vision and attitude of tolerance is both transferred to fan attitudes and behaviours at conventions, and also contributes to fan enjoyment. Conventions can be described as constructing:

> social structures more accepting of individual difference, more accommodating of particular interests, and more democratic and communal in their operation. (Jenkins, 1992b: p. 213)

One fan recounted how she had enjoyed watching *Star Trek* on the television; she was impressed by its values and identified with the Vulcan-conceived concept of IDIC [Infinite Diversity in Infinite Combination]. "I like being accepted at conventions as I'm quite a shy person ... I get accepted, not put down" (Interviewee 17). In contrast to the seemingly intolerant attitudes amongst the detractors of *Star Trek* fandom, the fans themselves are "firmly committed to a politics of equality and tolerance" ... through the philosophy of IDIC (Penley, 1997: p. 98).

Acknowledgement

This paper would not have been possible without the openness of the convention attendees interviewed. Thanks go to them and to the convention organisers in Glasgow who gave permission for the research to be conducted. Thanks are also due to those who attended the Leisure Studies Association conference presentation in Cheltenham and to Ian Jones for their helpful comments on an earlier draft.

Notes

1 Acknowledgement is paid to Bacon-Smith (1992) for the choice of title for this paper, though her wording is slightly adapted here.

2 "Zines are noncommercial, nonprofessional, small-circulation magazines which their creators produce, publish, and distribute by themselves" (Duncombe, 1997: p. 6). Fanzines are probably the largest and oldest category of zines.

3 Commercially-driven conventions tend to be much larger than fan-run conventions, with fewer activities and concentrating upon guest talks, for example Albert Hall (London) Generations convention and the large Creation conventions in the US, with numbers in attendance ranging from a couple of thousand to 10,000.

4 Stebbins contends that this quality "springs from the presence of the other five [qualities]" (Stebbins, 1997: p. 119), these being: 'the occasional need to persevere'; 'finding a career in the endeavour'; 'significant personal effort based on knowledge, training or skill'; 'durable benefits or rewards'; and 'unique ethos developing in its expression' (Stebbins, 1997).

5 To date, four series of *Star Trek* have been created. In chronological order, the original series, *Classic Trek*; and three spin-off series: *The Next Generation*, *Deep Space Nine*, and *Voyager*.

6 Uniform is usually Starfleet/federation, or some of the alien races such as Klingon, Romulan and Ferengi. "Cons can represent a stage opportunity for costumers, where garments can be compared or copied, and fans can get ideas from other fan artists" (Joseph-Witham, 1996: p. 9).

References

Abercrombie, N. and Longhurst, B. (1998) *Audiences*. London: Sage.

Argyle, M. (1996) *The social psychology of leisure*. London: Penguin.

Ang, I. (1996) *Living room wars: Rethinking media audiences for a post-modern world*. London: Routledge.

Bacon-Smith, C. (1992) *Enterprising women: Television fandom and the creation of popular myth*. Philadelphia: University of Pennsylvania Press.

Barker, M. and Brooks, K. (1998) *Knowing audiences — Judge Dredd — Its friends, fans and foes*. Luton: University of Luton Press.

Bernardi, D. L. (1998) *Star Trek and history: Racing toward a white future*. New Brunswick: Rutgers University Press.

Boyd, K. G. (1996) 'Cyborgs in Utopia — the problem of radical difference in *Star Trek: The Next Generation*', in T. Harrison, S. Projansky, K. A. Ono, and E. R. Helford (eds) *Enterprise zones: Critical positions on Star Trek*. Boulder, Colorado: Westview Press, pp. 95–113.

Duncombe, S. (1997) *Notes from underground: Zines and the politics of alternative culture*. London: Verso.

Fiske, J. (1992) 'The cultural economy of fandom', in L. Lewis (ed) *The adoring audience: Fan culture and popular media*. London: Routledge, pp. 30–49.

Grossberg, L. (1992) 'Is there a fan in the house? the affective sensibility of fandom', in L. Lewis (ed) *The adoring audience: Fan culture and popular media*. London: Routledge, pp. 50–65.

——— (1997) 'Replacing popular culture', in S. Redhead with D. Wynne and J. O'Connor (ed) *The clubcultures reader: Readings in popular cultural studies*. Oxford: Blackwell, pp. 217–237.

Harrington, C. L. and Bielby, D. D. (1995) *Soap fans: Pursuing pleasure and making meaning in everyday life*. Philadelphia: Temple University Press.

Harrison, T. (1996) 'Interview with Henry Jenkins', in T. Harrison, S. Projansky, K. A. Ono, and E. R. Helford (eds) *Enterprise zones: Critical positions on Star Trek*. Boulder, Colorado: Westview Press, pp. 259–278.

Harrison, T. , Projansky, S. , Ono, K. A. , and Helford, E. R (1996) (eds) *Enterprise zones: Critical positions on Star Trek*. Boulder, Colorado: WestviewPress.

Heide, M. J. (1995) *Television culture and women's lives: Thirtysomething and the contradictions of gender*. Philadelphia: University of Pennsylvania Press.

Helford, E. R. (1996) '"A part of myself no man should see" — reading Captain Kirk's multiple masculinities', in T. Harrison, S. Projansky, K. A. Ono, and E. R. Helford (eds) *Enterprise zones: Critical positions on Star Trek*. Boulder, Colorado: Westview Press, pp. 10–31.

Hertenstein, M. (1998) *The double vision of Star Trek: Half-humans, evil twins, and science fiction*. Chicago: Cornerstone Press.

Hines, S. (1995) 'What's academic about Trek', *Extrapolation*, Vol. 36, No. 1: pp. 5–9.

Ingham, R. (1987) 'Psychological contributions to the study of leisure — part two', *Leisure Studies* Vol. 6, No. 1: pp. 1–14.

Jenkins, H. (1988) 'Star Trek rerun, reread, rewritten: Fan writing as textual poaching', *Critical Studies in Mass Communication* Vol. 5, No 2: pp. 85–107.

——— (1991) 'Star Trek rerun, reread, rewritten: Fan writing as textual poaching', in C. Penley, E. Lyon, L. Spigel, and J. Bergstrom (eds) *Close encounters: Film, feminism, and science fiction*. Minneapolis: University of Minnesota Press, pp. 171–203.

——— (1992a) *Textual poachers — television fans and participatory culture.* London: Routledge.

——— (1992b) '"Strangers no more we sing": filking and the social construction of the science fiction fan community', in L. A. Lewis (ed) *The adoring audience: Fan culture and popular media.* Routledge: London, pp. 208–236.

Jenson, J. (1992) 'Fandom as pathology: The consequences of characterization', in L. Lewis (ed) *The adoring audience: Fan culture and popular media.* London: Routledge, pp. 9–29.

Jindra, M. (1994) '*Star Trek* fandom as a religious phenomenon', *Sociology of Religion*, Vol. 55, No. 1: pp. 27–51.

Jones, I. and Lawrence, L. (2000) 'An investigation of identity and gender in *Star Trek* and Football fandom', in S. Scraton and B. Watson (eds) *Sport, leisure identities and gendered spaces* (LSA Publication No. 67). Eastbourne: Leisure Studies Association, pp. 1–30.

Joseph-Witham, H. (1996) *Star Trek Fans and costume art.* Jackson: Univ. Press of Mississippi.

Lewis, L. (1992) 'Introduction' in L. Lewis (ed) *The adoring audience: Fan culture and popular media.* London: Routledge, pp. 1–6.

LSA (1998) 1999 Annual Conference — 'JUST' LEISURE?, *Leisure Studies Association Newsletter*, No. 51: pp. 5–6.

McQuail, D. (1997) *Audience analysis.* London: Sage.

Penley, C. (1991) 'Introduction' in C. Penley, E. Lyon, L. Spigel, and J. Bergstrom (eds) *Close encounters: Film, feminism, and science fiction.* Minneapolis: University of Minnesota Press, pp. vii–xi.

Penley, C. (1997) *NASA/TREK: Popular science and sex in America.* London: Verso.

Projansky, S. (1996) 'When the body speaks — Deanna Troi's tenuous authority and the rationalization of federation superiority in *Star Trek: The Next Generation* rape narratives', in T. Harrison, S. Projansky, K. A. Ono, and E. R. Helford (eds) *Enterprise zones: Critical positions on Star Trek.* Boulder, Colorado: Westview Press, pp. 33–50.

Shaw, S. M. (1984) 'The measurement of leisure: A quality of life issue', *Society and Leisure*, Vol. 7, No. 1: pp. 91–107.

Stebbins, R. (1992) *Amateurs, professionals, and serious leisure.* Montreal: McGill-Queens University Press.

——— (1997) 'Serious leisure and well-being', in J. T. Haworth (ed) *Work, leisure and well-being.* London: Routledge, pp. 117–130.

Tulloch, J. and Jenkins, H. (1995) *Science fiction audiences.* London: Routledge.

Wagner, J. and Lundeen, J. (1998) *Deep space and sacred time — Star Trek in the American mythos.* Westport: Praeger.

Leisure Studies Association
LSA Publications

An extensive list of publications on a wide range of leisure studies topics, produced by the Leisure Studies Association since the late 1970s, is available from LSA Publications.

Some recently published volumes are detailed on the following pages, and full information may be obtained on newer and forthcoming LSA volumes from:

LSA Publications, c/o M. McFee
email: mcfee@solutions-inc.co.uk
The Chelsea School, University of Brighton
Eastbourne BN20 7SP (UK)

Among other benefits, members of the Leisure Studies Association may purchase LSA Publications at highly preferential rates. Please contact LSA at the above address for information regarding membership of the Association, LSA Conferences, and LSA Newsletters.

JUST LEISURE: POLICY, ETHICS AND PROFESSIONALISM

LSA Publication No 71. ISBN: 0 906337 81 X [2000] pp. 257+xiv
Edited by Celia Brackenridge, David Howe and Fiona Jordan

Contents

Editors' Introduction
.... *Mike McNamee, Chris Jennings and Martin Reeves* v

Part I   POLICY 1
Changing their Game: The Effect of Lottery Sports
Funding on Voluntary Sports Clubs .... *Richard Garrett* 3
Issues of Legal Responsibility in Organised Sport
and Outdoor Recreation .... *John Hunter-Jones* 19
Sport and Leisure Planning: the Need for Assessment
.... *Ari Karimäki* 33
Best Value in Leisure Services: a Philosophy or
a Quality System? .... *Christine Williams* 45
Fairness and Flexibility in the Scottish Leisure Industry
..... *Anna MacVicar, Margaret Graham, Susan Ogden*
and Bernadette Scott 57

Part II   ETHICS 75
Sport, Leisure and the Ethics of Change ..... *Alun Hardman* 77
Just Leisure, Ethical Fitness, and
Ecophilosophical Perspectives .... *Karla A. Henderson* 93
"Sorry Ref, I didn't see it" — The Limitations of Shields
and Bredemeier's Model of Moral Action ..... *Carwyn Jones* ... 105
The Ethos of the Game: Representations of the Good Game
and the Good Player among Junior Football Players
in Sweden .... *Matz Franzén, Per Nilsson, Tomas Peterson* ... 121
Ethical Leisure: The 'Dark" and the 'Deviant"
Disambiguated .... *Heather Sheridan* ... 131
Sport — A Moral Laboratory? .... *Graham McFee* ... 153

Part III PROFESSIONALISM 169
Applying the Principles of "Green Games":
An Investigation into the Green Practices of Event
Organisers .... *Graham Berridge* ... 171
The Professionalisation of Museum Volunteers:
An Ethical Dilemma .... *Margaret Graham* ... 185
An Examination of Coaches' Responsibilities for
Premature Athletic Disengagement of Elite Greek
Gymnasts .... *Konstantinos Koukouris* ... 211
The 'Hand of God'? .... *Claudio M. Tamburrini* ... 227

TOURISM AND VISITOR ATTRACTIONS: LEISURE, CULTURE AND COMMERCE

LSA Publication No 61. ISBN: 0 906337 71 2 [1998] pp. 211

Edited by Neil Ravenscroft, Deborah Philips and Marion Bennett

Contents

Editors' Introduction ......
............*Neil Ravenscroft, Deborah Philips and Marion Bennett*

I   Work, Leisure and Culture

Contrasting Roles in Business Development for the Tourism and
Leisure Industries: the case of Dublin and Glasgow ......
.... *J John Lennon*

Volunteering in an Urban Museums Service:
A Definitional Reassessment .... *Margaret Graham
and Malcolm Foley*

II   Identity and Commodification

The Legal Boundaries of Tourism: The State
versus the Marketplace in Defining
the Tourist ... . *Brian Simpson*

Activities, Holidays and Activity Holidays
in Scotland .... Malcolm Foley and Gavin Reid

Carnival and Control: The Commodification
of the Carnivalesque at Disneyland .... *Deborah Philips*

Re-defining the Role of Trading in a Museum Service ......
.... *Gayle McPherson, Malcolm Foley and Alastair Durie*

Leisure Consumption and the United Kingdom (UK) Zoo ......
.... *Philippa Hunter-Jones and Cheryl Hayward*

The Current Growth of Jewish Museums
in Europe .... *David Clark*

Consuming the Countryside: Postmodern Hedonism
or Responsible Reflexivity? ......
.... *Jim Butterfield and Jonathan Long*

Rural Recreation: Perspectives on Landholder Attitudes
and Public Access to Private Rural Lands ...... *John Jenkins*

III   Representation

Coastal Tourism as Comparative Consumption of Cultural
Landscapes .... *Daniel O'Hare*

From 'Gayety and Diversion' to 'Developer's Lorry'
— Representations of Bath ....*Judith E. Brown*

History as Leisure: Business and Pleasure at
Beamish ....*Jennifer Iles*

Index

THE PRODUCTION AND CONSUMPTION OF SPORT CULTURES: LEISURE, CULTURE AND COMMERCE

LSA Publication No. 62. ISBN: 0 906337 72 0 [1998] pp. 178
Edited by Udo Merkel, Gill Lines, Ian McDonald

Contents

Editors' Introduction .... *Udo Merkel, Gill Lines*
.... *and Ian McDonald*

I The Production Process

The Impact of Globalisation on Cricket
     in India .... *Ian McDonald*
Modernising Tradition?: The Changing Face
     of British Football ......
     .... *Raymond Boyle and Richard Haynes*
Sack the Board, Sack the Board, Sack the Board:
     Accountancy and Accountability
     in Contemporary English Professional
     Football Culture .... *Stephen Wagg*
FIFA and the Marketing of World Football ......
     .... *John Sugden and Alan Tomlinson*
As Charmless as Chain-saws?:
     Managing jet ski use in the UK ......
     .... *Jenny Anderson and David Johnson*

II The Consumption Process

What Happens if Nothing Happens? Staging Euro 96 ......
     .... *Vincent Miller and Jeremy Valentine*
A Case Study of Adolescent Media Consumption
     during the Summer of Sport 1996 .... *Gill Lines*
Read the Paper, Play the Sport: A Decade
     of Gender Change ......
     .... *Kay Biscomb, Kay Flatten and Hilary Matheson*
Mediawatch: Mountain Biking, the Media and the
     1996 Olympics .... *Graham Berridge and Julian Kaine*

GENDER, SPACE AND IDENTITY: LEISURE, CULTURE AND COMMERCE

LSA Publication No. 63. ISBN: 0 906337 73 9 [1998] pp. 191
Edited by Cara Aitchison and Fiona Jordan

Contents

Editors' Introduction .... *Cara Aitchison and Fiona Jordan*

I   The Construction of Gendered Space and Identity

Gender, Class and Urban Space: Public and
      Private Space in Contemporary
      Urban Landscape .... *Liz Bondi*

Gay Tourism Destinations: Identity, Sponsorship
      and Degaying .... *Annette Pritchard, Nigel J. Morgan,*
      .... *Diane Sedgley and Andrew Jenkins*

Gendered (Bed)Spaces: The Culture and
      Commerce of Women Only Tourism .... *Cara Aitchison*
      and Carole Reeves

Shirley Valentine: Where Are You? .... *Fiona Jordan*

Sub-cultural Strategies in Patriarchal Leisure
      Professional Cultures .... *Jean Yule*

II   Spaces, places, resistance and risk

Flexible Work, Disappearing Leisure? Feminist
      Perspectives on Women's Leisure as Spaces for Resistance to
      Gender Stereotypes .... *Eileen Green*

The Case for a Place of their Own: Queer Youth
      and Urban Space .... *Arnold Grossman*

Ecofeminism, 'Risk' and Women's
      Experiences of Landscape .... *Barbara Humberstone*
      and Di Collins

Sex and Politics: Sites of Resistance in
      Women's Football .... *Jayne Caudwell*

Gay Tourist Space and Sexual Risk Behaviour ......
      .... *Simon Forrest and Stephen Clift*

CONSUMPTION AND PARTICIPATION: LEISURE, CULTURE AND COMMERCE

LSA Publication No. 64. ISBN: 0 906337 74 7 [2000]
Edited by Garry Whannel

Contents

Editors' Introduction .... *Malcolm Foley and Garry Whannel*

I   Public or Private Funding

Last Chance Lottery and the Millennium City ...... *Graeme Evans*

The National Lottery in the UK: Sitting Pretty or
     Running Scared? The impact of having fun on
     developing coherent leisure policy
     in the public sector .... *Judy White*

A Cultural Enterprise? The Spread of Commercial
     Sponsorship .... *Garry Whannel and Deborah Philips*

UK Women's Attitudes to the National Lottery
     and the Implications for the
     Marketing of Gambling .... *Clare Brindley*

II   Commerce and Cultural Identities

The Contemporary Culture of Leisure in Japan .... *John Horne*

Consumer Sovereignty and Active Citizenship:
     An Analysis of Leisure World .... *Sharon Todd*

The Leisurization of Grocery Shopping ....
     .... *Cheryl A Cockburn-Wootten, Nigel J Morgan,*
     .... *Eleri Jones, Marilyn Thomas and Annette Pritchard*

Dance Clubs and Disco: The Search for the
     Authentic Experience .... *Mike Lowe and Ian Atkin*

London's New Private Social Clubs: Personal Space
     in the Age of 'Hot Desking' .... *Martin Peacock*

III Participation and Volunteering

Leisure and Culture; Consumers or Participants? .....
     .... *Stan R. Parker*

Volunteers in Uniformed Youth Organisations:
     A Study of the County of Sheffield
     Guide Association and the Sheffield
     City Scout Council .... *Nigel Jarvis and Lindsay King*

Volunteer Management and Satisfaction:
     A Case Study of the National Folk Festival .... *Julie Hodges*

Explanations for Declining Membership of the
     Guide Association .... *Lindsay King and Geoff Nichols*

POLICY AND PUBLICS

LSA Publication No. 65. ISBN: 0 906337 75 5 [1999] pp. 167
Edited by Peter Bramham and Wilf Murphy

Contents

Policy and Publics: Introduction
Peter Bramham and Wilf Murphy

I   Public Culture in Modernity

The Economics of Culture in a Pluralistic Society
.... *Sylvia Harvey*

Mega-Events and Modernity: International
Expositions and the Construction
of Public Culture
.... *Maurice Roche*

II   Planning Public Sport and Leisure

Progress towards Shaping a Safety Culture
in the Leisure Sector .... *John Hunter-Jones*

The Search for a Level Playing Field:
Planning and Sports Stadia
Development ....*Sarah McIntosh*
.... *and Fiona Simpson*

III Leisure Capital, People and Places

The Experience of Unemployment and the Use
of Leisure Capital .... *Francis Lobo*

Survival of Industry and the Countryside, and
'Green' Leisure Development in
Post 'Resort Act 1987' Japan .... *Yohji Iwamoto*

IV   Leisure and City-Centre Regeneration

Leisure Property as an Indicator of the Changing
Vitality and Viability of Town Centres:
A Case Study
.....................................*Martha Rowley and Neil Ravenscroft*
The Myth of the 24-hour City ...... *John Spink and Peter Bramham*

LEISURE, TIME AND SPACE: MEANINGS AND VALUES IN PEOPLE'S LIVES

LSA Publication No. 57. ISBN: 0 906337 68 2 [1998] pp. 198 + IV
Edited by Sheila Scraton

Contents

Introduction .... *Sheila Scraton*

I   **Accelerating Leisure? Leisure, time and space in a transitory society**

Beyond work and spend: Time, leisure and consumption
[summary]... *Juliet Schor*
Tourist Landscapes: Accelerating transformations
.... *Adri Dietvorst*

II   **Meanings and Values**

Ethics in leisure — an agenda for research
..............................*Mike McNamee and Celia Brackenridge*
Camping and caravanning and the place of cultural
meaning in leisure practices *David Crouch and Jan te Kloeze*
Leisure, play and work in post-modern societies:
Liminal experiences in male adolescents ...*Dirck van Bekkum*
Authenticity and real virtuality .... *Frans Schouten*
Half crown houses: The crisis of the country
house in post-war romances .... *Deborah Philips*

III   **Transformations of time and space**

Electronic manipulation of time and space in
television sport .... *Garry Whannel*
'Staying in' and 'Going out': Elderly women, leisure and the
postmodern city .... *Sheila Scraton, Peter Bramham,
and Beccy Watson*
Leisure in Bulgaria: Changes and problems ......*Maria Vodenska*
New lives for old: Young people in post-independence
Armenia and Georgia .... *Kenneth Roberts,
Aahron Adibekian and Levan Tarkhnishvili*

IV   **Leisure Participation in Time and Space**

Inappropriate or inevitable? The role of the law in
planning for the illicit leisure activities of
young people .... *Brian Simpson*
Play through the Lens: Children's photography of after-
school play .... *Chris Cunningham and Margaret Jones*
Participation in free-time sport recreation activities: Comparison
of Gdansk Region, Poland and Guildford, United Kingdom
.... *Barbara Marciszewska*
Leisure preferences of Polish students with disabilities ......
.... *Wieslaw Siwiński*

LEISURE, TOURISM AND ENVIRONMENT (I)
SUSTAINABILITY AND ENVIRONMENTAL POLICIES

LSA Publication No. 50 Part I;
Edited by Malcolm Foley, David McGillivray and Gayle McPherson (1999);
ISBN 0 906337 64 X

Contents

Editors' Introduction .... *Malcolm Foley,*
.... *David McGillivray and Gayle McPherson*
Notes on the Contributors

I   **ENVIRONMENT, INVESTMENT AND EDUCATION**
Leisure and Green Political Thought .... *Jim Butterfield*
European Leisure and Tourism Investment
    Incentives: Changing Rationales in the
    UK and European Community .... *Graeme Evans*
Social Paradigms, Living Styles and Resource
    Policies .... *Thomas L. Burton and Robert Kassian*
Professional Hosts' Perceptions of Garden Festival Wales:
    A Qualitative Approach to Festival Impact Studies
    .... *Fiona Williams and David Botterill*
Greening the Curriculum: Opportunities in
    Teaching Tourism .... *Angela Phelps*
II   ENVIRONMENT AND Policies FOR SPORT
Quiet: Please: Sport in the British Countryside .... *Mike Collins*
The Hosting of International Games in Canada:
    Economic and Ideological Ambitions
    .... *David Whitson and Donald Macintosh*
The Social Benefit of Leisure Park Development: Environmental
    Economics of Fukuoka Dome, Japan
    .... *Koh Sasaki and Munehiko Harada*
III ENVIRONMENT AND THE IDEA OF SUSTAINABILITY
The Nova Scotia Envirofor Process: Towards Sustainable
    Forest Management or Placation by the
    Multinationals? .... *Glyn Bissix*
Measuring Sustainability in Tourism: Lessons from a
    Study of Chepstow for Other Walled Towns in Europe
    .... *David M. Bruce and Marion J. Jackson*
Eco or Ego Tourism? Sustainable Tourism in Question
    .... *Brian Wheeller*
Outside In and Inside Out: Participatory Action
    Research with an Embryonic Social Movement Working for
    Change in Tourism .... *David Botterill*
'Sustainable Tourism' — Or More a Matter
    of Sustainable Societies? .... *David Leslie*

LEISURE, TOURISM AND ENVIRONMENT (II) PARTICIPATION, PERCEPTIONS AND PREFERENCES

LSA Publication No. 50 (Part II)
Edited by Malcolm Foley, Matt Frew and Gayle McPherson
ISBN: 0 906337 69 0; pp. 177+xii

Contents

Editors' Introduction
About the Contributors

I. **MARKETING DREAMS OR NIGHTMARES**

Cultured Tourists? The Significance and Signification
of European Cultural Tourism ....*Greg Richards*

Alternative and Mass Tourists:
Will They Ever Go Away? ....*Brian Davies*

Correlations between Clusters based on the
Ragheb and Beard Leisure Motivation Scale
and the Attributes of Desired Holiday Locations...................
.... *Chris Ryan*

The Effects of Development on the Visitor's Perception
of Unique Natural Resources...
.... *Alan Jubenville and William G. Workman*

II. **TRENDS AND TRANSITIONS**

Tourism in Our Own World: Scottish Residents' Perceptions
of Scotland as a Holiday Destination ....*Brian Hay*

Patterns of Tourist Role Preference Across the Life Course...........
.................................*Heather Gibson and Andrew Yiannakis*

Dynamics in Camping Styles? The Background
of Change and/or Repetitive Behaviour
of the Camper in the Netherlands ....
.... *Erik Hout, Jan te Kloeze and Han van der Voet*

III. **DISCOURSE AND SELF-DISCOVERY**

"Provincial Paradise": Urban Tourism and City Imaging
outside the Metropolis ....
....................................*David Rowe and Deborah Stevenson*

The Influence of Wilderness Experience on
Self-Actualization .... *Won Sop Shin*

From Bushmen to Bondi Beach: The Social Construction
of 'Malestream' Images of Australia in Tourism
Advertising .... *Georgia Young and Peter Brown*

The Travelog in Popular Women's Magazines...............................
.... *Beverley Ann Simmons*

LEISURE: MODERNITY, POSTMODERNITY AND LIFESTYLES

LSA Publications No. 48 (LEISURE IN DIFFERENT WORLDS Volume I)
Edited by Ian Henry (1994); ISBN: 0 906337   52 6, pp. 375+

Contents

Modernity, Postmodernity and Lifestyles: Introduction
    Ian Henry

I: Modernity, Postmodernity and Theory in Leisure Studies 1

Leisure and the Dreamworld of Modernity
    Chris Rojek 3

Europe's Unification Project and the Ethics of Leisure Studies
    Eric Corijn 13

Los Angeles and the Denial of Leisure in the Entertainment Capital
    of the World
    John Fiske 27

'Leisure'?According To Who?
    Louise Bricknell 39

The Figurational Sociology of Sport and Leisure Revisited
    David Jary and John Horne 53

II: LEISURE, THE CITY AND THE NATION-STATE 81

Leisure and the Postmodern City
    Peter Bramham and John Spink 83

Same City, Different Worlds? Women's Leisure in Two
    Contrasting Areas of Tyneside
    Graham Mowl and John Towner 105

Changing Times, Changing Policies
    Peter Bramham, Jim Butterfield,
    Jonathan Long and Chris Wolsey 125

Cultural Activities in Greece:Tradition or Modernity?
    Alex Deffner 135

Young People and Football in Liverpool
    Ken Roberts 157

Leisure Systems in Europe and Their Economic and Cultural
    Impact in Comparative Perspective
    Walter Tokarski 173

III: SOCIAL STRATIFICATION AND LEISURE LIFESTYLES 179

Ageing and Mass Media
    Concepción Maiztegui Oñate 181

Leisure and the Elderly: A Different World?
    Alan Clarke 189

(continued)

Qualitative Assessment of Work and Leisure in the Lives of
　　Retired Male Faculty Returning to Work
　　Gene C. Bammel, Rebecca Hancock,
　　and Lei Lane Burrus-Bammel 203

A Life Course Perspective and Sports Participation Patterns
　　among Middle-aged Japanese
　　Junya Fujimoto and Munehiko Harada 209

No Room for Children —The Changing Dimensions of Provision for
　　Children's Play in Urban Areas
　　Barbara Hendricks 217

'Having the Time of Our Lives' — Is Leisure an Appropriate
　　Concept for Midlife Women?
　　Myra Betschild and Eileen Green 227

An Integrated Model of Women's Leisure Constraints
　　Karla A. Henderson and M. Deborah Bialeschki 243

Factors Influencing Ethnic Minority Groups' Participation in Sport
　　Bob Carroll 261

Leisure Constraints, Attitudes and Behaviour of People with
　　Activity Restricting Physical Disabilities
　　Rick Rollins and Doug Nichols 277

Differences in Leisure Behaviour of the Poor and the Rich in the
　　Netherlands
　　Johan van Ophem and Kees de Hoog 291

IV:　CHANGING LEISURE FORMS AND POSTMODERNITY 307

Collective Self-generated Consumption: Leisure, Space and Cultural
　　Identity in Late Modernity
　　David Crouch and Alan Tomlinson 309

Intimations of Postmodernity: the Cocktail Cult
　　between the Wars
　　A. V. Seaton 323

It began with the Piton. The Challenge to British Rock
　　Climbing in a Post-Modernist Framework
　　Dan Morgan 341

The Modularisation of Daily Life
　　Hugo van der Poel 355